This book belongs to

_____

The Fruit of the Spirit

of the

BroadStreet
P U B L I S H I N G

BroadStreet Publishing Group, LLC
Racine, Wisconsin, USA
BroadStreetPublishing.com

The Fruit of the Spirit

© 2017 by BroadStreet Publishing

ISBN 978-1-4245-5393-8 (hardcover)
ISBN 978-1-4245-5394-5 (e-book)

Devotional entries by Claire Flores, Rachel Flores, Cate Mezyk, and Carole Smith

Stock or custom editions of BroadStreet Publishing titles may be purchased in bulk for educational, business, ministry, fundraising, or sales promotional use. For information, please e-mail info@broadstreetpublishing.com.

Design by Chris Garborg at garborgdesign.com
Typeset by Katherine Lloyd at thedeskonline.com
Compiled by Michelle Winger

Printed in China

17 18 19 20 21 5 4 3 2 1

The fruit of the Spirit is love,
joy, peace, forbearance, kindness,
goodness, faithfulness,
gentleness, and self-control.
Against such things there is no law.

GALATIANS 5:22-23 NIV

Introduction

When everything else in life demands
your attention, spend time in God's Word
and find the love, joy, and peace you need
each day. God delights in every moment
you choose to spend with him.

This one-year devotional provides
you with godly wisdom and insight to
strengthen your faith and encourage your
spirit so you can bear God's wonderful fruit.

Be refreshed and inspired as you spend
time pondering the fruit of the Spirit. Let
your heart be filled with the peace that is
abundant in God's presence.

January

You have put more
joy in my heart than
they have when their
grain and wine abound.

PSALM 4:7 ESV

January 1

ALL IN LOVE

Let all that you do be done in love.
1 Corinthians 16:14 esv

Humans are emotional beings. We are motivated and impacted by our feelings and those of others. We speak harshly out of anger, embark on adventures because of curiosity, lash out in embarrassment, and give to those in need through empathy. Emotion is a gift, but if we allow ourselves to be overly driven by our human passions, they will misguide us. We can't trust our emotions to drive us—they are too unpredictable.

As followers of Jesus, we can check our hearts and continually remind ourselves to act in love. Everything God does is motivated and backed by overwhelming love for us, and that's the example we follow. Acting in love is always the right course of action; it neutralizes any sinful attitude or motivation. The positive effects of love on our lives are undeniable; they bring us closer to God and more into his likeness.

Lord, love doesn't come naturally to me in every situation. Thank you for enabling me to do all things out of love through your love in me. Help me to always check my heart before I react to any situation, so I respond and act in love.

7

January 2

ETERNAL MIND-SET

In this you rejoice, though now for a little while,
if necessary, you have been grieved by various trials.
Though you have not seen him, you love him. … Though you
do not now see him, you believe in him and rejoice with joy
that is inexpressible and filled with glory.
1 PETER 1:6, 8 ESV

Possibly the hardest thing about the Christian life is developing an eternal perspective. Our humanity is naturally short sighted, and we struggle daily to see what's beyond our immediate circumstances.

And yet, an eternal mind-set changes everything. It frees us from worry and anxiety to rest in peace and calm, knowing that the hope of glory remains, regardless of trials to come. No matter how long a certain wilderness feels in our lives, we will be redeemed and restored.

Lord, I often struggle to remember your eternal plan.
I grieve and worry over the hardships in my life:
those situations that make me wonder if there's really
a light at the end of the tunnel. Please switch my
perspective and remind me that you are always in
control. What I'm going through here is temporary, and
you have prepared for me a glory that will outlast time.

January 3

THE GIFT OF EMPATHY

*Rejoice with those who rejoice,
and weep with those who weep.*
ROMANS 12:15 NKJV

Empathy is one of the greatest gifts we can give to another person. It's a way of sharing the load, coming alongside someone in both pain and joy. It reminds all involved that no one walks alone.

Empathy is acknowledging that, without going through specifically what the other person is going through, you know how they feel. We are all human, and we all know what it is to cry, laugh, and experience pain or happiness. There is great power in our understanding of one another; even a small effort can be life changing for someone else in triumph or crisis.

**Lord, help me to be sensitive to the lives of those
around me. Let me have compassion for their pains
and genuine joy for their victories, sharing their sorrows
and reveling in their successes. I know that empathizing
with others will make me a better friend, spouse,
parent, sibling, and child.**

January 4

WALKING IN PEACE

Jesus said, "Peace be with you!
As the Father has sent me, I am sending you."
JOHN 20:21 NIV

Worry comes far too easily for many of us, but it was never God's intention for worry to be a driving force in our lives. We are visible expressions of an invisible God, and walking in peace is one of the loudest ways to share him with others. Peace from God brings confidence and security, and it shows the world what it means to be a follower of the God who's in control of everything.

When we step away from peace and allow anxiety to consume our minds, we lose a very important part of our relationship with Jesus. Peace is an easier way to follow him. We don't falter or hesitate to obey when we are able to trust without concern. Jesus sent us to do a work that is greater than anything we can see here on earth. By going forward in peace and trust, we help accomplish work that lasts for eternity.

Jesus, it's hard for me to be at peace. I worry about so many things, and that can stem from questioning whether or not you can handle everything in my life. I do trust you, but I need your help translating that trust into a constant peace. Thank you for being gracious to me and leaving your peace with me.

January 5

COMPREHENDING PERFECT FAITHFULNESS

Teach me your way, Lord,
that I may rely on your faithfulness;
give me an undivided heart,
that I may fear your name.

PSALM 86:11 NIV

We have a hard time fully grasping the faithfulness of God because we aren't capable of perfect faithfulness. In this verse, David asks God to teach him how to rely on God's faithfulness. What he is saying is that he doesn't understand it deeply enough to trust it completely.

When we remove the distractions and the hesitations from our hearts, focusing instead on the never-changing, always-trustworthy God, we can finally comprehend what it means to trust and fear him. When we learn the depths of his reliability and the completeness of his faithfulness, we won't hesitate to fall into his arms. We will know and understand what it means to have a heart focused on him.

Lord God, I want to know the depths of your faithfulness. Help me understand your character to such a degree that human failure doesn't stop me from trusting you. Unify my heart and focus on you, not on the world. I want to fix my gaze on you so I can trust you with my whole heart.

January 6

STAND FIRM

"Because you have kept My command to persevere,
I also will keep you from the hour of trial which shall come
upon the whole world, to test those who dwell on the earth."
REVELATION 3:10 NKJV

Multiple times throughout the Bible, God asks us to stand firm. While we often look for some sort of action we can take to prove our dedication to God, the truest test of our commitment is our ability to stand firm and continue in his love.

We don't earn our faith or God's favor. Once we've accepted what he's already done, the rest is about perseverance. He promises to bless us, not only with his presence, but also in keeping us from the trials that are coming to the whole world. He promises to protect us and keep us close to his grace. By enduring small trials in this life, we are saved from the greater trials that will come.

Thank you for your faithfulness, God.
Keep me standing firm in your truth. When I begin
to falter, hold me steady, so I may stand firmly
planted until the day of your salvation.

January 7

HIS GLORY

A man's discretion makes him slow to anger,
And it is his glory to overlook a transgression.
PROVERBS 19:11 NASB

"Love keeps no record of wrongs" (1 Corinthians 13:5). We've heard it a million times. Still, record keeping comes more naturally than forgiveness. When someone does something that's wrong, our natural reaction is to seek justice for our hurt. We know we are right, and we want to prove it.

Rushing to anger solves nothing. It takes a disciplined heart to stop, wait, and find a better way. You may think that being visibly right will elevate you. It might bring you glory, or you could be seen in the light you have always wanted. Your glory is in overlooking the wrong that was done to you. Since God sees everything, he knows when you are right and others have wronged you. He will bring you glory in his way and time. It will be far better than any glory you could have sought out for yourself.

Jesus, give me patience when I've been wronged.
Let me not rush into trying to prove my side of things
or taking my own glory. Give me slowness to anger,
and grace to overlook others' offenses.

January 8

POWERFUL KINDNESS

I will tell about the LORD's kindness and praise him for everything he has done. I will praise the LORD for the many good things he has given us and for his goodness to the people of Israel. He has shown great mercy to us and has been very kind to us.

ISAIAH 63:7 NCV

The Bible says that the kindness of the Lord leads people to repentance: not his anger, not his wrath—his kindness. There is power in kindness: a power that moves souls and changes lives. We can subconsciously equate kindness with weakness, but it's the exact opposite.

The Israelites turned their backs on God too many times to count. But what we see time and time again in their story is that God was still good. He showed them mercy; he gave them good things. He was kind to them. This did not mean that consequences and trials didn't come upon Israel, but the people knew God's promises and trusted him. In the same way, we can trust God and turn to him often, confident that his mercy is present, even in suffering.

God, I sometimes miss your point. I assume that you're angry with me or that I've distanced myself too far from you, but your arms are always open wide to me. No matter how many times I turn my back on you, you're still constant in mercy.

January 9

I WILL SEE HIS GOODNESS

I remain confident of this:
I will see the goodness of the LORD
in the land of the living.
PSALM 27:13 NIV

"It will be okay." Parents soothe fretful children, professors console students, and spouses and siblings calm each other with those words. There is nothing more reassuring than a confident hope: a knowledge that what is coming is better than what is. We struggle with many difficulties through our lives, but hearing that it will be okay can be the difference between getting through it, and giving up.

God gives you a beautiful promise of hope to speak during the hardest of times. You can be confident that better things are coming. God has blessed you, and he will continue to bless you. You know you will see, firsthand, the goodness of a loving God in the land of the living—a glorious heaven. There, the living will not just be getting by, or barely getting through; they will be truly alive. They will taste and see that the Lord is good to them.

God, you are infinitely good. Thank you for promising your goodness and your faithfulness to me. No matter how hard things get, give me confidence that I will see you and be alive with you.

January 10

RELENTLESS, PASSIONATE LOVE

I will show my love to those who passionately love me.
For they will search and search continually until they find me.

PROVERBS 8:17 TPT

You can always tell the measure of love by the lengths that love will go for others. Relentless passion and continual pursuit showcase love's endurance. The one who gives up easily is one who never truly loved.

The depth of our love and desire for God is similarly exposed. How easily are we deterred from pursuing him? Do certain tasks and items distract us from seeking his presence? When we truly long to know Jesus personally, we won't be stopped. Despite distraction or worry, we continue to seek him, pressing deeper and looking harder. We yearn for him in a way that won't allow us to stop searching. We do not seek in vain, because he promises to show his love to those who love him passionately and seek him continually.

God, let my love for you be so passionate and so true that other affections do not deter me. Let me set you as the greatest love of my life, the one thing I seek more fervently than any other. Help me to grow in my love for you. Continue to reveal your love to me.

January 11

IN EVERY SEASON

"Teaching them to observe all that I have commanded you.
And behold, I am with you always, to the end of the age."
MATTHEW 28:20 ESV

Life is made of seasons. For many of us, different people take part in each of those seasons. Your family was more than likely there from the beginning, followed by friends through school and college, and then maybe your spouse and kids if you got married and started a family. You lived a whole life before meeting your spouse and another before raising your children. Rarely do we have another person who was there through every moment of our life.

But God is the one who knows you in every season and every moment, more intimately than anyone else. He sees everything that makes up your heart: all the experiences and decisions that have come together to create your unique outlook and character. He is the ultimate faithful one—the one who is there through every season of your life, and he will be with you forever.

God, thank you for being with me through every season. I know that you understand me fully because you know everything I've gone through, even the pieces I've told no one about. Thank you for your faithfulness to me.

January 12

ANSWER GENTLY

A gentle answer deflects anger,
but harsh words make tempers flare.
PROVERBS 15:1 NLT

In the middle of an argument, the most difficult thing to do is to answer gently. To begin with, most of us find ourselves in arguments because both parties believe they are right. Gentle answers sacrifice the desire to make the other person see things our way. It's humility in its purest form; it feels like less than we deserve.

When two people are simply trying to prove a point, are either of them prepared to learn? In the heat of argument, neither is teachable; each is too busy trying to prove an opinion, and no one wins. If Jesus' birth and life on earth showed us anything, it's that humility and lowliness—not pride or a pedestal—are the eternal victors.

God, when I'm fighting with someone, I want to be right, not proven wrong. It's so hard to let go of a point and humble myself. You humbled yourself in front of the people you created. The ones who were supposed to bow to you insulted and spat on you, but still you served them. Thank you for your example of love and humility; give me the courage and strength to follow it.

January 13

TOUGH OBEDIENCE

Servants, be subject to your masters with all respect,
not only to the good and gentle but also to the unjust.
1 Peter 2:18 esv

It's easier to serve people we admire. We look up to them, and we long to catch their attention by doing good for them. However, if God is going to be glorified in us, we have to serve both those we love and those who are hard to love.

Sometimes, we have bosses, superiors, and authorities in our lives who don't lead well or fairly. Still, we have been placed under them by God, and we must serve and respect them. We have to remember that our one true authority is God, and he will see and reward our gentle obedience to his will.

Heavenly Father, I ask today for your grace to
submit to those in authority over me when I have
a hard time respecting them. You are my true master.
All the work and service I give to others is given to you.
When I struggle to serve, remind me of these truths.

January 14

KNOW WHO YOU ARE

Be still, and know that I am God.
I will be exalted among the nations,
I will be exalted in the earth!
PSALM 46:10 ESV

God never loses confidence in who he is. When we falter, become flustered, or wonder how a situation is going to work out, he reminds us to be still and remember him. Who is he? What is he worthy of? At the end of it all, we know he will be exalted in every nation, and everyone will bow to his name, as is his due.

No matter how difficult life gets, how hidden you feel, or how lost you become, don't forget who you are. You are created in the image of God, and in the end, you'll live forever with him through faith and grace. Don't worry about the present when you know who holds the future. Be still, remember who he is, and remember who he created you to be.

Jesus, help me to be still and remember who you are.
Your power and your glory are not lessened by
the turmoil in this world. You have a plan and
a purpose for all of it, including me.

January 15

LAYING DOWN BEING RIGHT

Work at living in peace with everyone, and work at living
a holy life, for those who are not holy will not see the Lord.
HEBREWS 12:14 NLT

No opinion is valued by anyone more than by the person who holds it. We arrive at our varying opinions in different ways—some shaped by the life we've lived, people we've encountered, wrongs done to us, or convictions we sometimes can't fully explain. Opinions come as we are shaped in life, and they shape us in return.

And while our opinions become an important part of us, how we express them to others is a delicate matter. We can alienate or bond with those with whom we share our opinions. This has been dramatically demonstrated by social media. There, opinions spew from the protective mask of a computer screen, the fallout feels leagues away, and offenses hide between the miles that separate people. God asks us to fight for peace and to work at living well with those around us, because when we lay down the need to be right and pick up the need to be loving, God is glorified and seen.

**God, I fight daily with my desire to voice my opinion.
I feel that I'm owed that platform, and I often justify the
harsh words I use to deliver it. Remind me that I am a
walking representation of you. I do not want to confuse
someone about your love or grace because I failed to
demonstrate those in my desire to speak my mind.**

January 16

READY TO FORGIVE

For You, LORD, are good, and ready to forgive,
And abundant in mercy to all those who call upon You.
PSALM 86:5 NKJV

Sometimes, we forget that Jesus already won our forgiveness. We forget that the full work was done on the cross. There is nothing we can do or have to do to get his grace. Still, we sometimes tiptoe to God, wondering if mercy will be given. Have we gone too far for his grace this time? Again and again, he reminds us it is finished. We are forgiven and free.

The beautiful truth in this relationship is that the grace of God is never permission for mockery of God. The knowledge that forgiveness comes readily sparks a desire in our hearts to not need it. Once grace has been tasted, we don't want to sin. Will we still struggle with our desires? Of course. Our greatest desire, however, will be to flourish under the mercy and compassion of our Father.

Lord God, thank you for the cross. Thank you for your sacrificial forgiveness and mercy, which accomplished their work a long time ago. I'm humbled by your great love, and I want nothing more than to please you and bring you glory. Give me the courage to repent freely, and give me the strength to resist future temptation.

January 17

DESTROYED DEFENSES

If you live without restraint
and are unable to control your temper,
you're as helpless as a city with broken-down defenses,
open to attack.

PROVERBS 25:28 TPT

We often use the phrase *I have a temper* as though it is unique to some of us. Unfortunately, a temper is a built-in feature. We all have one. The question is, do we have control of it?

Everyone comes up against people and situations that push them to the edge. One irritation follows another, feeding our anger. If we let that rage go, allowing ourselves to be overtaken by it, we destroy our defenses. We can no longer say that we were in the right—because we weren't. We lost control. Anger is a dangerous sin. While it isn't above grace, it's not without consequence. There are often casualties of anger, and the damage is done before we've had a moment to think.

God, I'm heartbroken over how easily I can lose my temper. Anger boils over so quickly, and I am blind in the moment. Through your Spirit, I know I can overcome it. Give me the grace and the power to restrain my anger and demonstrate your kindness.

January 18

STILLNESS

Be still in the presence of the LORD,
and wait patiently for him to act.
Don't worry about evil people who prosper
or fret about their wicked schemes.

PSALM 37:7 NLT

Distraction lurks everywhere. In the data age, there are a million screens, people, and gadgets fighting for our attention at any moment. It takes great amounts of effort and intention to stop, focus, and be still. In these fought for moments of stillness, we hear the voice of God the loudest.

When we quiet the sound of our surroundings and look away from attention grabbers, we can fully and clearly hear what he has to say. It's not for us to worry about what's going on the world. In fact, getting caught up in the sins of others takes our attention away from what God is trying to do inside of us. God will act. He will shine his glory on those who have lived in righteousness, and he will have his say against those who have turned their backs on him. We do not command that justice. God alone will decide and carry out his plan. We must just be still, and listen for his summons.

God, I have bought into this lie that I have to busy myself in order to bring you glory and further your kingdom. You didn't ask me to execute your justice— you asked me to be still and to wait for you to act. Make your will clear in my life, and give me the strength to do whatever you ask.

January 19

ALWAYS THE BETTER WAY

Hatred keeps old quarrels alive,
but love draws a veil over every insult
and finds a way to make sin disappear.
PROVERBS 10:12 TPT

It's strange how we all struggle with memory until we're offended. Then, suddenly, we can remember every detail clearly, every word or action that hurt or distanced us. Maybe it's because we feel a deep emotional connection to the things that hurt us. Insults damage us deeply, leaving marks that aren't easily erased.

Love has the power to heal the hurt. Love covers a multitude of sins, both those we've done and those done against us. When we make the conscious, albeit painstaking, choice to love past offense, our hurt evaporates with the insult. Love has the power to raise us up when we've been knocked down, and it can restore what hatred tried to destroy.

Lord, it's never easy to let go of something
that has offended me. Sometimes, I hold onto
my pain in an attempt to find my own justice for it.
Remind me that love is always the better way.
Give me the strength to choose love.

January 20

GETTING DIRECTIONS

Where there is no revelation, people cast off restraint;
but blessed is the one who heeds wisdom's instruction.
PROVERBS 29:18 NIV

Imagine you told a little girl that, someday, she'd get a prize, but you didn't tell her why or how to get it. That child probably won't do what you want her to do in order to earn the prize. All people, not just children, need directions. They need an end goal and instructions for getting there.

When you find yourself directionless, your guard comes down, and you are most susceptible to failure. You have to continually look to your guide and the directions laid out in Scripture. Without its instruction and hope, what reason will you have to stay on the path toward righteousness? Be diligent in your pursuit of revelation. Cast vision for yourself daily, and always hold it up to the standard of God's plan for your life.

Lord, help me to be mindful of my own direction
or lack thereof. Don't let me become apathetic
in my walk with you. I want to be a person
of vision, hope, and intention.

PEACE OF A PURE LIFE

I am saying this for your benefit, not to place
restrictions on you. I want you to do whatever will help you
serve the Lord best, with as few distractions as possible.
1 CORINTHIANS 7:35 NLT

"You're missing out," people might say to you when your Christian faith tells your heart to stop. God doesn't set parameters for us because he wants us to miss out on something. He sets them because he doesn't want us to miss out on his goodness. He knows how easily sin can derail a person, and he understands how quickly distractions of the flesh can separate someone from the rewards of the Spirit.

God's desire for us is for undivided, content hearts, focused on him. He doesn't want us at war within ourselves. He wants us to live in peace—his peace, which comes with a pure life.

God, remove the distractions from my life that are keeping me from your goodness. Help me not to dismiss your law as you wanting me to miss out. Help me to trust that, when you speak to my spirit, you want the best for me. I want a heart full of you, with no room for distractions that take away from our relationship.

January 22

INTERNAL TOOLS

God is working in you, giving you the desire and
the power to do what pleases him.
PHILIPPIANS 2:13 NLT

Have you ever noticed that the longer you say no to a specific sin, the easier it is not to give in to it? That's because you are not designed to be at war with sin forever. God is at work in you, giving you a stronger desire for righteousness as well as the capable power to do what is right.

When your struggle with sin feels like more than you can handle, and you feel the weight of temptation is crushing you, remember that you aren't fighting alone. God is working within you, giving you the tools to overcome sin and walk in perpetual freedom.

Thank you, God, for the knowledge of your presence in me. Daily, you are shaping me into the person I want to be, one who lives a pure life before you. Your tools create kindness, gentleness, patience, and ultimately victory. When I beg for purification, you've already begun the work. When I ask you for freedom, you're already breaking the chains. Continue this work in me.

January 23

STUMBLES, NOT FALLS

The LORD directs the steps of the godly.
He delights in every detail of their lives.
Though they stumble, they will never fall,
for the LORD holds them by the hand.
PSALM 37:23-24 NLT

Don't ever doubt God's intimate interest in you. Not even for a second. He created you, and he cares about your story as he adds new paragraphs every day. He feels your pain, sees your joy, and lavishes his love on you throughout it all.

When you stumble, you won't fall. You might feel as though you've been laid low. You might feel as though your future is crashing down around you, but he's never stopped holding it all together. He doesn't just know what you are going through, he delights in it. He sees the end, and he knows that everything works out. You will stumble, you won't fall. Don't lose sight of that incredible truth.

God, thank you for holding my hand through life. Thank you for directing my steps. Sometimes I feel so alone, but the truth is that I never am. When I look back on my life, I can see your faithfulness at work. Continue to lead me, and let my hand remain in yours.

January 24

A SINGLE SOUL

*"In the same way, I tell you there is more joy in heaven
over one sinner who changes his heart and life, than over
ninety-nine good people who don't need to change."*

LUKE 15:7 NCV

It's easy to get caught up in the big moments of faith
that sweep us away. We are drawn to the biblical stories of
thousands of souls saved, bodies healed, and demons cast out.
The stories of just one are less glamorous. Let's say a ministry
invests money, time, and energy into opening a coffee shop,
only to shut it down two years later. Those involved might
wonder, Was it worth it? Did the money, time, and effort save
one soul? Would that make the shop worth it? God would say
yes.

We want signs and wonders to define a great ministry.
The coffee shop is a failure to us, but heaven rejoices over the
faithfulness of those Christians and over the one new believer.
When we grasp his love and pursuit for the one, we can understand the joy in salvation. Let's dwell on the length that Christ
will go for one soul, and what he did to save us. Let us realign
our thinking of true ministry to capture the joy of heaven over
the one.

**Jesus, thank you for pursuing me. Give me a desire
to pursue others with the truth of the gospel,
whether a group or a single soul.**

January 25

SOUL CARE

When your heart overflows with understanding
you'll be very slow to get angry.
But if you have a quick temper,
your impatience will be quickly seen by all.
PROVERBS 14:29 TPT

Anger is a symptom. When we don't connect to and deal with a problem, anger tells us that it is bubbling under our skin. If you find yourself in a constant state of anger, it's time to tend to your heart. The wellspring of life flows from your heart. Is Christ's life flowing from your heart, or is it anger from bitterness, control issues, depression, anxiety, or pride?

Here in Proverbs, a heart overflowing with understanding slows anger. Does your soul need care? Are you pulling water from an empty well? If you continue on that path, you will pull up anger. It is important to take care of your soul to produce a life of patience. What restores you? Where are your still waters? It is not selfish to take care of yourself. To have patience with others, you must be patient with yourself. Allow yourself to rest in God's presence. Understanding your soul is key to a heart that draws from a well of life and brims with understanding, not anger.

Jesus, I repent of anger in my heart.
Refresh my wellspring, refresh my soul,
and let me draw from living waters.

January 26

RUN STRONG

Since we are surrounded by so great a cloud of witnesses,
let us also lay aside every weight, and sin which clings so closely,
and let us run with endurance the race that is set before us.
HEBREWS 12:1 ESV

Once every two years, the whole world turns its eyes to one place. Not toward a catastrophe or war, but toward inspiration at the Olympics. The crowds near and far support their favorite athletes, cheer on underdogs, and admire the winners. Four years later, beloved athletes can find trouble. They could be forgotten by the crowd that once held them so high.

We, too, run a race. It's important to notice the cloud, the innumerable number of "athletes" that have gone before you. They have run this race, and they have finished well. This is not a crowd that will turn against you, but a gathering of faithful witnesses. They cheer loudly for your endurance in faith. They are a crowd clothed in the righteousness of Jesus, encouraging you to discard your filthy robes and run free. The race requires patience, and you have an audience full of people cheering you on.

Thank you, God, for those who have gone
before me. Thank you that we can run the race well
in your strength. Continue your work of patience
and endurance in my heart.

January 27

OVERFLOWING SPIRIT

"I know your deeds, your love and faith,
your service and perseverance, and that you are
now doing more than you did at first."
REVELATION 2:19 NIV

Being filled with the Holy Spirit is not a one-time thing. When you become a believer, the Holy Spirit comes to dwell inside you and should be like a cup of water that is so full it sloshes out on everything around it. Is that how people would describe you?

Such overflowing people exist; you can probably think of a few. It's evident and real. This person is not tied to agendas, schedules, and to-do lists, but is willing and open to the Spirit's call. God is moving in our world, and our job is to partner with him. Lay down your agenda today, release your grip on your day planner, and grab hold of God's outstretched hand. He wants to use you in mighty ways.

Lord, I repent of running my life based on my agenda. Thank you for working in this world. Can I partner with you today? Show me the moments where you want me to slow down and speak truth or act in your name.

January 28

FAITHFUL COMPLAINT?

*You know that these troubles test your faith,
and this will give you patience.*

JAMES 1:3 NCV

Patience cannot be defined as waiting. When you are waiting for a friend to come over, but you are casually reading a book or enjoying the rest of your dinner, you do not need patience. It produces no discomfort for you. However, if you are in discomfort, then you show patience by not complaining. Can you be patient and complain? In situations that involve suffering, situations that are not petty or pointless, the answer is yes. Several times, the psalmist cries out to God. The writer was being tested. Still, the complaints reveal patience, because they speak to the sovereignty of God over the pain. They speak for the faith of the writer that God was in control of it all.

If you are in a season of suffering, do not be afraid to bring your requests to God. It's not impatience to ask him, like the psalmist, "How long, O Lord?" It is an awareness of the one who is in control and is producing more fruit in your life.

**God, even in my discomfort, I acknowledge your
sovereignty over my situation. Help me to endure
hard times, knowing you are in control.**

January 29

SIMPLE HOSPITALITY

The people of the island were very kind to us.
It was cold and rainy so they built a fire
on the shore and welcomed us.

ACTS 28:2 NLT

Hospitality is a vibrant and beautiful spiritual gift that is often overlooked. In Acts, the apostles appoint seven Spirit-filled people to attend to the hospitality needs of the community. In Hebrews 13:2, we are told our hospitality might entertain angels.

Hospitality is all about little gestures. It is the cozy warmth of home, that tears down a traveler's protective walls, allowing peace to fill their hearts. It meets simple needs. Through crackling fires, fresh beds, and clean water, kindness shines. Scripture tells us that God's kindness leads us to repentance. May our simple, hospitable kindness reveal the grace of Christ and lead others to repentance. Isn't that what every gift is for, what every fruit is about? That all would see and know the saving grace of God.

Dear Lord, thank you for the hospitable welcome
into your kingdom. How can I show kindness
to others today? Please open doors and provide
opportunities for me to offer simple hospitality.

January 30

NEW WINE, NEW JOY

You have put more joy in my heart
than they have when their grain and wine abound.
PSALM 4:7 ESV

Imagine you are a new farmer or a winemaker. The first clearing of the land breaks all the soft skin on your hands. The dropping and covering of each seed into the dirt is done with a whispered prayer of hope. When the rain does not fall, you plead. When it comes, you breathe a sigh of relief. When waters rise too high, you hold your breath, each heartbeat a prayer. This crop is your life.

You partnered with God to bring life, but it is out of your hands. The heat comes, and what was tiny grows large. The air cools, moods shift, and the time comes: harvest. Goodness is collected and joy found, bubbling over like the cup of new wine in your hand that, months earlier, was merely a dream. Grain and wine abound, and your hope is fulfilled. We find joy in life in this fact: our hope is fulfilled in Christ. His life, death, and resurrection won victory for all humanity. Our joy is founded on that unshakeable hope. Rejoice today: Christ is your Savior, and he has restored you to his kingdom.

Thank you, Jesus, for restoring me!
You bring joy to my life and heart, and I praise you
for the work you are doing in me. Remind me of
this fulfilled hope, today and always.

January 31

WORK FOR PEACE

Stop doing evil and do good.
Look for peace and work for it.
PSALM 34:14 NCV

We often feel powerless against evil. It surrounds us, pressing against our lives in the news, our neighborhoods, and our homes. Sin permeates our world. Even with Christ's promise, it is hard to feel victorious when we see so much failure around us.

We can't take a passive stance against evil. Through Christ, we have the power to stop it in ourselves and share goodness instead, which always triumphs. Peace isn't something which comes gently and unexpectedly. It's something we can work for, fight for, and pursue. We can truly be at peace with God and with those around us. We can do good, love others, and follow God's plan for our lives. Will we be perfect? No, but we can work toward it by the grace of God.

Dear Lord, thank you that I can do something about the evil in this world. Thank you that I have the power, by your Holy Spirit, to do good and choose peace. Give me the strength to work for peace in my life and trust you with all the rest.

February

Since we have
been justified through
faith, we have peace
with God through our
Lord Jesus Christ.

ROMANS 5:1 NIV

February 1

NO LONGER A SLAVE

We know that our old life died with Christ
on the cross so that our sinful selves would have
no power over us and we would not be slaves to sin.
ROMANS 6:6 NCV

Sin has a powerful grip, and you may feel you cannot break free of it. You try to overcome it again and again, but the temptation is too strong. You are exhausted, weak, and discouraged.

As a child of God, the truth is that sin has no power over you. You are not a slave to sin or your flesh. You are created in the image of the God who conquered death. The old you—the one who was powerless to resist temptation—died on the cross with Christ. You are not that person anymore. You've been given the Holy Spirit and the power to overcome any evil thing that comes against you. Put away your defeated mindset, and think of yourself as you are in Christ: powerful, strong, and victorious against sin.

Jesus, I am weak without you. I cannot walk away from sin's temptations. Remind me that I am not without you. I have your spirit inside of me, and through you I have the power to conquer sin. Help me to walk in that victory, sure of myself and of you within me.

February 2

LORD OF HEAVEN'S ARMIES

"This is what the LORD of Heaven's Armies says:
Judge fairly, and show mercy and kindness to one another."
ZECHARIAH 7:9 NLT

Isn't it interesting that God is described as the "Lord of Heaven's Armies" in this verse? When you think of the leaders of the greatest armies in existence, what comes to mind? Scenes of battle? Violence and valor, clashing armies and glinting armor? The commands following this great title aren't anything of the sort. The Lord instructs us to judge with fairness, be merciful, and share kindness.

This is the beautiful paradox of the nature of God. He is mighty, fearsome, and powerful, but he is also lovely, faithful, and trustworthy. He is a God who daily leads us—his army—into the world for a battle that isn't flesh and blood; it is a spiritual war for the souls and lives of all people. We don't fight with weapons made by human hands, but with powerful, heavenly weapons that can win souls.

Lord, give me the strength to be kind and to judge others with fairness rather than anger. Help me to be merciful when others are wrong. I want to be a light in a dark world, and I want to draw people to you, not push them further away. Thank you for your greatness and your gentleness.

February 3

INHERENT GOODNESS

For you, O Lord, are good and forgiving,
abounding in steadfast love to all who call upon you.
PSALM 86:5 ESV

We all approach God for different reasons, with different matters on our hearts. Sometimes, we come to him in joy and thankfulness. Other times, we come with our heads bowed low, nearly crushed by shame and sorrow. No matter how we come, he meets us the same way—with goodness.

God is full of love for us, his children. He doesn't receive us with quick anger or frustration, but with a love that is steadfast and unchanging. God isn't just good some of the time; goodness is his nature. Whether he is passing righteous judgment or granting undeserved grace, he is good. Because of his perfect character, we can wholly trust him.

Thank you, God, for your inherent goodness.
I never fear unfairness when I come to you.
Thank you for your steadfast love and for always
responding to me in goodness. Help me understand that
goodness, so I won't hesitate to come to
you first in every situation.

February 4

HEAVENLY REWARDS

Be patient, therefore, brothers, until the coming of the Lord.
See how the farmer waits for the precious fruit of the earth, being
patient about it, until it receives the early and the late rains.

JAMES 5:7 ESV

There is a prevalent message in today's culture that whispers sweet and appealing lies: rights to luxury and self-indulgence. You deserve it, Christian! God wants you to have it and to be happy. This whisper takes away the sweet truth of a God who rewards us and injects the poisonous lie that enjoyment must be immediate.

God wants to reward you. That is truth. He promises rewards to the faithful, and he keeps his promises. Those rewards are often not on this earth, and why would we want them to be? Earthly rewards are enjoyable, but they can be destroyed by moth and rust. Heaven's treasures are eternal. To lean into the pull of God's kingdom, not the tug of instant gratification, requires enduring patience. When you are tempted to give into temporary satisfactions, remember the rewards that wait for you in heaven. Know that your loving Father is waiting with more than you could think to ask for. Let that spur you on in your works and actions, motivating you to live with a kingdom-driven mind-set.

Develop patience in me, God! Grant me endurance
to wait for the gifts you have in heaven and
not be satisfied with temporary things.

February 5

WHAT DEFINES YOU?

*The believers were filled with joy
and with the Holy Spirit.*
ACTS 13:52 NLT

Do you ever try to describe someone to another person
and then wonder how people describe you? Usually we start
with physical features before throwing in a few characteristics.
What about "Christian"? That simple descriptor has negative
connotations in a lot of minds. In Acts, the first Christians are
described as full of joy and the Holy Spirit. The two go hand in
hand. To be full of true joy, you must be full of the Holy Spirit.
You choose to value God's presence in daily life. Joy is not
circumstance based; it's an inner confidence in the sovereign
control of Christ.

What defines you? Circumstances? Do waves and crashing
waters shape you like a canyon void? Or is the Holy Spirit
shaping you into fullness: a pillar of strength and a beacon for
your family and community?

**God, I don't want to be crashed around by the waves.
Define and mold me with your Spirit.
Open my eyes to whatever changes I need to make,
and let your life live in me.**

February 6

LOVE IS A MARATHON

Dear children, let us not love with words
or speech but with actions and truth.
1 JOHN 3:18 NIV

Hollywood's portrayal of romance can be a dangerous trap for relationships. True love is far from mushy, sweeping moments and more like a grueling race. Look around you. Marriages flounder, friendships crack, and parents are cut off from their children. Those who once professed love loudly now say, "I just don't love you anymore."

Love is a marathon. It has exhilarating moments, like a runner at the starting gate, full of expectation. It's in the middle—when muscles burn, sweat pours, and it isn't fun anymore—when you find real love. Real love is a choice of forward motion and daily momentum. It's not the frosting on the cake; it's the necessary ingredient that might not taste good alone.

God, thank you for the people you
have placed in my life. Help me to love well,
to love long, and to be loyal to those around me.

February 7

RESTORED

The LORD is my shepherd; I shall not want.
He makes me lie down in green pastures.
He leads me beside still waters.
He restores my soul.
He leads me in the path of righteousness for his name sake.

PSALM 23:1-3 ESV

Find a verse in the Bible where it says you have to say yes to one more project, you need to hustle, pull yourself up by the bootstraps, or just get over it. You're not going to find them, because God is not a taskmaster. He's not demanding, and if you think he is, you may be disguising your own demands in what you think is the voice of God.

What God does ask of you is this—take a Sabbath, once a week. Lie down in a beautiful, nourishing surrounding. Put down that burden; it's too heavy. Do less. Be restored, deeply and inwardly. Performance-driven lies, fueled by the enemy, drive us into the ground. God wants you in green grass, reflected in a still lake, with golden light on your face. Don't view the fruit of the Spirit as another task. Rest in the gentle nature of your Father, and let him restore everything you need for Spirit-filled living.

Lord, take my to-do lists and my tasks. Let me know what's from you and what I am putting on myself. Lead me to your Sabbath of still waters and green pastures that I may rest in you.

February 8

LET JESUS LEAD THE WAY

"To him the gatekeeper opens. The sheep hear his voice,
and he calls his own sheep by name and leads them out.
When he has brought out all his own, he goes before them,
and the sheep follow him, for they know his voice."

JOHN 10:3-4 ESV

In your town, you know the roads. You are familiar with your surroundings and know how to drive in rain or snow. A route you drive often is so familiar that you can predict every bump. When you are in strange territory, it is raining, and one headlight is out, anxiety and fear creep in. GPS can help with this, sure, but often satellite connection fails us. Our life journeys can feel the same way—dark, lonely, and uncertain.

The beauty of today's verse is that no road is untraveled, because Jesus has gone before you. He knows every scenario that is hurtling your way. You can live in peace with this promise. In fact, you are not even the one driving! When you surrender your life to God, the Holy Spirit guides you, and Jesus goes ahead of you. Your path is made straight and bright. If you ever feel life is a dark, unfamiliar street, stop driving, pull over, and let the one who has gone before you gently lead.

Jesus, thank you for going before me and knowing
the right path for me. Lead me in your will.

February 9

FELLOW PILGRIMS

Keep on loving one another as brothers and sisters.
Do not forget to show hospitality to strangers, for by so doing
some people have shown hospitality to angels without knowing it.
HEBREWS 13:1-2 NIV

Sometimes, the hardest person to love is the person sitting next to you in the pew. Fellow Christians have special exhortation from the apostles to show love to one another, for it is by this that we witness to unbelievers. Members of the body of Christ are strangers to this world, pilgrims journeying to our true kingdom. To show love and hospitality to your fellow Christian is to overlook theological differences and work together for the cause of Christ. As long as the cross of Christ is preached, different methods of worship and preaching are permitted.

Treat your fellow Christians with respect and humility, knowing that their salvation is more important than personal pride. Handle each other gently, and act in accordance with the Spirit. Today, take time to pray for the person in the pew. Maybe next time you are at church, invite a fellow believer over for lunch. Let gentleness bring unity to the body of Christ.

Help me, Father, to see your children the way
you see them. Bring unity to the body of believers,
and use me to fill the church with love.

February 10

DEAL KINDLY

You empower me for victory with your wrap-around presence.
Your power within makes me strong to subdue,
and by stooping down in gentleness
you strengthened me and made me great!
PSALM 18:35 TPT

God has dealt kindly with you. Do you believe this, or did your heart scoff at that sentence? If you scoffed, perhaps you immediately listed times when you thought God wasn't kind at all. A spouse with cancer. A wayward son. A backstabbing friend. A sour business deal. You got the short end of the stick, and you don't appreciate it.

We can't write about each trial every person faces. However, when God humbled himself and took on human flesh, he was dealing kindly. When he endured suffering and sin with you in mind, he was dealing kindly. When he gave you the Holy Spirit, your comforter and guide, he was dealing kindly. It is by no virtue of our own that God deals kindly with us. To him, we owe every success, blessing, and breath. Don't let bitterness erase the gentleness of your spirit. Instead, dwell on all the ways that God has dealt kindly with you.

Father, you are kind, loving, and good.
Help me to notice all the ways you have
blessed me with your kindness.

February 11

ONLINE JUDGMENT

"Look at the proud! They trust in themselves, and their lives are crooked. But the righteous will live by their faithfulness to God."
HABAKKUK 2:4 NLT

Social media. It's so easy to scroll and compare, compare, compare. We take our lives and measure them against the picturesque moments on our screens. We see the lives of nonbelievers and wonder why we aren't as successful, attractive, or liked. Look past the filters and hashtags. When you talk to them, you might find their true fruit in broken relationships, pain, torn families, arrogance, rage, and so on. There is no set look for the life of a righteous or unrighteous person.

How do you know if you are blessed, on and offline? Jonah was a prophet that ran from God and didn't want to do his will, yet God gave him a second chance. Job seemed like he was a wretched man by outward circumstances, but God was pleased with him. Do not give in to the temptation to look to the right and to the left, making assumptions about others' standings with God. Instead, trust the calling God has placed on your life, and faithfully let him guide you.

Lord, I repent of comparing myself to everyone around me. Help me to focus on my relationship with you. Thank you for blessing me and welcoming me into your kingdom.

February 12

LIBERTY AND LOVE

I am allowed to do all things, but not all things
are good for me to do. I am allowed to do all things,
but I will not let anything make me its slave.
1 CORINTHIANS 6:12 NCV

When you repeat yourself, it's usually to drive your point home. You want to communicate with your audience that what you said needs to be remembered. In this verse, Paul isn't writing the same thing twice. He is laying out two steps for us to live by: love and liberty.

The actions in your life should be filtered through this question: *Is this loving?* When making decisions in gray areas, consider that question. Are you acting in true love for God and for your neighbor? Secondly, live by liberty. When swimming in that gray area again, the mistake we make is asking ourselves, *Should Christians watch that movie, or listen to this artist, or go to such an event?* We are asking the wrong question. We should ask, *Is this a master over me? Am I a slave to this, or am I acting in love and living in liberty?* Many things can control us. Choose with Paul to live freely in Christ.

Lord, I want to live freely in you!
Show me what holds mastery over me,
and help me to break free from bondage.

February 13

PEACE, BE STILL

He arose and rebuked the wind, and said to the sea, "Peace, be still!"
And the wind ceased and there was a great calm.

MARK 4:39 NRSV

Our lives are full of storms. Winds of circumstances outside our control, poor decisions, and relationships can toss us about on waves of change or tragedy. We can't see which direction is up, and we can't see a way out. When you're in the middle of a storm, it feels like it will never end. It seems it's getting stronger, while you're losing strength.

We serve a God who has the power to stand in the middle of the storm and say, "Peace, be still." A God who can stretch out his hand and command the highest waves and the fiercest winds. Our God always has, and always will, set all things right. Trust his power within you; it is stronger than any storm.

Heavenly Father, the stories of your miracles are displays of your power. I know you are still that awe inspiring, but sometimes I forget that you can work those same wonders for me. Thank you for being stronger than the storms I face. Help me to trust you in turbulent waters until you speak, "Peace, be still."

February 14

POWERFUL, GENTLE LOVE

Many waters cannot quench love,
neither can floods drown it.
If one offered for love
all the wealth of one's house,
it would be utterly scorned.
SONG OF SOLOMON 8:7 NRSV

We often underestimate love. We think it is a tame feeling we can conjure or suppress. Scripture tells us otherwise. Love is a force, more powerful than floods and raging waters, more valuable than all the wealth we could offer for it.

If we could comprehend the incredible power of love, we would understand how love itself compelled God to take up human form. How were we—in our imperfection, our sin, and our rebellion—worth everything God gave? We are worthy only through God, and nothing can buy, destroy, or replicate his perfect love. All we can do, in light of his powerful love, is accept it, without trying to purchase it or negate it. We can only accept it with humble thanks.

Thank you, God, for loving me enough to give up
everything. Your sacrifice shows the world that the
most powerful force in the universe is also the gentlest
and humblest. Help me to accept and rest in your love,
without trying to pay you or talk myself out of receiving
your gift.

February 15

PRAY FOR GLORY

We do not give up. Our physical body is becoming older and weaker,
but our spirit inside us is made new every day.
2 CORINTHIANS 4:16 NCV

There comes a moment when we realize that some things in life are outside of our control. Once you trip, you fall. Snow piles up, no matter how much we might desire the eighty-degree days to linger. Everyone gets old. We can mask it, hide it, or pay our way out of looking like it, but it's ultimately beyond our control.

However, you can control how you react to getting old, and this brings new energy. Perhaps age and experience give you calm during situations that shook you in your twenties. Troubles predictably come and go, but glory is eternal. You can choose how you react to the trials that come, and you can choose glory or grief. To choose glory is to choose to honor God with our actions and lives, to recognize his sovereignty and trust his wisdom. To choose grief is to wallow in self-pity, make your circumstances who you are, and refuse to move forward. Pray for glory. Glorified in Christ, we can face storms with resolve, knowing the story's end and what is to come.

God, I want to live in glory. Help me cultivate a
Christlike self-control in every situation.

February 16

PEACE AMIDST THE STRUGGLES

*"Peace I leave with you, my peace I give to you.
Not as the world gives do I give to you. Let not your
hearts be troubled, neither let them be afraid."*

JOHN 14:27 ESV

Have you experienced your name dragged in the mud? Was it public ridicule, online or in person? Have your ideas ever been mocked? Have you been betrayed by a close friend, or deserted by all at the moment you needed them the most? These are painful situations, and peace is the farthest thing from your heart.

Jesus faced all of this suffering in one overwhelming week, but he faced it with unearthly peace. It unnerved those around him, including Pontius Pilate. How amazing that this same peace is the peace he gives you! The world does not know true peace, only momentary tranquility rooted in temporary things. The peace that Jesus hands you, the peace of God, has a foundation on the fact that God redeemed you through Christ's work on the cross. This biblical peace is untouched by what happens around you; we see that in Jesus' resolve at his looming death. It is not the absence of trouble, sorrow, or danger, but a goodness of life unrelated to those things. May the peace of God rule in you, because you have peace with God.

**Thank you, God, that I have peace with you. Thank you
for dying on the cross to bring that peace. Help me to
hold your peace every day, in every situation.**

LISTEN TO GOD'S DIRECTION

Let him turn away from evil and do good;
let him seek peace and pursue it.

1 PETER 3:11 NKJV

Here you are, sitting in traffic. Who wants to? Nobody. Maybe your car is on the side of the road, one tire blown. Who has time to change a tire? Who wants to haggle with insurance and the tow truck? Nobody! Simple road analogies show us life's reality—a wide span of "road bumps" along our map of life can throw us into frustration and discord.

Jesus asks us to trust. He knows and routes the paths of our lives. A direct route does not build character and touch others, and God wants to use you in this world. Set down your agenda and look for his road map! When situations don't quite go your way, turn to peace instead of frustration. You have peace because you know that God directs our paths. This road bump is temporary, and it could lead to his work in your life. Trust that he knows the directions you need to take. Today, embrace every bump and detour, peaceful in the confidence that God wants to use you in the world. Peep through the clouds to find God's glory in the everyday moments.

God, thank you for faithfully watching over the world and all the paths in it. Give me peace in the knowledge that you are in control, and use my life to your glory.

February 18

PROCLAIM PEACE

Since we have been justified through faith, we have
peace with God through our Lord Jesus Christ.
ROMANS 5:1 NIV

How can we gain true peace? People have deceitful and restless hearts. We are full of unrighteousness; not one of us is clean. Humankind has rebelled against God since the beginning, and that rebellion stirs the pot against peace. Until every knee bows before the creator, this world will never know true peace.

Peace in our hearts begins with a peaceful foundation with our creator. No longer do we rebel for our freedom, because we have found true freedom at the foot of the cross. Many people say they wish for "world peace." As Christians, we have it! This is the gospel we have, the gospel of peace, and how blessed are the feet of those who spread it!

Take time to share peace with someone today. It can be a friend, neighbor, or someone in a coffee shop. Find confidence in the answer to one of the most sought out questions that people ask—how can we have world peace? Don't keep that answer to yourself. Joyfully shout it for all to hear!

Lord Jesus, thank you for the cross! Thank you for
your death and resurrection! I want to share this
with all around me. Soften the hearts of those
who hear, that they may hear truth.

February 19

STRENGTHENED BY TRIALS

"If anyone is to go into captivity, into captivity they will go.
If anyone is to be killed with the sword, with the sword
they will be killed." This calls for patient endurance
and faithfulness on the part of God's people.

REVELATION 13:10 NIV

This verse is borrowed, in a sense, from the Old Testament prophet Jeremiah. It was not an easy time for the Jews in Jeremiah's day, and the same is true for those who testify as followers of Christ. John doesn't ask Christians to take up swords, join political revolutions, or start a war. He asks followers to faithfully use the weapons they are equipped with, Christ's gospel and testimony, as they fight the true spiritual enemy.

Jesus' sacrifice on the cross is our steadfast power. It gives us reason and hope in a shaken, disaster-ridden world. God gives us daily opportunities to stand against evil, and it is our job to faithfully fight for him. Perhaps that fight is praying for a child who has rejected Christ, a friend living in sin, or a sickness plaguing a spouse. Through these battles, God promises sufficiency for you. He proves himself faithful over and over, nurturing our faith. Your confidence in Christ and his work on the cross will strengthen your endurance.

Lord, you are a good and faithful father to me.
Help me to stand in the gap for the weak
and innocent, bringing others closer to you.

February 20

AT ROPE'S END

This calls for patient endurance on the part of the people
of God who keep his commands and remain faithful to Jesus.
REVELATION 14:12 NIV

No one wants to be in a difficult situation, but we all
wonder what we would do if trouble came upon us or those
we love. Scenarios and responses play out in our heads. We
all hope to be a hero or the brave one. Trouble, hardship, and
persecution—even something as simple as things not going
our way—shine bright lights onto our true selves.

These things expose us, yet they also expose God, and the
lights always find him faithful. When disaster strikes, and
when the storm arises, he is found faithful. His faithfulness is a
truth you can tuck deep into your heart.

But what are you exposed to be? Do trials reveal patience
in you? Suffering can be a tool used to sanctify us. It an expose
sin and identify areas of growth. We can choose to let our
hearts be hardened by trouble, or we can remain soft, with
hearts unlocked by the work of the Holy Spirit. When you
are at the end of your rope, pray that he will soften your heart,
extend your rope, and empower you to patience by his strength.

Holy Spirit, I am at the end of my rope with
this situation. Lengthen my line! Thank you for
being faithful, that I may count on you when my
world shakes. Give me patience to wait on you.

February 21

THE LORD WHISPERS

After the earthquake, there was a fire, but the LORD was
not in the fire. After the fire, there was a quiet, gentle sound.
1 KINGS 19:12 NCV

Imagine a gentle white snow, or waves lapping up on the
shoreline. The Bible tells us that his voice is like the sound
of many waters, but our modern world is a flash bang world.
Headlines scream for us, phones buzz for attention, and there
is a constant calling to "look here!"

Do you know his voice? Can you hear it? With nature all
around us, the Lord has left us without excuse. If you're feeling
beaten and tattered, stop what you are doing.

Step outside. Seek his gentle whisper.

Think of the stillness of a first snowfall. Think of the peace
that water brings. Jesus has no need to compete with our loud
world, and he will not. He walks his own way, and that way is
one of stillness. The Father's desire is to speak to his children,
but he will not shout over the distractions that clog our hearts.
The Holy Spirit was sent to comfort and guide, but he will
not wrestle control away from what we have given precedence.
Gentleness is a surrender. May we accept the gentle, restful
ways of our God and reject the world that batters us.

Speak, Lord, I'm listening.
I'm here, quiet before you. Speak to me.

February 22

BELOVED GAZE

"I know what you do. I know about your love, your faith,
your service, and your patience. I know that you
are doing more now than you did at first."
REVELATION 2:19 NCV

Have you ever lived in a small town? The saying "everyone knows everybody" is true! Family names and reputations go a long way, for better or for worse. Some small-town citizens can feel their bad deeds follow them around, that it is hard to change in a close social circle.

For God, the universe is a small town. What is known about you before his throne?

He knows that you are clothed in righteousness and washed in the blood of the Lamb, forgiven and blameless. In Christ, you are not known as your old self, but as your new self, clean before God. Let this truth wash over you today. He has a new name for you, one that only he knows. He has prepared a place for you. All these things, let them wash over you as extravagant love! In his kingdom, you are known as beloved!

On earth, we patiently wait for Christ's return. Are you gazing back at your beloved, or have you forgotten who you are? In patience, keep your gaze remaining on Christ.

Jesus, you are beautiful and holy. Keep my eyes on yours,
and help me wait for your return with an expectant,
loving heart focused on you.

February 23

PEACEMAKER, TROUBLEMAKER

"Blessed are the peacemakers,
for they shall be called sons of God."
MATTHEW 5:9 NKJV

If you grew up with siblings, you will agree that almost every family has a peacemaker or mediator. Somewhere in the mix, one person just wants peace. Nature or nurture, if you didn't find this in your family, perhaps you see it in a friend or coworker.

What's interesting is that a true peacemaker is really a troublemaker. A true peacemaker is a person bold enough to confront issues, because true peace will not be found until problems hiding in darkness are brought to light. This is true of the gospel too. In an unashamedly sinful world, the gospel needs troublemakers, because they will have to point out sin! Our sins show us we need a savior who brings true peace. Don't regard witnessing as an always happy calling, telling people what they want to hear and handing out hugs and high fives. Being a peacemaker takes courage, because the world is naturally against you.

Blessed are you in God's kingdom. Continue to confront darkness and bring sin to light, even when the world is against you.

God, I want to be a troublemaker for you!
Use me as a bridge to bring the truth of peace
between you and those around me.

February 24

CELEBRATE GOD'S BLESSINGS

*For seven days celebrate the festival to the Lord your God
at the place the Lord will choose. For the Lord your God
will bless you in all your harvest and in all the work
of your hands, and your joy will be complete.*

DEUTERONOMY 16:15 NIV

When you hear the words *spiritual discipline*, what comes to
mind? Usual responses include prayer, fasting, and meditating
on Scripture. If someone mentioned celebrating, would you
rebuke them? Is that answer unspiritual, irreverent? Surprise—
God actually commanded us to celebrate, rejoice, and have
parties!

Joy is overflowing exaltation. When you see a beautiful
sunset, you want to grab your kids out of bed and share it with
them. When people graduate college, get married, or have a
baby, we celebrate. It is right to celebrate the goodness of the
Lord! It is an overflow of joy into the world around us. It's
okay to laugh, dance, and celebrate what God has done in our
lives. He is a good father! Gather around a campfire and sing
your lungs out. Take your partner's hands and spin around the
kitchen floor. Delight in a warm meal with true friends. These
things are pleasing to God and bring him glory.

**Thank you, God, for the abundance of blessing and joy
in our lives! We celebrate you and the wonder of who
you are. Let our rejoicing be a beacon for your glory.**

February 25

GIVE GOD AWE

So I said to the Lord God,
"You are my maker, my mediator, and my master.
Any good thing you find in me has come from you."
PSALM 16:2 TPT

Self-image is a common struggle among people of all shapes and ages. Christian circles today often push back against this thought by emphasizing how treasured and wonderful we are to the Father. While true, taking the self-worth in without any teaching on the majesty of God is like eating hot sauce while ditching a good meal. The meal is wonderful by itself, while hot sauce enhances the flavor. Hot sauce by itself is not filling or satisfying, and your stomach will not thank you.

Christian, you are beloved of God. However, God is awe-inspiring and majestic. He is creator and master of the universe, holy and righteous. We need to turn our eyes first upwards, to our heavenly Father in awe, instead of grasping inwardly for self-worth. The solution to insecurities of self is security in the proper holder, and that is in God. Lift your eyes and find the goodness in God. Self-forgetful worship is a healthy habit. Christ in us is our hope. Spend time today finding awe in God and thanking him for being who he is.

God, you are majestic and wonderful! I am in awe of you. You have created this world, created me, and apart from you I have no good thing. Blessed be your name!

February 26

CHRIST IN US

Does your life in Christ give you strength?
Does his love comfort you? Do we share together in the spirit?
Do you have mercy and kindness?

PHILIPPIANS 2:1 NCV

Are you the type of person who loves making lists and crossing out completed tasks? This is a good passage for you! Paul presents to us a spiritual check-up. Imagine you are at Dr. God's office, sick with some ailment like anxiety, boiling anger, addiction, or fear. He asks you a series of questions, as doctors do, to get past your symptoms and to the heart of the issue. If you answered no to any of the above questions, the cure is in the verse!

It is the first phrase, *life in Christ*. Christ's life, lived out through us, is the cure to lack of mercy, kindness, strength, and comfort. Notice his life is in us, not beside us. This requires death of self, letting Christ and his fruit live through us. Take a self-examination. Is living pride killing the kindness in your life? Drown it in Christ. Is it not wanting to surrender a certain want or habit? When you are not dead to self, a life of kindness cannot come alive. Today, ask Christ to live life in you and through you.

Kill me with kindness, God! May I drown my old self every day and release my life to you. I repent of holding on to pride, wants, and other weights on my heart. Make me alive in you!

February 27

BE FILLED

The Lord protects everyone who loves him,
but he will destroy the wicked.

PSALM 145:20 NCV

Love in marriage is marked by a promise; couples exchange lifelong vows at the altar. Psalm 145 is full of God's promises to us. He promises to be near to those who call, lift up those who have fallen, show goodness and compassion to all, fulfill the desires, and protect his people. He promises intimacy, protection, goodness, compassion, and fullness.

Bride of Christ, this is your heavenly groom. He desires intimacy with you. He wants to protect and shield you. He yearns to bring you back with compassion when you stray, and he seeks you out to love you. He longs to fill your life.

Are you empty? Broken? Feeling unwanted, unloved, like you will never be enough? He can banish that emptiness with his presence. What are you in need of today? The love of Christ is a full, immeasurable cup that can satisfy every need. Today, let Christ fill you and protect you. Be alone with God today, vulnerable before him, and let him fulfill you. He desires you, meditate on his love.

When I am empty, O God, fill me with your love.
Wrap me in your arms today, and let me know
how much you love me.

February 28

LEADING LIKE A MOTHER

*Even though as apostles of Christ we could have used
our authority over you. But we were very gentle with you,
like a mother caring for her little children.*

1 THESSALONIANS 2:7 NCV

Leadership is a hot-button topic today. Rows of book-shelves are dedicated to its practice. But when did you last see a leadership book that had to do with motherhood? First off, let's get one thing out of the way—we are all Christian leaders, because Christ has called us all to make disciples. So you—yes, you—are a Christian leader. How is leadership like motherhood?

Two things. Mothers create. They create space inside of themselves for new life. Christians leaders need to facilitate rebirth in Christ. The Holy Spirit is responsible for that transformation, but we are responsible for creating space where the gospel can be heard. Second, we are to be like mothers by holding people close, living in close proximity with them, nurturing them, and letting them go when they mature. That is discipleship. Christian leaders must embrace the gentle spirit of a mother who only has a few and can give fully to those she has. As a Christian leader, no matter your age or gender, how can you look more like a mother and less like a corporate CEO? Ask the Lord for changes that need to be made.

**Lord God, may I lead today like a mother, pouring your
grace and message into those around me.**

March

This is how God
showed his love toward us
in that while we were yet
sinners Christ died for us.

1 JOHN 4:9 NCV

March 1

GOD IS LOVE

Anyone who does not love does not know God
for God is love.
1 JOHN 4:8 NKJV

It is those closest to us that can hurt us the most, those who dwell under our roof, share our table, and hear our hearts. John uses the word *love* forty-four times in this book, but almost as frequent is the reference to "your brother." Your brother means any other believer, and like family, they can be the hardest to love. We expect the godless to act godless, but pain from a fellow believer cuts deep.

When we have been wronged, even after forgiveness has been sought and amends made, the enemy wants to widen that divide. Disunity in the body of believers tears holes in the body of Christ, and nothing could please Satan more. Daily, we need to pray for love for each other. Daily pray for your fellow believer's good and well-being, even when grudges and frustrations come to mind. God is love for your brother. If you don't love our brother that you can see, touch, and hear, how can you profess love for a God that you can't? God and love cannot be separated. Seek and give forgiveness today wherever it is needed.

Lord, help me to forgive and to love as you love.
Change and soften my heart towards
my brothers and sisters in Christ.

March 2

MIND GAMES

*Let the peace that Christ gives control your thinking,
because you were called together in one body to have peace.
Always be thankful.*
COLOSSIANS 3:15 NCV

Our minds can be a baseball field with baseball-like thoughts hurtling every which way. Maybe you have your mitt out, ready to catch, or maybe you get hit with a thought out of left field. Instead of allowing your thoughts to be set statements of truth, take thoughts as information, and then determine your response. Your response should be determined through this lens; earlier in Colossians, Paul says we are new creations. As new creations, we need to learn to let our thoughts be and not to let them knock us down.

In God's eyes, we are dressed in the righteousness of Christ. Is your baseball thought God-honoring? Is it a credit to you, in light of your status as a new creation? With these questions in mind, you can accept that thought as truth and act on it, or dismiss it as a part of your old, sinful nature. Do you desire peace with other Christians? Within the body of Christ, view others as new creations as well, and honor your thoughts about them to promote peace.

**Lord, help me to guard my thoughts and surround me
in truth. Lead me through sometimes muddy fields, that
I may know what is truth and what is not. Your Word
is truth, and I desire it more than anything else!**

March 3

GOD'S CONSTANCY

*May they obey you and follow you
in the pleasant paths of love and faithfulness!
For your love surround them as your truth takes them forward.*

PSALM 25:10 TPT

There is a phrase in our culture right now—*all the feels.*
Basically, it's warmth, happiness, and melancholy, a bittersweet
mix of emotion. If you just read this verse for your devotion
today, you saw only joy. "Pleasant paths of love and faithfulness" sounds like a Hallmark card! One would assume that
things are going pretty well for David. Open your Bible and
read the whole psalm. In verse 25, he states his current condition: lonely, afflicted, distressed, full of troubles. Not quite the
Hallmark card from earlier.

What the author is doing is remembering who God is
more than what situation he may be in. Circumstances ebb
and flow, but God is constant. He is constantly righteous,
constantly just, and constantly loving. This is the essence of
his being; there is nothing temporary in God. You can know
pleasant paths by knowing God. By Christ's life lived out
in you, it does not matter what your circumstances are. You
remain on paths of love, knowing God's faithfulness.

**God, my circumstances may swirl and crumble
around me, but you are faithful! Surround me in
your love, and keep my eyes lifted to you.**

TREASURE FAITHFULNESS

*I was overjoyed when some of the friends arrived
and testified to your faithfulness to the truth namely
how you walk in truth.*
3 JOHN 1:3 NRSV

Steadiness is not sexy. It is tried and true, an old family recipe or route map. It is worn from seeing the storms in life and rough from not hiding away. It fades against what is flashy and new in this world, antique wood next to new granite. It is quiet at times, loud at others, a tree with roots spread deep and wide. It often says no to a new course, confident in the path before it.

Faithfulness is not sexy. Our world lets you replace everything, from spouses to material goods, in the blink of an eye, but faithfulness is a quality treasure in the kingdom of heaven. To be faithful is to endure, a quality we see Jesus praise Christians for in Revelation. Don't be swayed by the flashy, catchy pop bang antics of the world. God's Word is true, steady, and reliable, and it can guide your every move in life. Stay close to the truth of his Word, that you may be found faithful in the final days.

Jesus, the world flashes around me—keep my eyes on you. I want to be found faithful in the end. Strengthen me with your endurance, that I may finish this race well.

March 5

BE CONFIDENT IN TRUTH

*True, some of them were unfaithful, but just because
they were unfaithful, does that mean God will be unfaithful? Of
course not! Even if everyone else is a liar, God is true.
As the Scriptures say about him, "You will be proved right
in what you say, and you will win your case in court."*

ROMANS 3:3-4 NLT

Have you ever heard someone say that they don't believe
in the church because some Christians did not meet a certain
standard? Yes, the church is to be God's light to the world, but
the church is not full of perfect people who don't sin or make
mistakes. We are all in the process of sanctification, renewed
daily in Christ. The whole message behind the fruit of the Spirit
is that it's not about us, but about Christ's life lived out in us.

Your measuring stick is Christ, and all the inches you need
have been provided through his death on the cross. Seek a
life modeled on his. Christianity does not rise or fall from
the actions of Christians. It is all based on Christ, and he has
proven true. You can rest in confidence in the work of your
Savior. There is nothing better than being confident in the
truth, and the truth is that Jesus Christ has clothed you in
righteousness. Today, tell someone else about your confidence
in God; tell others he is mighty to save.

**God, help me to share your goodness and praise your
mighty acts! Let me sing of your faithfulness and love.**

March 6

THE PEOPLE OF KINDNESS

He has told you, O man, what is good;
and what does the LORD require of you
but to do justice, and to love kindness,
and to walk humbly with your God?
MICAH 6:8 ESV

Do. Love. Walk. These are verbs, action words. Kindness is a visible fruit of the Spirit, more than a state of mind or something we keep internal; it's a response. The love that the Spirit gives us creates kindness. The Greek word used for kindness is *chréstos*, while Greek for Christ is *Christos*, very close in pronunciation and spelling. When the early church hit the scene, there are some early writings that refer to Christians as "the people of kindness."

Is that how someone would describe your congregation, as *people of kindness*? Does that phrase describe you? Think of all the early church faced in the unbelieving world, where in some cities there was maybe a hundred Christians for ten thousand people. Considering the obstacles they faced—persecution, along with diseases and famines—did they not have every excuse to be far from kind? Still, they chose to be a people of kindness. May we be known as the people of kindness as action, not afterthought.

Make my kindness active, Lord. Show me tangible ways
to share your gospel today. May I act in kindness
to all around me and bring glory to you.

March 7

WISE RESPONSES

Can you bridle your tongue when your heart is under pressure?
That's how you show that you are wise.
An understanding heart keeps you cool, calm, collected,
no matter what you are facing.
PROVERBS 17:27 TPT

Analyze Jesus and his disciples. Thomas was known for his doubting, cautious nature. At the other end of the spectrum was "act first, think later" Peter. Each disciple had his own personality. Now, think of Jesus. Doesn't the verse above describe him perfectly? When the wind swept down the mountainside and the waves roared, Jesus didn't flinch. When a demon-possessed, violent man got in his face, Jesus was calm. Jesus had self-control in tense and crazy situations because he knew who was in control. He had wisdom beyond all understanding because of his relationship with the Father.

Are you lacking in control over your reactions, words, or deeds? Take a look at your closest relationship. If it's not with God, make that change today. Pray for wisdom and an understanding heart. We want to be like Jesus, who only does what he sees the Father doing. Spend effort and time on gaining understanding from the Father, and let him teach you to be like him in the most difficult of situations.

Lord, fill me with your spirit, that I may act with self-control. When I'm facing trials and the road is rough, give me your wisdom! I want to know you.

DEMONSTRATE FAITH TO THE WORLD

Patient endurance is what you need now, so that you will continue in God's will. Then you will receive all that he has promised.
HEBREWS 10:36 NLT

Patient endurance by the saints is a common Bible occurrence. Take Joseph, who patiently endured when his family, driven by jealousy, sold him into slavery. He held on to God's promises, and he became powerful in Egypt. Hannah was barren, but she was full of patient endurance because God made her a promise, and he kept it. In Jesus, who patiently endured the cross, the most difficult and agonizing of deaths, he kept his promise to the world.

You can flourish in the fruit of the Spirit when you stay in one spot; your faith will remain shallow if you run from resistance. Maturity comes with staying as your roots grow deep into the soil of a God-honoring life. This isn't displayed in working your own power to fix the situation. Instead, it is a quiet confidence in the promises that God has given you. What does he promise for your marriage, children, best friend, neighbor, and your healing or your restoration? Write them down, post them in plain sight, and rejoice in waiting under the wings of a faithful God.

Lord, I will keep your promises before my eyes. Give me patience in knowing you are at work and in control.

March 9

DWELL ON THE GOSPEL

This is how God showed his love toward us in that
while we were yet sinners Christ died for us.
1 JOHN 4:9 NCV

Is the gospel still applicable to you? What if you have
moved into deeper theological territory? Few of us would
admit it, but we often space out when we hear Romans verses
or John 3:16 because we have heard them so often. Be encouraged to dwell on the gospel. Hear it again and again, letting it
crack away another layer of your dry soul.

God created humanity and desired a relationship with his
creation, but they disobeyed God, and that one sin changed
the world. God had a plan to redeem us, and his Son came to
be God with us. Resisting every temptation, he gave his life to
conquer death and sin, bringing us back into right relationship
with the Father. He was raised on the third day and sits at the
Father's right hand. He wants to clothe you in righteousness
and give you the place prepared for you. Through the Holy
Spirit, you are welcomed into his kingdom with open arms!
You are the lost sheep that was found! Heaven and the Father
rejoice and dance over you (Zephaniah 3:17). May you hear his
song and rest in his love.

Thank you for the beauty of the gospel, Lord. Thank you
that it ends there, and that I have nothing to prove.

March 10

THE GREATEST INVESTMENT

We also have joy with our troubles, because we know
that these troubles produce patience, and patience
produces character, and character produces hope.

ROMANS 5:3-4 NCV

Gordon B. Hinckley once said, "You will come to know that what appears today to be a sacrifice will prove instead to be the greatest investment that you will ever make." In the financial world, a risk-free investment is too good to be true. Spiritually speaking, there is such a thing. What is painful to give to God? Whatever you just can't release your grip on, go ahead and let go. You are not just giving up for the sake of giving up—you are investing. You can give confidently, knowing that God will make a greater return than you ever could.

In your hard times, he is returning to your patience. When you feel like your patience is measured small, he is returning to you character for your life! When your character is being tried, what's coming back to you is hope—beautiful, joyful, love-inspired hope, and hope in God never disappoints. Don't be like a child who has a stick and refuses to trade it in for the prize they cannot see or imagine, when a new bike is around the corner. Trust in the investment that God wants to make in you.

God, I trust you! You are good. I rest in the truth
that you have good in store for me.

March 11

SOUL SICKNESS

I know how to live on almost nothing or with everything. I have learned the secret of living in every situation, whether it is with a full stomach or empty, with plenty or little. For I can do everything through Christ who gives me strength.

PHILIPPIANS 4:12-13 NLT

Isn't today's world always crying out for more? The bottomless belly of our generation cries out for contentment and never finds it in what we already have. "Divorce him, and get someone who appreciates you." "Sell your house and get a bigger one." Change your hair, update your wardrobe, buy the latest phone, work towards that promotion, get more likes on that picture. The bottomless belly will eat and eat, but can never be filled. It brings only soul sickness.

Soul health is found in contentment in Christ. We cannot get caught on the rat wheel of more. We must learn the discipline of contentment, which is the fruit of self-control. Its roots are found in gratefulness. The more you grow in being grateful, the more you weed out desires not meant for you. Practice today by finding three things you are grateful for. Jot them down or share them with a friend. Continue this practice, until you wake up one day to discover you have been living on the other, greener side all along.

Thank you, Jesus, for these three gifts. Thank you for all the blessings you give me. Grow contentment within me, and help me to learn to love my green grass.

CURRENT KINDNESS

"Let the one who boasts boast about this:
that they have understanding to know me,
that I am the Lord, who exercises kindness, justice
and righteousness on earth, for in these I delight,"
declares the Lord.
JEREMIAH 9:24 NIV

What do you think of kindness, what comes to mind? A mother's eyes as she sacrifices her time and sleep for a sick child? A stranger stopping to help when you drop everything on the sidewalk? Free coffee in the drive-thru? Some great saint serving in a distant country, giving out water and caring for the dying?

All of those are actions. In Jeremiah, God tells us to take pride in the fact that he takes action towards us! He might not tangibly buy you a free coffee in the drive-thru lane (through he uses people who do so), but he sacrificed his beloved—his Son—for you. His love in action towards you is always current and always around you. Lift your head, receive his kindness, and then boast about him! God's kindness toward you is real, active, and beautiful. When you notice him and brag about him, it brings glory to his name and leads others to him. Today, brag on God and his ultimate kindness—the sacrifice of his Son for you and his daily kindness.

You are a good Father who continually shows kindness to me. Thank you! Open my eyes to your kindness, and help me boldly share that kindness with others.

March 13

HEALING THROUGH LOVE

Your love is so extravagant it reaches to the heavens!
Your faithfulness so astonishing it stretches to the sky!
PSALM 57:10 TPT

From age thirty to forty-two, her health was in decline. It was an embarrassing issue, one that made even the smallest tasks difficult. Hospitals, clinics, specialty doctors—all turned her away with shaking heads. She was a health anomaly, and most just told her to stop trying, because she would be this way till she died. Hospital bills stacked up next to lists of tasks she couldn't complete. Written off by friends and family, so afflicted that no one wanted to touch her, she heard his name in a crowded place one day. Pushing past everyone who rejected her, who couldn't or wouldn't help her, she reached out and caught the edge of his shirt. She lifted her head as he turned, and …

Yes, this is a modern take of Jesus and the woman with the affliction (Matthew 9). How do you picture Jesus when he asks, "Who touched me?" Is he upset? Stern? He already knew she was healed. Perhaps there was a twinkle was in his eye as he watched her express her faith. He rejoiced with her; he loved her! Beloved, Jesus is turning his face towards you today, filled with utter love. Receive it.

Lord, do you look on me with love and kindness? I often see you so harsh, even when I know your love. Change my view, and let me see your face.

March 14

UNCONTROLLABLE ASSURANCE

Righteousness and justice are the foundations of your throne;
steadfast love and faithfulness go before you.
PSALM 89:14 NRSV

Life often brings us situations we cannot control. Perhaps it is an unplanned pregnancy, or you or your partner cannot have children. A spouse gets sick, or a family member dies. In such times, we look for any tiny aspect we can control, but the situation is out of our hands.

Though most of those situations make you feel hopeless, the faithfulness of God works in the same manner. It is a force that cannot be stopped or controlled. All of his attributes—his love, justice, faithfulness, and mercy—are unstoppable forces. Instead of leaving us hopeless, this out of control feeling grounds us. We cannot control or affect how faithful God will be to his promises to free us from sin and heal us, restoring our souls. We cannot change how deeply God loves each and every one of us. When you live a life with Christ, you live in a house built of righteousness and justice, surrounded by love and faithfulness. Doesn't that sound beautiful? There may be a situation where God seems to have abandoned you. Step into his house, his presence, and remember his faithfulness.

God, rescue me! I need to know you are faithful—
I need to know you are here! Make known your
presence and speak to me today.

March 15

LIGHT AND WARMTH

*"Neither do people light a lamp and put it under a bowl.
Instead they put it on its stand, and it gives light to everyone in
the house. In the same way, let your light shine before others,
that they may see your good deeds and glorify your Father in heaven."*

MATTHEW 5:15-16 NIV

Have you ever watched the sunrise from high place as light slowly encompassed everything around you? Shadows lift and dew falls away as the powerful warmth of the sun touches every aspect of creation. Each sinner and saint, poor or rich, young or old, feels the sun when it rises day after day. And the goodness of God is like the sunrise. It's there, day after day. Steady, bright, and warm, it's the opposite of what we want when we have sinned or are living in darkness. The sun isn't waiting for you to climb out of your dark hole so it can scorch you to death. It's waiting for your face to emerge and feel its warmth in the freshness of a new day. It wants to give you life.

God is not waiting to scorch you. He wants you to have life in the sun. Then, we can be a sunrise in the lives of others, encompassing them in warmth and brightness of Jesus' love, inviting them out of the darkness and into the light.

**Thank you, God, for the faithfulness of
the sunrise every day. Let me know your
warmth and share it with others.**

FINDING LOVE

There is no fear in love; but perfect love casts out fear.
Because fear involves torment but he who fears
has not been made perfect in love.
1 John 4:18 NKJV

Ever used the phrase *worried sick*? It's true; fear knots our being, and our minds become focused to the point of torment. God's love can calm your stomach and redirect your mind. We need to abide in his love. We can accept this phrase, but how do we apply it? A young girl on a camping trip prayed for God to show her his love. That night, she found a piece of driftwood, shaped like her first initial, on the shore. The girl took it home and hung it on her wall, delighted in his love.

Look for God's love and find ways to dwell in it. Perhaps you dedicate a notebook to daily write down the ways he displays his love. You could take pictures or talk to a friend every week about God's love in your life. The spirit of fear will often attack you with fear of lack. Will God come through? Will your needs be met? Maybe your fear of hurt has manifested in a need to control everything. Trust God. He is working for you, and you can trust him to rescue you. Put your fear to rest by finding tangible ways to abide in his love today.

Lord God, free me from fear and show me your love.
Let me rest in your presence.

March 17

RESPONDING IN PEACE

Do not take revenge, my dear friends, but leave room
for God's wrath, for it is written: "It is mine to avenge;
I will repay," says the Lord.
ROMANS 12:19 NIV

Think of missionaries who have had their families murdered, yet forgave the murderer, or Holocaust survivors who have forgiven their torturers. Though these stories are powerful examples of God's forgiveness in a person's heart, sometimes they are too far removed from our situations. We can't imagine what we would do. What does daily forgiveness look like?

When a friend stabs you in the back, walk away from the urge to rant on social media. When your spouse snaps at you, don't fight for the last word. We are called to live at peace with everyone. When our pride is wounded by another's deed, only God is a competent and righteous enough judge to handle the situation. The only thing you can control is how you react, and you are called to promote peace, give forgiveness freely, and love your neighbor. God's job is to be the avenger and enforce justice. Let him do his job while you do yours, and you will be rewarded for it.

Lord, my job is peacemaker—fill me with peace. I need forgiveness to reign in my life, but I cannot forgive without your power. Root up any bitterness in my heart, and make it soft soil before you.

March 18

THE LIFEBOAT

Do not be overcome by evil, but overcome evil with good.
ROMANS 12:21 NIV

It's a cycle. You struggle and fight your way to the top of the waves, only to get pushed back under again. Sometimes you catch a break, but another pounding is on its way. It's the cycle of drowning that will lead to your death; crashed into, pushed under, fighting, bob up, relief, starting over again. Sometimes, forgiving feels like that. You think you're over it, and then something triggers the pain still there. Anger, rage, disappointment, frustration—wave after wave hits you and pushes you down. Suffocated, you can't focus on life around you.

The goodness of God is a lifeboat, and he's reaching out his hand to pull you up. He wants you on the shore, not dragged down by the inevitable evil of this world. He wants you safe in his arms, in a warm blanket by a hot fire. When you are bobbing in a situation that hurts so much you can't breathe, cry out. Ask God to pull you to shore and help you forgive, again. Pray for goodness for yourself and for your afflicter, when you can. It is rough sea, but not one you sail alone. Let him pull you into the lifeboat, time and time again.

**Father, take my hand and pull me up. I want to
be near to you. Thank you for rescuing me,
and give me the strength to keep forgiving.**

March 19

SPEAK TRUTH

Remind the believers to yield to the authority
of rulers and government leaders, to obey them, to be ready
to do good, to speak no evil about anyone, to live in peace,
and to be gentle and polite to all people.
TITUS 3:1-2 NCV

When Paul is writing this to Titus, he mentions in chapter one that the Cretans are known as lazy, gluttonous liars. Were their rulers much different? These verses easily apply to modern governments. We are quick to rant on social media and share that photo or video that states our opinion against a leader, be it satire or fact. To be gentle, polite, not speaking evil—does that describe how we interact with others?

In the workplace, how do we interact with coworkers? What do we say about our bosses? Are you on call, ready to spring into action to do good? Or are you by the water cooler, slandering and cutting down others? Are you encouraging and sharing truth and life on social media? Or are you spinning your tires in another political debate? We are not to wait until the government is godly or the person is worthy to be gentle with our words. We are called now to keep our tongues tamed. Maybe today is the time to practice more keeping our mouths shut and our keyboards still, and instead exercise obedience.

This is hard, God! Controlling my tongue is difficult.
Give me grace. Help me to stay silent and not be
counted amongst the fools. Fill me with true,
godly wisdom.

March 20

JESUS' HEARTBEAT

He tends his flock like a shepherd:
He gathers the lambs in his arms
and carries them close to his heart;
he gently leads those that have young.
ISAIAH 40:11 NIV

How do you picture Jesus? Our perceptions of God, for-mulated by the world around us, are often misleading. When you picture him healing people, perhaps his face is stern as he demands people to get up and walk. As a shepherd, maybe you picture a bored, lonely youth surrounded by dumb, filthy animals. In order to gently lead, his face needs to be full of compassion and mercy, eyes brimming with love, a smile on his lips. That is who he is.

There are three things to remember about the gentle shep-herd; he provides, he protects, and he leads. For every need you have, God will provide. He is tending to you, aware of you, and ready to meet your needs. Every time your soul feels danger, or you know your life is under attack, remember you are close to his heart—just listen for the beat. Every time you feel directionless, he is ready to lead you. His leading does not push and shove you down the road. His is a gentle hand and a knowledgeable gaze into a future unknown to you that he has walked many times over.

Jesus, thank you for going before me and leading me
so gently. I love you, Lord! Help me to listen for your
heartbeat in my life.

March 21

CULTIVATE PEACE

I am in prison because I belong to the Lord.
Therefore I urge you who have been chosen by God to
live up to the life to which God called you. Always be humble,
gentle, and patient. Accepting each other in love.
EPHESIANS 4:1-2 NCV

If Paul is in prison and he is living up to his calling, the reader needs a self-examination. Today, we are pressured to have multiple callings—to have businesses, raise children, be great spouses, volunteer, minister, and look good while doing everything! It's time to stop. The character qualities and spiritual calling that we are to aspire to don't mesh with the work that entangles us.

This world is not humble, gentle, or patient. It's self-seeking, pushy, and instant. Nothing is more emphasized in Scripture than to walk as a person who has the life of Christ inside and lives for the kingdom. We need to remember how backwards that kingdom is! It is not a do-it-all, self-achievement glory march. It's a dying to self. It's sitting in prison. It's God working and us asking how can we move in sync to his rhythm. Today, stop the hustle. Turn off the channels that are demanding that you be more, and take hold of the character calling that Christ has for you.

Lord, what is my calling? Help me to walk in that and be released from the trap of comparison. Let me walk according to your kingdom ways.

March 22

FRUIT FROM PAIN

To all who mourn in Israel,
he will give a crown of beauty for ashes,
a joyous blessing instead of mourning,
festive praise instead of despair.
In their righteousness, they will be like great oaks
that the LORD has planted for his own glory.

ISAIAH 61:3 NLT

Pain is real. Whatever grief has met you on this journey of life, it does no good to suppress that pain, run from it, or nourish it. It will overtake who you are. Trials, pain, and suffering will come; let God move mightily for good. Let the pain be soil that nourishes a life full of the fruit of the Spirit! Let God be your gardener, growing love, joy, peace, and gentleness out of unlikely situations. The Lord has planted you, hurt one, for his glory. He wants to complete his good work in you by making you a shelter for others. He will grow strong gentleness and love in you, so you can share the glory that we are not alone; we have a God who loves us deeply.

Let the grief and the pain do more than just subside over time. Use your time and pain to bring glory to God. Grow into the love of Christ and spread your roots wide, so that you may be tall to the world outside, a beacon of the hope and glory of God.

I release my pain and grief to you, God. Use it as soil in my life. I love you, I trust you, and I know you are working for good within me.

March 23

LOOK FOR BLESSINGS

Oh, how great is Your goodness,
Which You have laid up for those who fear You,
Which you have prepared for those who trust in You,
In the presence of the sons of men!
PSALM 31:19 NKJV

Nothing moves us quicker out of our worldview, swirling around the god of self, than thankfulness to the true God. We can step outside of our world and into thoughts of him, by examining the goodness he shows in the world, from big to small, A to Z. It is then that we see God touching every area of our lives. He is not boxed up in the praise of our Sunday mornings or set down at the end of our Bible reading time. He is fluid and available, large and in motion, touching, moving, and breathing into the joints and ligaments of everyday life.

It creates an outworking of goodness in our lives when we acknowledge the goodness he has bestowed on us. We are moved to compassion when we thank him for moving in compassion towards us, and gratefulness stirs our hearts until they overflow. Spend time today in gratefulness and praise. Start little, start big. It doesn't matter. Position yourself outside of your world to see God at work around you.

Thank you, Lord, for the sunrise and the beauty of the world around me. Thank you for the food you have given me, the roof over my head, and the clothes on my back. Thank you for …

March 24

TRUST THE ONE

Trust in the LORD, and do good;
Dwell in the land, and feed on His faithfulness.
PSALM 37:3 NKJV

Nothing can push us in a wrong direction faster than fear. We make hasty judgments, slam shut the doors of our hearts, and focus on surviving at all cost when fear comes into play. Our insecurities are our shaking knees as we stand on the edge of the cliff, wondering if God is there. Fear and insecurity go hand in hand; one often stems from the other.

God is calling us to trust in him, and trusting in him brings goodness. We are not trusting him if we set up all the conditions around a situation. That is only a façade of trust, and it sets us up to fail when life isn't boxed and neat. The goodness of God is not conditional to our circumstances. Sometimes trusting is being still, sometimes it is waiting for his timing, and sometimes it is jumping off the cliff. When you trust, you see that his goodness is constant. You can wave goodbye to insecurity. Today, take time in prayer to tell God about your insecurities, and look into what your fears may be. Don't try to control the outcome, and ask God to change your heart to trust in him.

I trust you, God; free me from fear. I know you have only good in store for me. Help me to walk with you.

March 25

OVERCOME TEMPTATION

If you live according to the flesh you will die; but if by the spirit you put to death the deeds of the body, you will live.
ROMANS 8:13 NKJV

After life-changing events in her marriage, a woman faced temptation like she had never faced before. She had never been tempted to cheat on her husband. In ten years, she was either pregnant or with her children. Back at work, suddenly temptation smacked her in the face. Her husband had struggled for years with pornography, and she never understood his battle until she stood on her own front. Truly, it was a battle, a struggle in her soul between the voices that screamed, *No one will know!* and the truth that, in one night, she would rip apart the fabric of everything she had worked to build in the past ten years.

In the end, she stood firm and said no, and that battle ended in the death of her flesh. Discerning between lies and truth, she recognized a battle being waged in the spiritual realm. With the Spirit, she was able to step outside of herself long enough to see these things and to ask God for help. It is possible to say no. Jesus said no in the wilderness. Step outside of your temptation and see the battle around you.

Lord, I want to die to my flesh and live for you!
I confess to you I feel weak. Help me to know and
follow truth, filled with the Spirit, so that
I make choices that honor you.

March 26

TAKE OFF THE BAND-AID

He has said to me, "My grace is sufficient for you,
for power is perfected in weakness." Most gladly, therefore,
I will rather boast about my weaknesses,
so that the power of Christ may dwell in me.

2 CORINTHIANS 12:9 NASB

You take another drink. You flirt too long. You take one
… more … step towards that temptation. You feel powerless!
Desire overrides logic and your brain, shutting out all truth. So
much of addiction is a Band-Aid over the raw areas of our life
that we don't want exposed to the sunlight. We patch and fix,
throwing on Band-Aids of alcohol, sex, food, shopping, money,
or praise. An unrelenting master, addiction drives us straight to
our graves.

Christ is asking you to expose raw areas. Bring them to light!
Nothing can hide in the darkness. He is all mighty, all powerful,
and able to fill to bursting your weakest areas with his power.
Your powerless state is all your flesh-filled self has, but when live
by the Spirit, his power is what fills you up, inside and out. Let
his life flow through you. He can break every chain, but he will
also expose those weaknesses. Gladly! Pray it out loud!

Jesus, I struggle with _____, but your power heals,
restores, and clothes my shame in
your righteousness and crowns me with your name.
Bring me to light. Expose my raw areas,
and fill me with your Spirit!

March 27

GOD-HONORING SPEECH

The prudent keep their knowledge to themselves,
but a fool's heart blurts out folly.
PROVERBS 12:23 NIV

Have you ever lost control of your mouth? We should all raise our hands; saying too much is a universal problem. Even the quietest, most introverted people would agree that they have blurted when they should have remained silent. When the words coming out of your mouth would make your mama blush (or smack you upside the head), look to your heart.

Am I spreading that rumor (or "prayer request") to promote myself? Red flag. Am I preaching or teaching because I like being patted on the back? Red flag. Do I always know the answer to others' issues, even when there might not be an issue there? Controlling red flag. Your tongue and speech, what you want to blurt out, reveal the red flags in your soul. Take it as a direction from God to work on that area of your heart as you also keep your mouth shut. That may seem like harsh advice, but a fool is a harsh title. "Out of the abundance of the heart [the] mouth speaks" (Luke 6:45 ESV). God wants to purify the wellspring inside of you, and he asks you to draw from his well of cool, fresh water.

Jesus help me to control my tongue and clean
the wellspring in my soul. Let me draw from
your well of goodness.

March 28

PATIENT WARRIOR

Do you want to be a mighty warrior?
It's better to be known as one who is patient and slow to anger.
PROVERBS 16:32 TPT

This is for the parents trying to leave a legacy. This is for those with careers looking to leave their mark. This is for your kids, who are searching for purpose. This is for young people seeking a calling. This is for the old wondering if they have made a difference.

Maybe you want to be a prayer warrior, a dinnertime warrior, a justice warrior, a love warrior. The foundation to being a fighter is your character. Anger robs us of our character. It deteriorates soul from the inside out, and without strong character, you won't stand at all. The surefire path to getting wherever it is you want is your character. Build, labor, and love on it. It will require silent tasks, daily prayers, and constant repentance, but that is what might is made of. Don't let anger and other character sins rob you of the warrior you are supposed to become. Warrior, from prayer to justice, we need you! Ask the Spirit to build a firm foundation of Christ's character in you; it will last when the battle rages.

Jesus, I want be a warrior for you. I feel the calling to rise up and fight. Create an unshakeable foundation in me, and help me to work through daily anger to build character that lasts.

March 29

PRAY AWAY APATHY

The end of all things is at hand; therefore be self-controlled
and sober minded for the sake of your prayers.
1 PETER 4:7 ESV

Apocalyptic language can frighten people, including the visions of Revelation. We try to line up current events with what we read and end up focusing more on the scary unknown and less on our Savior.

There is no need to fear the end. Before our worry runs away with us, Peter, who stood by Jesus himself and heard him preach on the end (Matthew 24) tells us to focus. He tells us to pray for moral strength, that we are not ruined by end time stresses. Peter tells us that our main concern should be spiritual apathy! Apathy is a silent killer, and it describes the state of many of our churches today. Now, that is what should frighten us.

How is your prayer life? Prayer is the fire that burns away apathy. Is it only at mealtime? We need self-control to pray, and we must pray for self-control against the temptations ahead. Instead of focusing our efforts on controlling our behavior, let us increase our prayer life, asking the Spirit to take control.

Spirit, take control of my life. Fill me up again.
Help me to exercise self-control in this world.

March 30

ADVENTURE OF LIFE

*Make it your goal to live a quiet life, minding your own business
and working with your hands, just as we instructed you before.
Then people who are not believers will respect the way you live,
and you will not need to depend on others.*

1 Thessalonians 4:11-12 NLT

We want to know our grand adventure, but we burn out
trying to match our gifts and talents with every moment.
This shames the ordinary. Living in small-town America as a
churchgoing mechanic or grocer isn't enough anymore. Hear
this: a place is only as big and exciting as God is to you. The
presence of God brings eternity to your surroundings.

Your calling is to know God and make him known, part-
nering with his work in you. When we say life is an adventure,
it is, but that adventure can be found in folded laundry, clean
kids, and a loving spouse. That adventure can be paperwork,
computers, and fluorescent lights. Bigger is not always better.
Some people are called to be pastors; all are called to share the
gospel. Some are called to serve the sick overseas; all are called
to take care of the Samaritan on the road. God wants to do
amazing things, right where you are, whether in a small town
and the inner city.

**Jesus, I'm sorry for getting caught up in my
calling rather than your presence. I am willing to
lead my quiet life anywhere. Show me how to know
you and make you known.**

March 31

DEVOTION

*Until I come, devote yourself to the public reading of Scripture,
to preaching and to teaching.*
1 TIMOTHY 4:13 NIV

Part of our role as believers is to encourage one another
with Scripture. The pages of the living Word of God are fresh
air for your spirit. You breathe in the words on the page, and
they give you nourishment. The Bible is our armor, protecting
us from the day and what it might bring, sending truth into
our hearts to equip us with tools we will need.

Not everyone has the gift of preaching and teaching, but
God gives us opportunities to share his message, which is what
we do until Jesus comes back. We spread the word about his
kingdom and the truth of who he is! Even in this busy world,
we should make time to dedicate to our study of the Word. It
takes practice and discipline to make this part of our everyday
routine, but it is so necessary to live a life for Jesus. Devotion is
a practice of self-control and brings honor to God.

**God, thank you for the tools you give me in the Bible.
Let its pages nourish my soul, and help me dedicate
time to you and your Word every day.**

April

Grace to you and peace
from God our Father and
the Lord Jesus Christ.

2 CORINTHIANS 1:2 NKJV

April 1

TEMPTATION IS POWERLESS

No temptation has overtaken you except what is common to mankind. And God is faithful; he will not let you be tempted beyond what you can bear. But when you are tempted, he will also provide a way out so that you can endure it.

1 Corinthians 10:13 NIV

There is no sin or temptation too great for God, friends. It can seem hopeless. It can feel endless when you're stuck in the middle of it. Remember that we serve a God of redemption! We serve a God who says, *Pursue me in this, and I will set you free. This is not beyond me. I am not powerless in this!*

Through the work of Jesus Christ on the cross, you are free from even the darkest sins. He can take weight you carry and toss it like a feather. Satan does not stand a chance against the creator of the universe, and God wants to free you. Look inside at what might need to be redeemed of, and ask God to help you endure temptation by your side.

God, sometimes my sin feels hopeless. Sometimes, I feel I'm the only one carrying this load. Sometimes, the temptation is too great. Remind me today, Father, that you are not beyond this. You see me, and you know my struggle and heart. I want to pursue you more than this sin. Remind me that you are here, cheering me on and redeeming my life!

April 2

PIECE BY PIECE

Do you see people skilled in their work?
They will work for kings, not for ordinary people.
PROVERBS 22:29 NCV

Building a large Lego set takes skill. You have to read the instructions, follow them exactly (even for tiny gray pieces that appear to have no purpose), patiently build layer upon layer, and have a vision for how the pieces will come together. If you put a piece in the wrong spot, take a breath, ready your teeth and nails, and pry them apart. It takes patience, endurance, and confidence. With hard work, you end up with a masterpiece.

Hard work feels good! When you put your heart and soul into something and see positive results, you feel joy in your accomplishment. The glory of hard work belongs to God. He often asks us to do things, and when we put our best effort forward, the reward is beautiful and fulfilling. Praise God for the work he gives you!

God, thank you for giving me endurance for hard work. Thank you for letting me see the value in what it means to accomplish tasks for your glory. I thank you for these opportunities, and I ask that I always keep you in the forefront of my life, whatever I'm working on.

April 3

FORTRESSES

Be my rock of refuge,
to which I can always go;
give the command to save me,
for you are my rock and my fortress. …
For you have been my hope, Sovereign Lord,
my confidence since my youth.

Psalm 71:3, 5 niv

Did you ever build a fort as a child? Perhaps it was blankets and stacked pillows in your living room, or a sheet over your bunk bed. Maybe you went bigger and a parent helped build you a tree house. If you built a fort in the woods, it was most likely made of sticks, boards, and whatever you happened to have around your house to serve as walls or the roof. When you were building, you made sure to have the basics; a solid floor, walls, and something over your head. The goal was protection and shelter.

Today, the fort we build is our relationship with our God. He is a fortress of rock, sturdy in the ground, unmoving. No one can destroy him. He is the solid ground beneath us, the walls of shelter around us, the roof that protects us. He will give us hope and confidence in his love, and he will not shake and crumble.

God, thank you for your constant protection and
support beneath me. Thank you for your never-ending
love and support. Thank you for sacrificing
yourself in your Son, because through him,
we can have this relationship.

April 4

SLOW DOWN

That you do not become sluggish, but imitate those who through faith and patience inherit the promises.
HEBREWS 6:12 NKJV

In today's culture, being busy has value. Overcommitted juggling conveys the lie that you are more important in life than others, that you are adaptable and balanced. In this rapid fire life, patience can be a difficult fruit to cultivate. Most of us are on the opposite side of sluggish—in fact, we are much too busy, and that can make us impatient. Always in a hurry, always busy, with little time, effort, or energy for the things that really matter in life. We are always on the go, and God tell us to slow down. God tells us to rest and prioritize the things of life that truly matter.

We are running a race for Christ, not for more stuff or more events. We are to be patient. Slow down. Have faith in God's promises.

Father God, help me to slow down today. Give me a patient attitude and heart towards the events weighing down my calendar. Give me wisdom on how to do the busy part of life well, without hindering the ones I love or my relationship with you.

April 5

SANCTIFICATION

Now may the God of peace himself sanctify you completely,
and may your whole spirit and soul and body
be kept blameless at the coming of our Lord Jesus Christ.
1 THESSALONIANS 5:23 ESV

There will come a day when our slates are forever wiped clean. Tears will no longer splash the table with grief, bodies will no longer be broken, hearts will no longer feel any pain, and our sinful human nature will not get in the way of a relationship with Jesus. There will come a beautiful day of redemption for the entire world, and there is a side you'll want to be on.

Get right with Jesus, friends. Commit your life to following him and communing with him, leading a life that glorifies his name. It can seem easier to do this life alone, separated from definitions of free will and sin, but this life is an eyeblink. Eternity is forever.

Jesus, I ask for your Holy Spirit to be with me today,
that I may live my life for you. In my conversations
with others, may I always give the glory to you,
and share your love with them.

April 6

PEACE WITH JESUS

*Grace to you and peace from God
our Father and the Lord Jesus Christ.*
2 CORINTHIANS 1:2 NKJV

True peace only comes from Jesus. His peace gets deep inside your heart and settles there, releasing any anxiety or fear you were carrying, any worry about what tomorrow might bring. When you live for God, you understand that his sovereignty makes worrying pointless. You are able to rest, knowing your steps are determined and your heart taken care of. It doesn't mean you get to do whatever you want and be lazy, but pursuit of a relationship with Jesus does mean freedom. He is freedom from baggage that can weigh you down and restrict you from living the life you were created to live.

God formed you with purpose, with your life in mind. Walking with Jesus allows you to live in that purpose and to pursue your mission wholeheartedly. This is his hope for us!

**God, thank you for being the perfecter of peace for me.
Thank you for purposefully creating me and giving
me a road map to follow. I ask for your help in forging
the way, that I may live that life fully. I want to release
all I carry at the foot of your cross.**

April 7

YOUR FACE

*Who have been chosen according to the foreknowledge
of God the Father, through the sanctifying work of the Spirit,
to be obedient to Jesus Christ and sprinkled with his blood:
Grace and peace be yours in abundance.*

1 PETER 1:2 NIV

Brothers and sisters, God's desire is for you to feel loved, cared for, adored, and cherished. He wants you to have peace in every situation you might face. He wants you to experience the mercy Jesus gave us with his work on the cross. This can only be accomplished in relationship with Jesus. Hear that. This peace and love can only be accomplished when you devote your life to Jesus.

There are many reasons to follow Jesus as your Lord and Savior, but peace is a big one. Life happens, relationships and plans go wrong, and we often search (and fail) to find peace in things or people. The world can give temporary peace, definitely, but then it dissipates, leaving behind an even larger hole to fill. It can only be filled by Jesus' redeeming love and saving grace.

**Jesus, I invite you into my life, today and every day.
Fill me with your Holy Spirit, and remind me of who
you are. I want you to be Lord of my life, but often
I fail. I need you to pick me back up and remind me
of the love you have for me. You died on the cross
for the world—for me. You saw my face when
you died. Thank you, Jesus.**

April 8

RICH PROMISES

Mercy, peace, and love be yours richly.
JUDE 1:2 NCV

To be rich is to have plenty, to want nothing, and to be full of all you've ever desired. This verse in Jude is powerful because God has desires for us. He does! He desires us to feel his perfect mercy, peace, and love, and to feel them all richly. Not just a little, not just a sprinkling—no, a flood of gifts, absorbed into who we are.

This is attainable through hope in Jesus. It doesn't mean we won't have hard moments, tough situations, or trying times, but Jesus has promises of redemption and mercy, peace, and love. There is the promise of true joy that comes each morning, of the purposeful path that he puts us on, and the guarantee that he will never abandon us. His desires are for us to feel these things richly, fully, and often.

**God, thank you for being a God of redemption.
Take this broken life of mine and fill it with your
mercy, peace, and love. I don't want to fill my life with
temporary riches that don't matter; I want to be full
of matters of the heart. Guide me in this journey,
Father God, to find them through your Son.**

April 9

ARE YOU TIRED?

*"I know you are enduring patiently and bearing up
for my name's sake, and you have not grown weary."*
REVELATION 2:3 ESV

Life with Jesus is the most rewarding relationship there is!
He fills our spirits with gifts only he can give. He promises us
eternal reward in heaven. His Spirit lives inside of us—what a
gift! On the flip side, following Jesus can be difficult. There is
persecution. Our hearts are constantly warring between good
and evil, as the enemy does not want you in a relationship with
Jesus. There is the sorrow that comes with loved ones who hav-
en't yet seen the light, even after years and years of prayers. The
wish to be socially and culturally normal fights with the desire
to live a radical life for Jesus.

God will not let you grow weary. He will encourage you,
uphold you, and give you more endurance than you need. If
you're feeling tired, sit in his presence. Rest a while with him.
Cast your anxieties and cares on him, and he will release you
from them.

God, thank you for your endurance. Thank you that
you won't let me grow weary in our relationship. I know
that you will give me all I need and more to make it
through all seasons of life. I want to continue to speak
your name, doing things out of love for you, and yet
I can't keep pace if I'm not walking with you.
Help me to start each day with you first!

April 10

KEEP THE FAITH

By continuing to have faith you will save your lives.
LUKE 21:19 NCV

This life goes by quickly. In the span of eternity, this life is an eyeblink and soon ends. Every thing and every person dies. We have assurance, however, in Jesus Christ that our lives will not end when everything here does. Our spirits will live forever with him in eternity if we commit our lives to him in servitude and faith.

This is not an easy task. Rewarding, yes, but often difficult in this sinful world. You may want to give up if you're off a spiritual high and not "feeling" God. You may want to follow the sin that has been tempting you. Jesus reminds us to have faith. Keep your faith. Doing so will "save your lives" and bring you into eternity with him. Stay the course, brothers and sisters, and pursue God with fearless faith.

God, I want to follow you above all else. When I feel my faith is lacking, I ask for an abundance from you. Give me faith and assurances as my king. I want to follow you, that I might live in eternity with you. Thank you, Father, for your incredible gift of eternal life!

April 11

GENERATION TO GENERATION

Teach older men to be self-controlled, serious, wise,
strong in faith, in love, and in patience.
TITUS 2:2 NCV

Have you ever had a grandparent or older friend help you through a situation? Did they give you advice or tell you a relatable story? They have experienced the life we haven't yet encountered. Each experience, shaped their hearts a little differently, filled their knowledge tanks a bit more, and gained new wisdom. Fruits of the Spirit are learned early on, but then they are nourished, pruned, and weeded inside and out. They are never perfected, but time refines and sharpens them into beauty.

Having an older person to counsel you is wise and fortunate. They have learned much over the years, and we can glean nuggets from their knowledge for situations we face. God can relay so much through his people, and we should seek counsel from the generations that have gone before us.

Father, thank you for giving me people that I can gain
wisdom from. Help me to seek them out and be bold
in my questions. Use them as vessels in my life, Lord,
and continue to refine their hearts as they grow
in relationship with you, as I do.

April 12

FAITHFUL RULES

I have chosen the way of faithfulness;
I set your rules before me.
PSALM 119:30 ESV

Faithfulness requires following rules. It means keeping promises and truths at the forefront of your mind. To be faithful means to pursue loyalty, no matter the cost. This is true of your ultimate relationship and loyalty to Jesus. Choosing to follow him means following some rules. They are laid out in the Book of Life for us to use as a road map, but it can be difficult to adhere to them. With God's grace, we have a choice to follow good and God, or the enemy and evil without him.

Studying the Bible and memorizing the rules it lays out is a strong way to remain faithful. Opening the living and active Word of God is like turning on the GPS in your car. He guides, never leading you astray, and as you follow his Word, you remain faithful in your love and relationship with him.

Jesus, I want to be faithful to you. I want to choose you, time and time again, even when I am tempted. Help me adhere to your rules, follow your guidelines, and live a life worthy of you.

April 13

BRAVE COMMANDMENT

Jonathan had David reaffirm his oath out of love for him,
because he loved him as he loved himself.

1 SAMUEL 20:17 NIV

Perhaps one of the easiest commands to understand is one of the hardest to attain: love your neighbor as yourself. Loving someone as much as you love yourself means treating them as you would treat yourself. It means taking care of them as you would take care of yourself. It requires sacrifice to put their needs above your own. Take a few minutes to think about what those sacrifices would look like in your life.

It is brave, truly brave, to love others as much as you love yourself. It takes courage, grace, understanding, and selflessness to act out this commandment as God asks us to. It is not in our nature to think of others first; it is a learned trait, one we need to prune and nurture. We will fail and stumble, and we will, undoubtedly, forget to put others first. But with God's help, we can do our best to remember and serve others in the most selfless way possible.

God, I want to love others more than I love myself. Even on my worst days, when I don't think too highly of myself, I still prioritize my needs above others. I'm a selfish human being, Father, and my flesh wants to keep living this way. By power of your Holy Spirit, rescue me and teach me the right way to love.

April 14

SHELTER AND REFUGE

But let all who take refuge in you be glad;
let them ever sing for joy.
Spread your protection over them,
that those who love your name may rejoice in you.

PSALM 5:11 NIV

Have you ever been caught in a horrible storm and needed to find shelter? As a child, maybe your parents had to pull over under a bridge to protect your car from hail. Maybe you were caught in a tornado and went down to the basement to be safe. Maybe you've been threatened by something that made you seek protection from law enforcement or a teacher you trusted. Seeking shelter is "taking refuge," and we usually remember why we needed safety. Often, that memory is embedded in our souls as a time of rescue.

God says he is our refuge in times of trial. He is our safety net, always willing to catch us and put us back down safely. He gives us shelter, yes, but he also gives protection and guidance. He is the one who saves us when we are beyond saving.

God, I praise your name today for the way you have rescued me! I rejoice and sing for the love you have for me and the protection you give me. Thank you, Father God, thank you!

April 15

CELEBRATING PROMISES

It was a time of happiness, joy, gladness,
and honor for the Jewish people.
ESTHER 8:16 NCV

Celebrations are a beautiful time in life. No matter who
or what you are celebrating, being in a room full of people
smiling and laughing together over a happy event is a good
time. You can probably envision a moment like that now: the
yummy food, the fancy attire people are wearing, the happy
noise, the beautiful toasts of honor, and the togetherness that
comes with being in one room, united, for a cause.

In this verse in Esther, the Jewish people are celebrating! It
was a great time of joy, because God's promise was delivered
to them. They could see that faithfulness and devotion to God
had allowed them to prosper, as he said they would. God's
promises are evident when we follow his commands, when we
live a life worthy of him, and when we are faithful.

God, I desire to live a life worthy of you! I want
to seek you first. I know that your promises do
come true, and I trust in them. Help me to see joy
in all you've given and entrusted to me. Let my life
be a celebratory one, Jesus, in all I do!

April 16

THE JUST GOD

It is a joy for the just to do justice,
But destruction will come to the workers of iniquity.
PROVERBS 21:15 NKJV

We don't often like to talk about the God who will come to judge. That God is all about justice and morality. We don't like to dive deep into the promise that he will make right every wrong thing done in this world, that sinners will be judged and decisions made. We don't like to talk about that God because we have minimized sin in our world.

We have made little of sin, wanting to focus on the love of God rather than that other side of him. We like fairness, we strive for equality, and we desire graciousness. The things we don't want to discuss? They don't go away just because we choose to ignore them. God will come to judge the living and the dead. It's time for a soul check. Spend some time with God and lay those sins at the foot of the cross. Repent and choose a holier life. Your God, both loving and just, will bless you for it.

God, forgive me. Forgive me for making light
of the sin in my life, stuffing it away so I don't have to
deal with it. I want to release it, repent of it, and be
forgiven. As much as you are a just God, you are loving
and desire this for me too. Help me to see
my waywardness and come back to you!

April 17

MANY REWARDS

"Rejoice in that day and leap for joy,
for surely your reward is great in heaven;
for that is what their ancestors did to the prophets."
LUKE 6:23 NRSV

There are many rewards in this life. Acknowledgment for a job well done at work. A diploma after years of school and hard work. A smile from a complete stranger after blessing them with a hot meal. An unexpected I love you from a child breaking up the mundane in your day. A salary increase to help with expenses. The joy you see in bringing people together for a common purpose. A complete healing from cancer. A positive pregnancy test.

Still, none of these can compare to the reward in heaven. They don't even scratch the surface of a life in eternity with Jesus. Yet at times, we put more work into these earthly rewards than we ever put into the greatest heavenly one. We prioritize the immediate reward here and forget about what this life is all about. Christ has done the work; remember to live in thankfulness every day.

Jesus, I want to remember that you promise a life with you if I follow you. I want to set my eyes and focus on eternity. I love this life you've given me here, Father, and I want to do this life well, but I want to make sure my priorities are with you first.

April 18

PERFECT PROSPERITY

"Peace and prosperity to you, your family,
and everything you own!"
1 Samuel 25:6 nlt

Do you know that God delights in blessing you? When he says he loves you, he is saying that as a Father to his children. Do you know, in your heart, that it is a perfect, unconditional love God loves you with? Do you know that God is for you and wants what is best for you?

He desires peace for us in everyday moments, tough moments, and mundane and static moments. He desires us to find worth and value in every aspect of our lives: in the children we are given, the roof over our heads, the things we own, and the jobs we hold. His truth, that perfect love and peace, is ours. Let us pursue him and put him first. This is our greatest blessing.

God, I know that you see me and my family.
I know that you are for me and love me unconditionally.
I know that you desire peace for my home and love
abounding for others. Let this truth seep deep down i
n me to the places that I can't quite reach on my own,
and let it settle on my heart.

April 19

LOVING HAND

But the meek shall inherit the land
and delight themselves in abundant peace.
PSALM 37:11 ESV

Our greatest peace comes from peace in and with God. The world cannot give us this peace with possessions, counseling, or relationships. Peace of mind, a supernatural peace that transcends all humanly things, can only come from God. God knows our every step, every day, and every hair on our heads. He knows the motivation in our hearts and the hard work we put into our jobs and families.

He sees you, friend, all of you, and loves you. He loves us with a special kind of love that we can't fully understand, and it is not ours to know. It is God's, for him to determine. Let us remember that God will make all good for us. He will give us plenty and not leave us in want. He will reward us with the heavenly rewards of eternity.

God, thank you for your loving hand that I can't fully comprehend. Thank you for seeing me, completely and intimately, and loving me despite my flaws. Thank you for giving me a supernatural peace amidst troubling and distracting circumstances. Continue to fill me in the way only you can.

April 20

ON OUR KNEES

Pray for the peace of Jerusalem!
"May they be secure who love you!"
PSALM 122:6 ESV

It is not easy to be at peace with the way our world is headed. Every day, shootings, drowning children, simmering wars, refugees, and other tragic events flood our screens. There are few stories of help, love, and giving. This is a world that desperately needs Jesus, a world that is failing in our humanness. Our world cannot survive without the love of God intervening, and it is painful to watch our earthly home crumble into ruin.

In these times, it is easy to feel helpless. We feel ill equipped to teach our kids, make changes, or take any action towards solution. What we can do? We can pray. We can pray for our nations, for our leaders, for our active Christian missionaries who are seeking out unreached people. We can get on our knees and pray for deliverance. This is, by far, our greatest tool; we have a God who hears our desperate prayers.

God, thank you for hearing me. Thank you for knowing my broken heart for this world and for promising redemption in the coming age. Thank you that you will make all of this right someday. Until your return, may I hold on to that glorious hope and fall on my knees in prayer.

April 21

GIFT IN THE HOLY SPIRIT

This is the One who gives his strength and might to his people.
This is the Lord giving us his kiss of peace.
PSALM 29:11 TPT

Do you know that the same Spirit that created the heavens and the earth lives inside of you? Let that sink in. The Spirit of God, who created everything and everyone, can rest in your life, giving you words and supernatural strength, power, and love. What a mind-blowing thought! Why do we have such power?

God informs us that the power of the Holy Spirit is a gift to us. He can give us supernatural strength, granting us a mighty hand to conquer anything in his name. The Spirit was given to us as a gift when Jesus was here, and now that Spirit is accessible to us all, anytime we need it. Similar to a kiss, gentle and yet powerful, this is a gift that changes the world.

God, I thank you for the gift of your Spirit.
I praise your name for the strength and peace that comes
from only you. It isn't of me, but it is for me. Your Spirit
is mine to use, and I'm forever grateful for that selfless
and powerful gift. Help me to use it in the right ways,
Father God, continually glorifying your name!

April 22

A FATHER'S TEACHING

*"All your sons will be taught of the Lord;
And the well-being of your sons will be great."*
Isaiah 54:13 NASB

We are taught certain behaviors and morals from those who raise us, the parents and parent-like figures in our lives. At some point, we start to make conclusions for ourselves, but the foundation laid early in our lives is the base upon which all other decisions are made. Sometimes those opinions and foundational values go against the desires of God, and we wrestle with that upon salvation.

God says we can be "taught of the Lord." He is above anything we've previously learned, and he can redeem any parts of our lives that need saving. He is a God of redemption and a Father that loves to reteach his children through the words in the Bible. The Bible is an exceptional tool for us to discover what God thinks, and what we think, about certain issues. Just as we were taught by an earthly father figure, God is our true and heavenly Father. All instruction should come from his Word.

**God, thank you for the guiding gift of the Bible!
Thank you that my past does not need to define
my future, and things I may have learned wrong
can be made right. Teach me your ways
as I seek you in your Word.**

April 23

REBUILT

To knowledge self-control, to self-control perseverance,
to perseverance godliness.
2 PETER 1:6 NKJV

We are works in progress. Each soul is a broken person that God is transforming from the inside out. Layer by layer, we are molded, shaped, restructured, and put back together. Our hearts are pruned as God brings them out of the dark and into the light, trimming off pieces where necessary. Our character is tested, strengthened, and preserved.

As we gain insight into the knowledge of God and who he says he is, we can add to our building supplies. We each have a little pile of tools, and we need them to survive and conquer this world in the name of Jesus. Each time we gain knowledge, we are better equipped to handle certain situations, and God adds more and more fruit to our base understanding.

God, thank you for being my master builder.
When I crumble or crack, you don't give up on me.
Give me new knowledge of you, and continue
to form and strengthen me in the toughest
of times and weakest of moments.

April 24

GIVING THE OTHER CHEEK

Or do you show contempt for the riches of his kindness,
forbearance and patience, not realizing that God's
kindness is intended to lead you to repentance?
ROMANS 2:4 NIV

You were probably taught at some point in your life that if someone wrongs you, the best way to react is to shower that person with kindness. They may have hurt you, but you do not repeat the behavior. In fact, you do the exact opposite. This methodology does not seek revenge; it shows the world a different way, one that requires loving others instead of hurting them. It would be nice to follow up with all of those people you treated kindly. Did you impact their lives? Did they pay forward how you treated them? Did they think about you when they went to hurt someone else, changing their minds because of your example?

God constantly showers the world with kindness. All of the good we have is from him, and he wants us to fall to our knees in reverence and awe of him, understanding we can't do anything without him. Today, remember that all the goodness in life has a maker, a designer who has chosen it all for us, and he desires us to pour it out to others.

God, I want to remember your kindness when
I'm blessed by something or someone. Even when others
hurt me, make your love the focus of my mind and heart,
that I may share it with them.

April 25

KINDNESS IN TROUBLE

On the way, Naomi said to her two daughters-in-law, "Go back to your mothers' homes. And may the LORD reward you for your kindness to your husbands and to me." … "The LORD bless you, my daughter!" Boaz exclaimed. "You are showing even more family loyalty now than you did before, for you have not gone after a younger man, whether rich or poor."

RUTH 1:8; 3:10 NLT

If you have time, take a moment to read Naomi's story in Ruth. After moving to a foreign country, her two sons die, and her daughters-in-law remain with her, showing great loyalty and kindness to her in her grief. She urges them to go back to their mothers' homes. Not only that, she sends them off with a blessing from the Lord! Later, Boaz recognizes that kindness in Ruth, Naomi's daughter-in-law, and both women are blessed for their kindness in trouble.

May we all be quick to show such kindness when we can't see clearly in our grief. May we put ourselves in others' shoes, viewing the situation from eyes other than our own. May we bless others in the name of Jesus and send them on their way if that is in their best interest.

God, thank you for examples like Naomi in the Bible. I want to put others before myself and seek to understand their perspectives before jumping to my own conclusions. Above all else, I want to show kindness, Lord, in love for you.

April 26

OUR GREAT COMMISSION

Solomon answered,
"You have been very kind to my father David,
and you have made me king in his place."
2 CHRONICLES 1:8 NCV

We have a big job in the world today, a job that has been handed down generations upon generations. This task requires selfless servitude to God and an understanding what must be done to expand his kingdom. We are obligated, as believers of Christ Jesus, to carry on the good work of bringing others into the kingdom of God through a relationship in Christ Jesus. It requires a great deal of patience, love, and understanding.

We can learn from others before us. We can learn from leaders in the world today who follow Jesus. We can gain insight into how to best show the love of God to the unbelievers in the world. Through the power of the Holy Spirit, they will see the light of Jesus—the true way to everlasting life.

Father, I want to learn from others before me.
I want to soak up the knowledge of the Bible
and use that as a guide for a life worthy of following You.
There is much work to be done, and I desire
to do my part for your kingdom. Give me insight
into how I should live for you, Jesus!

April 27

CONFRONTATION

*"Behold, your servant has found favor in your sight,
and you have shown me great kindness in saving my life. But I
cannot escape to the hills, lest the disaster overtake me and I die."*
GENESIS 19:19 ESV

We are saved through faith in Christ Jesus. And we are saved by grace, from no undertaking of our own. We are not worthy of this great saving and redeeming power, but God loves us beyond comprehension. When we accept Jesus as our Lord and Savior, our slate is wiped clean. We start anew. Still, we are not perfect, and our flesh is often weak. We sometimes choose the enemy over Jesus, and continue life in an evil way.

God says that sin leads to ruin. God will make right all of the evil in this world someday, and we need to rest in Jesus alone. We must not run; we must face the enemy head on, in the name of Jesus, and fight for freedom. Fight with Christ so that sin's chains will be broken forever. Jesus promises this freedom, and so much more, in a life lived for him!

Jesus, help me confront the enemy today in
your name and tell him he is not welcome in my life.
May I not try to run but fight him with your help.
You are my Savior, Redeemer, and friend, Jesus,
and I'm grateful for the kindness and love
you show me every day, even in my sin.

April 28

FLYING IN FORMATION

Your flock found a dwelling in it;
in your goodness, O God, you provided for the needy.
PSALM 68:10 ESV

Have you ever watched geese flying through the evening light? They are always together, flying in V formation, with a leader to guide them. It really is beautiful, their ability to come together as a team to fly towards a common resting place in water or sun. The collective term for geese is *flock*—a flock of geese, flying together, for a common purpose.

Friends, this is how the body of Christ needs to fly: together, united, and with a goal in mind. Providing meals to the homeless, helping orphans and the elderly, sharing the gospel with unbelievers on the street, serving others in your congregation, sending a word of encouragement to someone, and showing kindness and love through the power of the Holy Spirit—there are countless tasks. We can do some on our own, but together, with Jesus at the head, we can do immeasurably more.

Jesus, I am so grateful to be a part of your family! I want to serve, selflessly and graciously, everyone I encounter in my day on your behalf. Help me to see your children as you do and bless them through my words and actions.

April 29

REARVIEW MIRROR

"And now arise, O Lord God, and go to your resting place,
you and the ark of your might.
Let your priests, O Lord God, be clothed with salvation,
and let your saints rejoice in your goodness."

2 Chronicles 6:41 esv

We have a faithful and true Father. The God we serve created us from ash and built us with intention. You were no accident, child of God; you were not created out of convenience or misunderstanding. You were created in love, and God wants to save your life through his Son, Jesus Christ.

Jesus was the ultimate sacrifice from God—himself. He came to live a perfect life and die in our place. God's greatest desire is that your old life be in your rearview mirror. The path you were walking on is now behind you, and before you is a life lived in communion with him. You are clothed in salvation and righteousness through Christ's blood on the cross. Wear it in humility, thankfulness, and kindness.

Jesus, thank you for sacrificing yourself on the cross
so I could be free. Thank you for giving me clean robes
to wear, an anointing from you that I don't take lightly.
Give me eyes to see what you have ahead for me,
God, that I may I never look back.

April 30

FAITHFUL COMPANION

And the heavens will praise Your wonders, O LORD;
Your faithfulness also in the assembly of the saints.
PSALM 89:5 NKJV

Have you ever had a dog? A dog that follows you around wherever you go and whines when you head for the door without her? A dog that jumps up and down in excitement when your key turns in the lock because he knows you're home and staying put? A dog that is so loyal, you know she would do anything to protect you?

God jumps in excitement when you spend time with him. God sings along with you when he hears your voice praising his name! God cries when you walk away from him and rejoices when you come crawling back, broken and ashamed. He picks you up off the floor and wipes your eyes and slate clean. He whispers words of love and forgiveness into your heart and tells you that you are loved, cherished, beautifully made, and purposefully formed. Take comfort in his faithfulness today.

God, you are faithful, loving, and true.
Your admiration of me is unfathomable, and I'm not
worthy of this love. Thank you that, through your loving
eyes, you deem me worthy of your love. I'm so grateful
for your faithfulness, God; help me spend
my life following you.

May

"Blessed are the gentle,
for they shall inherit
the earth."

MATTHEW 5:5 NASB

May 1

FAITHFUL REWARD

*"The LORD rewards everyone for their righteousness
and faithfulness. The LORD delivered you into my hands today,
but I would not lay a hand on the LORD's anointed."*
1 SAMUEL 26:23 NIV

In 1 Samuel 26, David, future king of Israel, is running
for his life from King Saul. When God gives David the upper
hand, he does not kill Saul; instead, he trusts that the Lord,
who anointed Saul to be King before David, would work out
the situation for his good.

Following Jesus is grueling work. It is beautiful, too, but
convictions of the heart, persecution from loved ones or friends,
and misunderstanding make it difficult to remain pure in a
sinful world. Remember the joy that is yours when you pursue
Jesus and follow his lead! When you're holding on to him in
the middle of a crisis, remember the good he has promised you.
This is only the beginning! The eternal reward is coming soon.
Your reward in heaven is filled with more than you can comprehend. Do not grow weary; rest in Jesus, trust him, and watch as
he rewards you for your faithful devotion to him.

**God, I want to remain faithful to you even when it's
difficult. I want to press in instead of lean away, trusting
in your eternal reward promised to me. Remind me that
my faithful devotion to you is necessary and purposeful.
I love you, Lord!**

May 2

BAD HABITS

And the Lord's servant must not be quarrelsome but kind to everyone, able to teach, patiently enduring evil, correcting his opponents with gentleness. God may perhaps grant them repentance leading to a knowledge of the truth.
2 TIMOTHY 2:24-25 ESV

Breaking a habit can test our patience. It could be a habit that you've had since a kid, and you realized how much it was affecting you as an adult. As you've been doing it for years, it can take years to break. It may be a disease like alcoholism or an eating disorder that has controlled your life for far too long, and you want to be freed from it. The enemy can take small and large habits or diseases and use them to negatively affect our lives.

We need to be patient in enduring and overcoming the enemy as we strive to destroy evil work in our lives. We certainly can't do it alone; we need Jesus to come in and radically break our bonds. As our redeemer, he wants us to see the truth of how our habits affect us and how the enemy has used them to derail us.

Jesus, help me to see the truth of this bad power over my life. I want to be patient in my understanding of how this has affected me and gentle in my recovery. I ask in your name, Jesus, that you take this from me, and redeem all areas of my life.

May 3

INCREASED CAPACITY

Not given to drunkenness, not violent but gentle,
not quarrelsome, not a lover of money.
1 TIMOTHY 3:3 NIV

We've all been there. Someone said or did something at just the wrong moment and it takes everything in you not to snap. You want to lash out in anger, say something hurtful back, or do something cruel, just to see them in pain. Sometimes, it is truly only by the grace of God that you don't. In our human-ness, we sometimes don't have the capacity to stop ourselves, but God always does.

We can ask for God to give us a greater capacity for his goodness. We can pray to him to increase our gentleness, to give us an abundance of patience and understanding. We should not give in to the temptations of this world, instead focusing on his fruit and the nourishment of our spirits.

God, I can think of someone right now that I have held a grudge against. I've wanted to say something hurtful to someone, and there are situations I can't let go. I release them to you, Jesus. I let go of any anger I'm harboring, looking instead towards your truth and love. Lord, please increase my capacity for all your good gifts.

May 4

TWO KINDS OF LAW

Gentleness, self-control.
There is no law that says these things are wrong.

GALATIANS 5:23 NCV

All our lives, the law is our abiding government. The law tells us what is right and wrong. The law is a moral compass to use in gray and confusing situations. For an unbeliever, these national and global laws are the only rules to follow, the one gauge for living an upheld life. But for the believer, there is government law and another, higher law—the law of God. The spiritual, good, biblical law God he wrote for us. This is the law we as believers are to abide in and many of our fruits are perfectly agreeable to the law of God, goodness and self-control being two of them.

If you are practicing goodness and self-control hand in hand, you won't stray far from an upheld life lived for God. God is delighted when we work with what he has given us— our gifts and the fruits of the Spirit—for his glory.

God, I want to be a fruitful servant for you!
I want to follow the principles you have laid out for me,
seeking goodness and self-control in all areas of my life.
I can't do this in my human flesh, and yet you
hold me close. Keep me in line, Jesus, through
your love and words from the Spirit.

May 5

WORDS AND DEEDS

Now may our Lord Jesus Christ himself and God our Father,
who loved us and by his grace gave us eternal comfort
and a wonderful hope, comfort you and strengthen you
in every good thing you do and say.
2 THESSALONIANS 2:16-17 NLT

Our words can have a big impact. What we say matters. How we live our life is telling of who we live for. Still, our words and deeds often fail us. There are many situations we face where we can't find the words. We aren't sure exactly what to say. We know that nothing we do will help, so we feel helpless and unworthy. What can we do?

We can pray. We can ask for the Holy Spirit to intervene on our behalf and give us words and action. He is eternally comforting, supernaturally hopeful, and he can bring strength when all human strength fails. God wants us to speak goodness and mercy, bringing hope to the lost and broken. Often, it is not within our reach to know how to do that, but God knows. Rest in that truth. Trust his words through the Holy Spirit, and know your goodness comes from him.

God, I'm not worthy to be delivering your messages, but people here need you. I want to be a vessel for you to use, however you see fit. Guide me in my conversations, give me the words I need, and help me pursue the lost with goodness and faith.

May 6

INHERITANCE

"Blessed are the gentle,
for they shall inherit the earth."
MATTHEW 5:5 NASB

God supplies all of our needs. He gives us life, breath, and blessing upon blessing upon blessing. He wants his children to inherit the earth in gentleness and love, not with bitterness or judgment. Leave the judging to God. We are to be gentle in our love to others, in our grace to unbelievers, and in our daily interactions with everyone we encounter.

He blesses us on earth today in countless ways, and we also know we have a spiritual inheritance with him as our Savior. We also know what is to come—an eternal inheritance reserved for those who love Jesus and follow him. What a beautiful gift from God!

God, let me be gentle in showing your love to all people. Soften my attitude, any judgments I may have, and any self-righteousness on my part. Give me ears to hear and eyes to see your children the way you do. I want to love wholeheartedly through your Spirit and help others inherit the kingdom with you in eternity!

May 7

LOVE WELL

With all humility and gentleness, with patience,
bearing with one another in love.
EPHESIANS 4:2 ESV

Did you ever have a super sweet teacher growing up? You knew that you could do no wrong, and if you did, you'd get a gentle and loving reminder of how to act instead of making the choice you just did. She radiated kindness and became an important part of your childhood because of the way she lovingly helped shape you. Even now, you may think back on her and feel the corners of your mouth going up into a smile—she evokes that much emotion in you.

This is how we ought to behave towards our brothers and sisters. We are all seen as equal in the eyes of God, and yet we sometimes think of ourselves as better than the next person. God loves us equally and unconditionally, and he wants us to love one another with gentle and humble spirits, patient as our neighbors work through whatever they may be going through. He tells us to love; love one another well.

God, I want to be a light for those stuck in the dark.
I want to show them that a life with you with you allows
us to act differently, in humility and gentleness, no
matter what we are facing. I want to love my brothers
and sisters well; please help me achieve that goal.

May 8

AT THE TABLE

Rather, he must be hospitable, one who loves what is good,
who is self-controlled, upright, holy and disciplined.
TITUS 1:8 NIV

Wonderful love and conversation happens around the table. A delicious meal, people coming together, music on, forks and hearts ready—what a beautiful picture of fellowship! The gift of hospitality is one that can stretch you, if you're uncomfortable opening up your home. You might jump to wrong conclusions about your house being too small or untidy, your food not being interesting enough, or your kids creating the wrong ambiance for the meal.

Let that all go. Open your front door! Commune with others around a table, engaging in holy conversation that is pleasing to the Lord, eating food graciously gifted to you from the Father, and open your heart to the people seated around your table, countertop, or porch. There is always room at the table for Jesus to be present in your home.

Jesus, I want to be disciplined in my learning and growing of my gifts, and that includes hospitality. I want to give all in my pursuit of your children's hearts as you use me in their lives. Help me to shed any insecurities I have and invite some people over in love. Give me grace, Father, for myself and my home.

May 9

CALLED TO LEAD

Therefore an overseer must be above reproach,
the husband of one wife, sober-minded, self-controlled,
respectable, hospitable, able to teach.
1 TIMOTHY 3:2 ESV

Being a leader in the Christian faith is a big job. It requires devotion, sacrifice, and strict guidelines. This doesn't mean just pastors, deacons, or elder boards; this is for anyone who is seen as an example to follow in the Christian faith. This could be parents to children, a friend to another friend, or a coach to a team. This is anyone who wants to abide in the love of God and maintain his guiding principles while teaching others about his love. Surprise—we are all Christian leaders in this secular world!

The greatest part about this life of service is that God doesn't let you walk it alone. He doesn't abandon you and leave you to figure it out. He gives you the fruits of the Spirit to bring nourishment and richness to your work. He gives you nurturing, growing gifts to lean on, wherever you feel called to go in his name.

God, I can't teach or lead on my own. I don't want to,
because I know I'm not qualified. I can't do this
without you, and I ask that you give me the tools I need
to shape my life into one that leads unbelievers to you.
I want to be a vessel for you, Jesus, and I need
your strength and guidance.

May 10

YOU ARE WORTHY

I am unworthy of all the lovingkindness and of all the faithfulness
which You have shown to Your servant; for with my staff only
I crossed this Jordan, and now I have become two companies.
GENESIS 32:10 NASB

In our human brokenness, we are not worthy of God's love and devotion, but he claims us as we are. He knows each of our names. He tells us we are loved and cherished, despite our human weaknesses and propensity to sin. His love is unconditional, his grace overflowing. If you're feeling unworthy, remember God doesn't require much—just you.

He is faithful in his promises to you as his son or daughter, and his desires for his children are boundless. He will never stop loving you and cheering you on. His loyalty to you is perfect and relentless. You are his forever and ever. He has parted seas, burned bushes, and sacrificed his only Son out of love for his people. He has done them for you.

God, remind me of my worthiness in you. I want to see myself through your eyes as Father and creator. Encourage me in my walk with you, despite my great flaws. It is so easy to get lost in the busyness of today and think you're not present as you were in the Old Testament, but you are here. You are always available through the power of your Holy Spirit and Jesus' work on the cross. Do not my faithfulness to you waver, God!

May 11

HOW WOULD JESUS LOVE?

I led them with cords of human kindness,
with ties of love. To them I was like one who lifts
a little child to the cheek, and I bent down to feed them.

HOSEA 11:4 NIV

Jesus Christ loves all little children! This can be a difficult to remember when we see videos of starving kids all over the world, bombs going off, buildings collapsing on nine-month-old babies, or parents losing children to cancer. There is so much hurt and sorrow in the world that we lose sight of the Jesus who walked on this earth, blessing children, walking and playing with them, feeding and clothing them, and ultimately sacrificing himself so that those children, and all of us, could walk in freedom.

At the core of Christianity is kindness and love, and these principles should continue to be the focal point. We don't have all the answers; we aren't meant to. God will answer them all on the last day. But for now, with what we have, we should love wholeheartedly and without restraint. We should shower people with kindness and love, without judgment. There will be a time and place for that, but we learned to love from Jesus, and his love is limitless.

Jesus, I want to follow your example and truly love others, especially those that are more difficult to love. Give me the strength and willingness to walk with them, eat with them, and help them if they need it, just as you would have done, Lord. You are my role model, and I'm so grateful for your teaching!

May 12

LEGACIES

God can point to us in all future ages as examples of the
incredible wealth of his grace and kindness toward us,
as shown in all he has done for us who are united with Christ Jesus.
EPHESIANS 2:7 NLT

Everyone leaves some sort of legacy for someone. It may be a grandparent passing down the family farm to their grandchildren, a mom giving her wedding dress to her daughter, or a friend blessing another friend with something meaningful. Whatever it is, it leaves a special impression on the receiver, and it's treasured. Jesus came as a baby, walked the earth as a sinless and perfect man, and died on the cross for our salvation. That is his legacy, his mark, and we are forever saved for it.

Our calling is to tell others about the kind and gracious love that Jesus showed when he suffered and died on the cross. We share the beauty of his resurrection and his gift of the Holy Spirit. United with Jesus, we can do the impossible, and we should shout that truth from the rooftops! Let his message be your legacy.

Jesus, today I want to remember the legacy you have
left for me—the saving grace of your work on the cross.
I desire to complete my calling and share this gift with
others, to your glory, and instill hope in the lives of
broken people. My legacy is to love you and show
that love to everyone I know.

May 13

HUMBLE ARMOR

Let the righteous strike me;
It shall be a kindness.
And let him rebuke me;
It shall be as excellent oil;
Let my head not refuse it.
PSALM 141:5 NKJV

There was once a boy who was popular in school, but he was silently insecure about himself. In order to make himself feel better, he picked on the lesser to boost his own self-esteem. He was a tornado, destroying everything in his path and leaving a trail of hurt. Such people may be harder to find as adults, but they can be found in our neighborhoods and offices.

God's answer to these people in our lives is to give them the other cheek. "If someone slaps you on one cheek, turn to them the other also. If someone takes your coat, do not withhold your shirt from them" (Luke 6:29 NIV). It is not in our human nature to allow hurt in our lives, but God knows what is going on in the other person's heart. We turn the cheek and then get on our knees to pray. We can put on the full armor of God and not be destroyed, not even frustrated, by this kind of behavior. God will protect us, and we will come out strong!

God, I want to be ready and willing to give someone my other cheek if I'm hurt, but I know this choice isn't easy. Remind me that you are forever in my corner. Remind me that this sacrifice will not be in vain, and that all good deeds are done for you.

May 14

EXAMPLES

"Please swear to me by the LORD, since I have dealt kindly with you, that you also will deal kindly with my father's household, and give me a pledge of truth."
JOSHUA 2:12 NASB

The "pay it forward" movement is a noble one. You receive or witness a kind act, and it entices you to continue that kindness and bless someone else. You do good, hoping others will follow suit. We don't always notice the little ways this happens. There is the babysitter, who cleans your floors as a favor after the kids are in bed, or the teacher who stops to give each child a hug at the end of class. The coffee barista puts a little chocolate treat on top of your cup after she sees your toddler is with you. These are little miracles born out of kindness, and we often don't notice them.

When we do notice, it blesses our lives. Our hearts fill up just a bit more, and kindness gives us a smile that lasts all day. This is how God wants us to live. Bless others in kindness and love, doing the little, and when needed, bigger things in the name of Jesus.

God, thank you for people who have blessed me in big and small ways. Every act is a gift, and you show your love and kindness through many people. I want to be an example of your love to others with kind acts and servitude. Give me these opportunities, God, and help me to pay attention.

May 15

NO MORE CHAINS

We are slaves; yet in our bondage our God has not forsaken us,
but has extended lovingkindness to us in the sight of the kings of
Persia, to give us reviving to raise up the house of our God,
to restore its ruins and to give us a wall in Judah and Jerusalem.

EZRA 9:9 NASB

The ties that we have to our own sin, and the sins of others, are often described as chains. They are tough to break, difficult to carry, heavy, burdensome, and over time rust and cause sores and bleeding. The enemy delights in our chains.

God does not abandon you. He does not forsake you. He does not let chains of sin entrap you and swallow you whole. He defeats the enemy, breaking those chains, even those generations old. "No more!" he says, and shows us his mighty power in Jesus and his work on the cross. There is so much love in our redeeming Father, so much grace when we are walking in sin. God does not want sinful chains to hold us back from living the life he designed for us. He wants us to repent and be released! Be free!

God, forgive me of my sins and the sins of my family.
These chains are too heavy for me to carry on my own.
I lay them at your nailed feet, Lord. I give them to you
and ask that you break them forever. Release me,
and do not let the enemy have power over me any longer.
In your name, I ask for freedom.

May 16

GOOD AND FAITHFUL SERVANT

Solomon answered, "You were very kind to your servant,
my father David. He obeyed you, and he was honest
and lived right. You showed great kindness to him
when you allowed his son to be king after him."

1 KINGS 3:6 NCV

Someday, we will answer to God. This is not a scare tactic; it is truth. What a beautiful sound to our ears would these words be? "Well done, good and faithful servant! You have been faithful with a few things; I will put you in charge of many things. Come and share your master's happiness!" (Matthew 25:23 NIV).

"Honest" and "living right" are compliments we want to hear, yet we can't achieve them on our own. We are sinful by nature. Sometimes, we let this deter us from living our best. We feel the odds are already stacked against us and give up far too easily. Don't let the enemy win battles; we have already won the war. Get in the Word. Spend time with God. Seek him, and he will come knocking. Ask for wisdom and he will grant it. Ask for an increase of his Spirit, and he will give it to you. His wants are generous for you, and he pursues your heart.

God, I want to hear you say, "Good and faithful servant!" I want to know that I gave it my all and sought you. There is so much temptation and evil in the world; I can't win on my own. I need you, Jesus— I need you!

May 17

GOD'S FAMILY

To godliness brotherly kindness,
and to brotherly kindness love.
2 PETER 1:7 NKJV

Everyone in our lives are our brothers and sisters. We may not be related by blood, but we are all part of God's family. We are all precious to him, uniquely created, beautifully designed, and intricately, purposefully pieced together. Our family is one another, united together under the name of Jesus Christ, and the promise we have of an eternal forever with him. God's greatest desire is to see his children united in faith in his Son, Jesus.

We have work to do. As believers, we live a different way of life, one radical with love. When others stop to wonder why we are so kind and loving, we glorify the Father. Our greatest purpose should be to shower love and kindness to our brothers and sisters so that they ask, "Where does your joy come from?" It is such a simple, beautiful concept, and one believers should constantly pursue. In Christ, let us unify this family of God's together, forever.

God, I know it pains you to see us living separately from one another and apart from you. Help me to see the everyone in my life as my brothers and sisters. I want to shower them with the supernatural love and kindness that only comes from you. I want to help expand your kingdom. Show me how, Jesus!

May 18

PERFECT FORGIVENESS

Be kind and compassionate to one another,
forgiving each other, just as in Christ God forgave you.
EPHESIANS 4:32 NIV

Showing others forgiveness is imperative to living a life with less baggage. The weight of unforgiveness and ill feelings toward others can drag you down, make you feel awful, and be a hindrance to living your best life. Jesus Christ is our perfect example of forgiveness.

When we think of the way we sin, the things we do wrong in our humanness, the reasons we are so awful to each other, remember Jesus. He did the hard work for us. He suffered torture and abuse, was yelled at and spat on, then nailed on a cross and left there to die—for you. He did this for all of us, promising us freedom through his blood. He forgives us, time and time again, when we let him and others down. We certainly can forgive others in his name.

Jesus, I praise your name for the countless times you've forgiven me as I've walked in sin. I'm so sorry for the ways I let you down when temptation gets the best of me. I thank you for thinking of me when you died on the cross, for doing the hard work for me, so I can live a life of freedom and grace. Give me wisdom and guidance about how to forgive as you do.

May 19

TODAY'S TABITHAS

Now in Joppa there was a disciple named Tabitha
(which translated in Greek is called Dorcas);
this woman was abounding with deeds of kindness
and charity which she continually did.
ACTS 9:36 NASB

You may have a Tabitha in your life, someone who goes above and beyond in most situations. Someone who doesn't just say she loves Jesus; she shows his love in how she behaves, how she speaks, and how she serves and loves others. This person in your life is a bright, shining star, and your life has been enriched because of the countless ways she has shown the love of Jesus to you. What a gift of a person!

When we continually pursue and seek Jesus, we can grow to be this person too. Our gifts may be different, and that is okay. God will use you for his glory in other ways. He doesn't put boundaries on his gifts to us, and he doesn't limit us. He wants to increase our gifts! He wants us to use them for good and bless us through them. Tabithas act out of love for Jesus, and they are rewarded! They keep giving, serving, and loving because they feel his love when they share it.

God, thank you for the Tabithas in my life, those who have blessed me by loving me well. Thank you for the opportunities to be a Tabitha to someone else. Continue to show me how to love others like you do, Jesus. I want to love in your name.

May 20

INTIMACY WITH GOD

God demonstrates His own love toward us,
in that while we were still sinners, Christ died for us.
ROMANS 5:8 NKJV

God desires intimacy with you. He fashioned you to be sustained by him, to be holy and pure, faultless and blameless, fully accepted and completely bound up in his love. Jesus' blood has washed you clean, and nothing stands between you and those benefits. When you drift, you only need to call upon him and step back into this interaction of love.

You have been chosen to enjoy increasing measures of God's favor and grace. At this moment, take time to step into greater intimacy with Jesus. Bring everything to him, exchanging stumbling points for stepping-stones. Jesus relentlessly works for your good, and you have the opportunity to accept greater measures of his unconditional, limitless love.

God, thank you for your perfect love.
Please pour it into every area of my life that is thirsty
and dry. It is my goal to woo your heart, not because
you need it, but because I need it. I want to overflow
with love for you in the way you do for me.

May 21

JOYFUL LIVING OVERFLOWS

"I have told you these things so that you will be filled with my joy.
Yes, your joy will overflow!"
JOHN 15:11 NLT

Before this verse, what had Jesus told his disciples? He told them that the key to a joy-filled life is love. If you keep God's commands and abide in his love, you will be complete in him, and your joy will be full.

This is not about racing to do good or act righteously. It does not mean that we can achieve this on our own. It does not mean that sadness or pain results from failing this command. We desperately need Christ. This is about abiding in him. Out of the overflow of being loved, we love God back, and we love others as well. In loving this way, we cover all other commands, and we are filled with joy as a result.

God, I come to you in humbleness. Will you please
journey with me into your love? I want to abide with
greater love and a purer commitment of my life to you.
Let me be your servant of love, and let me experience
your purest joys firsthand.

May 22

JESUS, NOT JUGGLING

You will keep him in perfect peace,
Whose mind is stayed on You,
Because he trusts in You.
ISAIAH 26:3 NKJV

Navigating our obligations in life is like juggling glass inside a room of bouncing rubber balls. We wear ourselves out trying to manage our own affairs while avoiding mishaps with others. What mayhem and stress! How can you succeed in such an environment? Peace seems impossible.

Jesus is the Prince of Peace, and he has all we need. In his presence, our hearts settle, and our focus switches from juggling to Jesus. We can rest when in his presence. Refreshed, we then step back into the world, still abiding in him. Carry Jesus into the world. The room of rubber balls fades away, and God takes care of the juggling through us. The first ball is always that restorative intimacy with Jesus. He adds others, important commitments. Unimportant ones vanish or reappoint themselves elsewhere as God guides us to screen what is not necessary or profitable in his plans for us. Our partnership with Jesus brings us peace, and we are blessed. Jesus is our focus, and we have always been his.

Jesus, I am formed in your image, and you are peace.
I will abide in you this day. Let us, later, pick up what
is important and let the rest be. Help me focus on our
relationship. Thank you for being my peace.

May 23

FAITH TO HOPE

If we hope for what we do not see,
we wait for it with patience.
ROMANS 8:25 ESV

Hope springboards from faith. Faith expresses confidence in the unseen truths; it is a prerequisite to all spiritual understanding. How powerful it is! Hope takes this faith and looks forward into the future, and in this we cultivate patience.

In times of need, your faith produces hope that drives you forward, patiently. You see your position more clearly through Christ's eyes as you consider his faithfulness and its impact toward your potential. You confidently expect good in your future, because you know all things will pass except faith, hope, and love. Therefore, you patiently work forward in God's plan for your life, fueled with resolve, doing what is in your hands to do.

God, you have given me ample reason to hope!
Your faith transforms my future, directing me even now.
Please help me follow you, patiently, every day.
Remind me of my blessings, that I may exalt you
and keep you in mind all day. Help me to be patient
and wait on you as you fulfill your promises to me,
revealing the glory of your goodness.

May 24

MEPHIBOSHETH

David said, "Is there still anyone left of the house of Saul, that I may show him kindness for Jonathan's sake?" … And David said to him, "Do not fear, for I will show you kindness for the sake of your father Jonathan, and I will restore to you all the land of Saul your father, and you shall eat at my table always."
2 SAMUEL 9:1, 7 ESV

After winning Israel, David wanted to show kindness to the family of the previous king. David's treatment of Mephibosheth, Jonathan's son and Saul's grandson, is a picture of Jesus bringing people into his presence and them. Jesus, like David, combs through your circumstances, identifying the means by which he can bring you into his joy.

God always blesses us as we step into his presence. He is more joyful, fun, inspiring, and engaging than anyone else. He made each of us unique, and he made us for joy. Jesus doesn't want you to wait for heaven's blessings. He wants you to experience joy now. He wants you to experience a life well-lived. Today is a day of blessing, and Jesus has invited you into it.

Jesus, I am blessed by the richness of your kindness and grace. Please enliven my heart toward your blessings. I am excited to start this new day with you. Show me your kindnesses, that I may recognize them and praise you. Show me where you have studded my life with kindnesses. They are nectar for my soul, sweet and satisfying. I bless you, Lord. Thank you for your kindness!

May 25

MILK NOURISHES ALL

Rid yourselves of all malice and all deceit, hypocrisy, envy, and slander of every kind. Like newborn babies, crave pure spiritual milk, so that by it you may grow up in your salvation, now that you have tasted that the Lord is good.

1 PETER 2:1-3 NIV

As we experience the goodness of God, we, too, want to be good. The natural response to God is to ascribe to his holiness. God's pleasure rests upon people who seek him and his will, acting for his glory. We start simply, as children or newly reborn adults, with the spiritual milk of God's word. This is like Sunday school.

From milk, we move on to confirmation class, tackling the harder concepts of Christianity. As our hearts become more tender to what pleases the Lord, we are distressed when we sadden him. We are comforted, our hearts further softened, by his loving responses. How could we resist this holy and wonderful God? No matter where you are in your spiritual journey, return to his simple promises for assurance.

God, thank you for your holiness and tender goodness. I commit my days to you, and step into your goodness by kneeling before you, arms outstretched, holding nothing back.

May 26

PROMOTED

His master said to him, "Well done, good and faithful slave.
You were faithful with a few things, I will put you in charge
of many things; enter into the joy of your master."
MATTHEW 25:23 NASB

Faithfulness brings exponential rewards in the kingdom of God. Not only do we receive the joy of obedience, but we receive more rewards from the trust God ably places upon us. All of us can look forward to the day we stand before God and, by his grace, the gates of heaven.

Here on earth, the application of that increased trust can come into our lives in the forms of greater responsibility and influence. It could look like promotions and prestige, earthly responses to the glory God has placed upon us and we have ably carried. When such earthly blessings come our way, let us accept them with humbleness and gratitude. Let us use our new gifts to further glorify our Lord, always looking ahead to the final day.

God, thank you for your faithfulness. You have
longed to give me certain gifts. Guide me through
the opportunities you present. Show me where you
want your faithfulness to make a difference in me.
I choose to accept your challenges; help me
see them through to completion.

May 27

WHERE LOVE AND GOODNESS MEET

Always be humble and gentle. Be patient with each other,
making allowance for each other's faults because of your love.
EPHESIANS 4:2 NLT

Where love and goodness meet, there is gentleness. God, the embodiment of all of and all goodness, breeds all the gentleness we need. It is contagious in the heart of a believer, inspiring tenderness toward all.

However, we are still sinful humans as well as saintly believers. Sometimes, it is hard to work up enough love and goodness for gentleness. In such situations, we can ask God for gentleness, and he will often respond by settling into our hearts his perspective on the matter. Whether it be through his Word, another believer, or in quiet darkness, he will make his gentleness known to you.

Kind and comforting Holy Spirit, train me into
gentleness. Enlighten me, that my heart may grow
more compassionate every day. I know you are steadfast;
you never leave me, even when my gentleness runs dry.
Persistently develop me, so I may treat others
with your signature gentleness as a result
of your love and goodness.

May 28

ATTRIBUTES OF GOD

But you, Lord,
are a compassionate and gracious God,
slow to anger,
abounding in love and faithfulness.

PSALM 86:15 NIV

If the Lord deserted us each time we botched it, we would all be lonely indeed. How fortunate that he is not like that! Steadfastness and dedication are in his nature. He provides avenues of intimacy for us all.

Looking back over our lives, we can pinpoint moments when the Lord placed his weighty presence, his favor, and his mercy on our lives. We receive these graces, not because we deserve them, but because God is good and willing to bless us wherever we are. It isn't that he wants us to stay in the muck. He is simply always present, and he wants to help us. This is how he grows the fruit of the Spirit in us, and it starts with self-control. To the rest of the world, this is foreign, but God will always grow his children into forms of righteousness using self-control. This fruit will reveal itself to the world in our work and homes.

God, you created me to be responsible in the world, not to give into it. Please gift me with your self-control, and teach me to walk fruitfully in it. When it is my lifestyle, I will reliably bless you and others around me.

May 29

EXTEND FORGIVENESS

"Forget about the wrong things people do to you,
and do not try to get even. Love your neighbor
as you love yourself. I am the LORD."
LEVITICUS 19:18 NCV

The injustice we feel when poorly treated is natural. However, we are not to let injustices provoke us. In fact, God's plan for dealing with injustice is to love and forgive unreservedly. This doesn't make us chew toys, at the mercy of sin's teeth. It makes us powerful.

Consider the love God has lavished upon you. Examine who he is and what he has done for you. Contemplate the high value he places upon you, even in your imperfection, and how very much he esteems and cares for you. God's love is forever, and knowing how he cares for you allows you to have a healthy perspective on what love is. It gives you power over the both the wrongs you do and those done to you.

Lord, sin is a heavy issue. You never hold it over my head when I have sin, even if I have really hurt people. Thank you for forgiving me even though I don't deserve your kindness. Help me extend forgiveness and freedom to the people in my life, cutting all the strings of conditions on my love or forgiveness. Thank you for making all of us free. Bring to my mind, Jesus, the people you want me to bless and forgive right now.

May 30

RECEIVE WISDOM

But the wisdom from above is first of all pure. It is also peace loving, gentle at all times, and willing to yield to others. It is full of mercy and the fruit of good deeds. It shows no favoritism and is always sincere. And those who are peacemakers will plant seeds of peace and reap a harvest of righteousness.

JAMES 3:17-18 NLT

Wise choices bring about peace and righteousness, along with a host of other spiritual fruit. These build trust and strength in our relationships. Spiritual fruit grows because your actions tend to the seeds of wisdom the Holy Spirit plants in your life. When God's peace is obvious in your life, your seeds of peace will grow in the soil of others' hearts. You will also grow in favor with God and man!

People enjoy the company of wise, peaceful people. They bring rest and clear minds to every situation. When considering our relationships, we must always remember that the Holy Spirit dwells within each one of us. He offers us all we need to create peaceful relationships that are worthy of the high calling God has placed on our lives.

Heavenly Father, there exists no wisdom like yours. My best plans can fall short, but yours never do. Help me live in wisdom, and give me faith to walk in your ways. Then, your peace will seep into my surroundings. I relinquish my understanding for yours. Please, let your Holy Spirit move upon me.

May 31

DRAWN CLOSE

To those who by patience in well-doing seek for glory
and honor and immortality, he will give eternal life.
ROMANS 2:7 ESV

God has power over souls, and that means nothing can take you out of his hands. Jesus gives you victory as you trust him, follow him, and stay in loving communion with him. Jesus speaks love over you, and he wants you to live in that love. You seek glory, honor, and immortality by seeking Jesus. He wants you nearer every passing day, to become closer to him than you have ever been.

In this closeness, you understand that God's nature is to give good gifts. Glory, honor, and immortality are good gifts. Patience is a good gift. Patience protects your heart as you move from glory to glory. Troubles will come. Storms destroy, nations fall, and people let us down. Patience gets us through each trial, moving us ever closer to Christ. Move in wisdom and trust your Lord by asking him for patience.

Jesus, I want everything you have for me.
Protect my heart. Draw me in. I dedicate myself to you.
Keep me in your love, and keep me focused on you.
Do your work in my life, and help me to patiently
live out your plans for me.

June

Now faith, hope, and
love abide, these three;
but the greatest
of these is love.

1 Corinthians 13:13 esv

June 1

BAPTIZED IN KINDNESS

We put no obstacle in anyone's way, so that no fault
may be found with our ministry, but as servants of God we
commend ourselves in every way: by great endurance, in afflictions,
hardships, calamities, beatings, imprisonments, riots, labors,
sleepless nights, hunger; by purity, knowledge, patience,
kindness, the Holy Spirit, genuine love.
2 CORINTHIANS 6:3-6 ESV

When we are baptized into God's family, Jesus' kindness
baptizes our hearts, and our repentance is made complete in
our changed lives. When we, in turn, show kindness to others,
walls break down, doors open, fellow believers are strengthened, and new converts enter into Christ's kindness. The cycle
goes on, and the circle ever widens.

We are the hands and feet of God. Jesus' kindness is
expressed in the members of his bride, the church. Let us be
kind to each another, as Jesus is kind. Let us share God's goodness in the world around us, wherever we go.

God, show me your kindness today. Continue to change
me from within. I want to be the difference in someone's
life. Thank you for your life, and for the opportunities
you give me to live as a baptized child of God.
Let your kindness pour from my heart.

June 2

GOD'S FINGERPRINTS

His divine power has given us everything we need
for a godly life through our knowledge of him who
called us by his own glory and goodness.
2 PETER 1:3 NIV

We are called to live in God's goodness. We add goodness to our faith, knowledge to goodness, and self-control to knowledge (1 Peter 1:5-6). Each fruit helps cultivate other fruits, and our spiritual fruit grows as we taste and see that the Lord is good. His goodness produces good things. If you dwell in goodness, you will live out that goodness; it becomes a facet of your identity. God has his fingerprints all over your life!

You are where you are today because of God and your relationship with him. How did you cultivate that relationship? By living his Word, conversing with him, and listening for his Spirit instead of talking over him. Relent to the Lord. Be intimate with Him. You will see growth of favor and goodness in your life. The wisdom and presence of God is expressed in his goodness.

God, I am ready to be with you. Express your
goodness in me. Show me who you are in your Word.
I yearn for your presence, and I will live and believe,
fully, what you say. Help me do this. I want to
always experience your goodness.

June 3

CARRIED

He passed in front of Moses, proclaiming,
"The LORD, the LORD, the compassionate and gracious God,
slow to anger, abounding in love and faithfulness, maintaining
love to thousands, and forgiving wickedness, rebellion and sin."
EXODUS 34:6-7 NIV

God carried Abram to become Abraham, Jacob to become Israel, and he will carry you to your new name in glory. That means you are in the middle: the middle of a wildly successful transformation that God has begun in you. He will not relent until you have grasped that victory for yourself.

The Lord passed before Moses on Mount Sinai, and he cried out his nature to Moses. Jesus, right now, wants to cry out who he is to you. He is faithful. He is good. He is everything you have ever needed or ever will need. Jesus is your master, your Savior, and your love. He will carry you to completion.

Thank you for your faithfulness, Lord.
Reveal yourself to me. I know that you are good, kind,
and compassionate. You are faithful; you have never
left me, and you never will. That is true of no one else.
You are the epitome of faithfulness, and you are my God.
You will see me through. Speak to me, Lord,
in the faithful way you always do. I love you.

June 4

GENTLE DISCIPLESHIP

For the love of money is a root of all sorts of evil,
and some by longing for it have wandered away from the faith
and pierced themselves with many griefs. But flee from these things,
you man of God, and pursue righteousness, godliness,
faith, love, perseverance and gentleness.
1 TIMOTHY 6:10-11 NASB

On a day of great deliverance from his enemies, David praised the Lord aloud, saying, "You have given me the shield of your salvation, and your gentleness makes me great" (2 Samuel 22:36 ASV). Greatness from gentleness? God's gentleness was a tool he used to build greatness in David's life. That doesn't mean he didn't discipline David. There were consequences for his sin. But David continued to be great because of his humble repentance and God's mercy.

You are God's tool of gentleness in this world, and in his gentleness, he makes you great. Today's verse alludes to the importance of your choice to be gentle with others. God disciplined David in gentleness, and he does it with you. Your own gentleness, as it develops, will elevate others so they have opportunities to spiritually prosper.

Holy Spirit, please teach me how discard the unworthy and pursue what really matters. Fashion within me a godly and gentle spirit. Show me where to direct this gentleness, whether toward myself or others. I wish to embody all aspects of your person. Please, make it so.

ON THE WAY TO SELF-DISCIPLINE

Gentleness, self-control; against such things there is no law.
GALATIANS 5:23 ESV

Self-control produces long-term benefits for those who have it and those around them. Still, we all experience situations where self-control slips through our fingers. The results are regrettable. We can avoid pain, misunderstanding, and anger by increasing this fruit of the Spirit. How can we grow in self-discipline?

The Bible says God has given you a spirit of self-control (2 Timothy 1:7). Yes, you already have it! With his assistance, you can continue to develop it. He will heal you when you stumble, strengthen you when discouragement strikes, and establish your new, Godly identity in your motives and actions. Instead of becoming weary at the thought of self-control, rejoice in it. This is a gift from your Lord, and each day is a brand-new day.

**God, thank you for self-control. Today, let's have fun
together, applying it and seeing what happens.
Keep me focused and eager to cultivate this fruit.
Thank you for the richness it brings, all of the
blessings it establishes and builds in my life.**

June 6

FLOURISHING LOVE

Now faith, hope, and love abide, these three;
but the greatest of these is love.
1 CORINTHIANS 13:13 ESV

Love is the only way to foster healthy growth. We know how to love because he first loved us; we respond in kind to the love we have received. When considering his love, we learn, more and more, who God is and what he has done for us. He puts a high value on us. He wholeheartedly esteems us, and cares for us deeply. This allows us to claim a healthy perspective of love.

This healthy perspective of love will not end with this world. It will continue with the saints into eternity. Invest in God's love. Make a point to understand it, live in it, and help it flourish on the earth. Let that love fuel you into sharing it, that many more people will see the greatness of God's love.

God, give me a heart for your love. Help me to see it
as the lasting investment that you have chosen to give
your people. Let me be at the heart of a great movement
that changes lives—the movement of your Son,
and the love he showed the world on the cross.

June 7

JESUS-CENTERED

You make him most blessed forever;
you make him glad with the joy of your presence.
PSALM 21:6 ESV

There is no sweeter place than the presence of Jesus. Life's trials take their proper place in the background when we rest in his embrace. Jesus is the King of Kings and Lord of Lords; he guides us in every situation, showing us which troubles to avoid and helping us withstand what must be passed through. He leads our lives well.

God's Word says we should enter his presence with thanksgiving, praise, and worship. His Word also says that in his "presence there is fullness of joy" (Psalm 16:11 ESV). This is why our cares lose their bite the moment we rest in him. If we are continually feasting upon his Word, seeking his face through thanksgiving and praise, and waiting upon him, we will never lack in regard to joy. We will ably assess life's trials from a heavenly perspective. Feast upon Jesus, so your cares cannot feast upon you.

Heavenly Father, as we travel each day together, let me always seek deeper intimacy with you, worshiping you with a heart of gratitude and a song of praise. I want to live life in a heavenly perspective and with a joy-filled heart. Give me eyes that focus on you in all situations.

June 8

EVEN WHEN MOUNTAINS FALL

*"I have told you these things, so that in me you may
have peace. In this world you will have trouble.
But take heart! I have overcome the world."*
JOHN 16:33 NIV

The world can be a distressing and disturbing place. Whether you are watching the news on TV or watching your own troubles swirl about you, we all expect inner turmoil to become a part of our lives at some point or another. When the world is shaking, it can be difficult to feel God's presence.

The good news is that Jesus isn't reasonable. He says that you will have peace in him even when turmoil shakes the foundations of your normal, even if mountains are falling into the sea (Psalm 46:2). Please know that God cares for you, and you always have inner sanctuary within him. His rest gives you peace: the peace that passes understanding and makes your circumstances cower. Keep praying, and continue to abide.

**God, you are everything I need. Give me this
space of time to rest within you, gathered into the
holy place. Reconstruct my mind-set, reform my heart,
and firmly ground me in alliance with your person
and your priorities. Thank you for being greater
than my human reason.**

June 9

GOODNESS

He said, "I will make all My goodness pass before you,
and I will proclaim the name of the LORD before you.
I will be gracious to whom I will be gracious,
and I will have compassion on whom I will have compassion."

PSALM 23:6 NASB

Two aspects of God are evident in this passage. Firstly, God has rights on his grace and compassion. He deliberately gives us gifts—in this case goodness, graciousness, and compassion. Secondly, God is willing to hold nothing back from us when he presents all of his goodness. He will bestow his nature and very person to bless us ... as much as we can handle.

If God was willing to reveal his personality, motives, and goodness to Moses, who carried his Spirit for only a season, then how much more is he willing to reveal himself to you, who holds him within your heart at all times? He is waiting for your response.

God, make me intimate with you! By the power
of your Holy Spirit, change my heart in your presence,
and open my eyes to see you clearly. I wait for you;
transform my life and take me on your holy journey.

June 10

HEARTS OF REVERENCE

In your hearts revere Christ as Lord. Always be prepared
to give an answer to everyone who asks you to give the reason
for the hope that you have. But do this with gentleness and respect.
1 PETER 3:15 NIV

Wherever we go, whatever we do, Christ is with us. It isn't impossible to spend the hours of our day in constant companionship with him. We are simply bringing our best friend alongside us through the day. Jesus is our best friend, but he isn't just keeping us company. He is keeping us, his children and people, with him through eternity.

When the one who keeps us is Jesus, we live in confident hope. At any time, you may be asked why or how you respond as you do in situations that bring others down. You aren't better than another who would make a poor choice. You are simply clothed in Christ; his loving presence is changing you. Let that humbleness make your response gentle and respectful.

God, I am not always gentle or respectful, but you dwell within me at all times. Help me cultivate a rewarding and fulfilling relationship with you—one that blesses you, me, and others as I adopt your gentleness.

June 11

FROM THE MOUNTAIN TO THE VALLEY

Beloved, if God so loved us, we also ought to love one another.
1 JOHN 4:11 ESV

While we were still sinners, Christ died for us. He lovingly leads us as he cares for our souls over mountains and valleys, in joy and sadness. His love overcomes our foibles; instead of condemning us in them, he uses them as springboards to call us further into righteousness. There no defeatism here! Jesus unlocks the greatness within each one us as he refuses to see forgiven blemishes that the world is quick to point out.

God now calls each of us to love others just as we have been loved. In response, we do love others. We overcome their foibles with love. We call them into righteousness, and we choose to see each human before us as God's object of love and a potential member of his pure, spotless bride-church.

God, your love eradicated my sins when you gave me the righteousness of Christ! If my sins and my identity are as far removed from one another as the east is from the west, then I cannot look at one and still see the other. Please transform me with this truth, conditioning my heart as I gaze upon you. Help me to follow your righteous intentions and encourage people toward you and your affections.

June 12

RELISH HIS PRESENCE

You will teach me how to live a holy life.
Being with you will fill me with joy;
at your right hand I will find pleasure forever.
PSALM 16:11 NCV

Doesn't this verse depict exactly how our relationship with Jesus works? We spend time with him, and he fills us with joy. We lay our heads on his chest, and as we listen to his heartbeat, ours beat in the same cadence and rhythm, skipping for the same pleasures. In his pleasure, we receive what we need: identity, sustenance, belonging, a way to live.

What a great God we serve! Let us relish his presence and joy. Take some extra time to pray today.

God, I think I know you pretty well, but there
is always more. Open my heart to beat with yours
today. In our quiet time, unravel the mysteries of your
enveloping joy. I want to understand you more and be
a better friend, child, and servant. Most of all,
I just want to be with you. Today, what shall I learn in
your presence? What joy and pleasure shall we share
together? I am so grateful that you love me, and I want
to love you deeply in return. I want to relish you. I want
to adore you in a way that is fitting of who you are.
I want to love you because you love me, and I want to be
with you because you fashion my heart in joy.

June 13

GOD'S PLANS BRING PEACE

"Agree with God, and be at peace;
thereby good will come to you."
JOB 22:21 ESV

Have you ever been confused about what to do when faced with a personal choice? Circumstances, logic, and perceived advantages can swirl decision-making into a confusing mess. The secret to managing the chaos is wrapped up in two truths: (1) God is kind to you, and (2) his way always brings you peace.

Whenever a decision isn't settling with you, ask Jesus to give you peace and guidance on what he would have you do. Many times, his choice will be one you didn't think of or previously discarded. When you swap over to his plan—unfavorable though it may first appear—you will have inner peace, and you will be glad for his outcomes in the long run.

God, give me the grace to agree with you
by following you in your peace. Thank you for offering
your guidance, even when it isn't what I want. I love
to spend time with you, and I know this helps me to
understand you. Thank you for your fellowship and
rest. Thank you for the peace you lead me into and the
goodness of my life as I step with you day by day.

June 14

AN EVER-FULL WELL

Preach the word; be ready in season and out of season; reprove,
rebuke, and exhort, with complete patience and teaching.
2 TIMOTHY 4:2 ESV

Patience—we all need it! Fortunately, the Holy Spirit, the third person of the Trinity, dwells within you as a believer. He is, singularly, the most patient person you have ever met. This means you always have at hand an ever-full well of patience.

Let Holy Spirit guide you in the spiritual race you are running. You will be amazed at how much stronger you are each season when you refuse anything but the victories God has ordained for you. You are his precious servant and child, and he grows you in all good fruit—including patience.

God, you are the well of life that dwells within me.
Remind me that I have all I need in you.
When times get tough, I need your fruit more than ever.
I know I can come to you and be transformed in your
presence. You are a good Dad, and your gifts are good.
Thank you for your Holy Spirit and for the kind
patience that grows in me.

June 15

THE HOLY SPIRIT KEY

As God's chosen people, holy and dearly loved,
clothe yourselves with compassion, kindness,
humility, gentleness and patience.

COLOSSIANS 3:12 NIV

Kindness is key to helping people open up to God's love and acceptance. In his kindness, God sent Jesus to show all the traits listed in today's verse. He now expresses his kindness to and through us in the person of the Holy Spirit.

Today, let Holy Spirit walk you through whatever it is that you need in the way of kindness, be it for yourself or for those around you. Be ready for a wonderful day, because this is your opportunity to be flooded with and changed by his tender and perfect kindness. He longs to take your hand and bring you along on his good intentions for your day, today and every day.

Holy Trinity, here is my hand—please, take it.
Show me your kindness, and let me feel your presence
in my life. I want to do what you want to do, whether you
are moving in or through me. Thank you. I praise you!

June 16

SATURATED WITH GOODNESS

"I will fill the soul of the priests with abundance,
And My people will be satisfied with My goodness,"
declares the Lord.
JEREMIAH 31:14 NASB

Jesus loves us with an everlasting love, continually spilling his goodness upon us. He wants us to overflow with his goodness in every aspect of our lives, and our thirst for his goodness leads us to seek him.

When you actively cooperate with Holy Spirit as he permeates your being and your life, you become increasingly hungry for him, drinking in more and more like a sponge, until you are saturated with his presence. This is when every parched area of your spirit receives the quenching rain of his presence.

You are designed to feast on the continual, daily flow of the Holy Spirit and his blessings in your life. You are designed to be satiated with God's goodness. You were meant to be satisfied.

God, satisfy my longing for you, and open me to commune with you in a deep and constant exchange. I believe you for your presence, your goodness, and your abundance. I believe you are my best friend, permeating my life in all aspects. Thank you! In humility, I place myself at your feet. Help me to delve into the intimacy you have prepared for me. May you be satisfied with me, too, my goodness and my joy.

COVENANT OF LOVE

*Know therefore that the LORD your God is God; he is the
faithful God, keeping his covenant of love to a thousand
generations of those who love him and keep his commandments.*

DEUTERONOMY 7:9 NIV

Through the blood of Christ, the faithfulness of God spans all generations and peoples, making us his righteousness and his hope of glory. He has your back! Following his will, you continually unlock this incredible mystery of faithfulness between you and Jesus, the master of your soul.

If you feel you have painted yourself into a corner, know that he not only has your back, but he knows in detail what needs to happen for you to break through. Press forward in prayer, and do not just give up or assume it is not in your hands to fix. Jesus is a masterful maker, and he uses your hands to complete his masterpiece in you. Reflect on that at the end of today's prayer.

**God, your faithfulness spans the breadth of heavens
and plumbs the depths of the seas! You are the Alpha
and the Omega, the beginning and the end! This I
hold in my hands: my faith in you. This you hold in
your hands: my life and my situation. Because nothing
escapes the grasp of your faithfulness, I rest in you,
running the race. I will give you my painted-in corners,
and I'll take your perspective and instruction.
Lord, I need your help and guidance in …**

June 18

PERSEVERE

If your boss is angry at you, don't quit!
A quiet spirit can overcome even great mistakes.
ECCLESIASTES 10:4 NLT

It is so tempting to give up when we know others are against us. It is even more tempting to quit and move on toward greener pastures when your supervisors and other authority figures are displeased with your performance levels.

Don't give up! If a soft answer turns away wrath, and the Lord is willing to help you move forward, you must also know you have the ability to give the opportunities you have one more shot. Be the steady employee who proves that fixing an issue makes a better impact on others than never having an issue. You have God's permission to excel. Jesus believes in you! He is heartily invested in your future.

God, at times I want to give up, but your Word encourages otherwise. I know you have a better perspective, and the wisdom you give comes straight from your throne room. Show me the wise choices before me, and help me to shine in my place of employment. It's often hard to keep a job, but you are wise, and I am able to be a very good employee with your guidance. I am listening, and I wait for you.

June 19

ROYAL CONTROL

To be self-controlled and pure, to be busy at home, to be kind, and to
be subject to their husbands, so that no one will malign the word
of God. Similarly, encourage the young men to be self-controlled.
TITUS 2:5-6 NIV

Home is a fortress for the heart, wellspring of growth
preserver of good morals and epicenter of family bonds that
last the lifetimes of its inhabitants. To be queen or king of a
house—whether it is a party of one or Buckingham Palace—is
vitally important.

Both husband and wife are subject to the true King, Jesus.
Everyone else in the household will follow suit after their
form; the king and queen show the kingdom how to honor the
King. The industriousness, self-control, and kindness of a godly
person is regal to behold, and it encourages like behavior from
others. Sometimes, your loudest sermons speak in the daily
actions and habits you undertake.

God, I confess I don't always do all the things this
verse encourages. I don't even try, sometimes. But you
said if I love you, I will keep your commands, and they
will not be grievous to me. Please help me, Lord.
Here I am, loving you and keeping hold of your promise
that this doesn't have to hurt. Show me how I can flow
in your love, expressing the self-control and everything
else that bubble forth from you in a healthy way.
Thank you for your love; you are my everything.

June 20

The Love Perspective

This commandment we have from Him:
that he who loves God must love his brother also.

1 JOHN 4:21 NKJV

When Jesus wiped our sins away, we no longer had to concern ourselves with the letter of the law. Jesus was perfect man and God for us, and we thank him and walk in his ways by trusting and living in communion with him.

When we live in constant communion with Jesus, we adopt his views on people, circumstances, and happiness, which lies with him. Baptized in his love, we realize we are valuable to God, and others are equally valuable. The inherent value of a person isn't based upon their actions, but upon their identity. We are humans, which means we are the only element of creation completely pressed into the mold and fashioned in the image of God.

When we love each other, we love God, and what we do to people, we do to him. It is good to treat others fairly and with love, recognizing their purpose and holding them to a standard of love and goodness. We love others because God loves us.

God, thank you for loving and valuing me. Let us—you and me, together—love people, today. Show me your perspective, and help me adopt your own ways as mine as we share life together throughout my days. You are precious to me. Help me be present and effective for people the way you would be on the earth.

June 21

RUN TO THE LORD

The humble also shall increase their joy in the LORD,
And the poor among men shall rejoice
In the Holy One of Israel.
ISAIAH 29:19 NKJV

This passage describes Jerusalem's response when God confused the plans of their besiegers. Jerusalem had sinned greatly, and in his love and concern for their current welfare and future existence, God authored their rebuke. Although painful, this rebuff ensured preservation and future blessings for Israel. We, too, share in these blessings through Jesus, our King.

God's rebuke for his people is not a casting away, but evidence of his fatherhood. If you are a child of God, you will endure discipline. You will emerge from it in a better state, even more in love with Jesus, and you will shine his glory as a result. You will, through God's address, throw off encumbrances that have prevented you from fulfilling your destiny in the kingdom of heaven. Run to Jesus in humility, and receive your reward. He is good!

Jesus, I'm running to you! I want you to be the boss, in charge of every area of my life, and I want your impact there, now. Please bring me through this. I am in your presence, ready to listen. I want to be beautifully broken, rejoicing because I came before you and honored you as true Lord. Thank you for your lordship.

June 22

FAITH AND PEACE

Those who love Your law have great peace,
And nothing causes them to stumble.
PSALM 119:165 NASB

It is so good to rest in the cradle of right living! No matter what happens around us, we have the peace of knowing we are in good standing with God, and he approves of what we have done. Even when we fall short, as humans do, we know we are still right with God, clothed in the blood of Christ.

Among all people, we who love and live in God are most blessed, no matter our current circumstances. Why? Because we are able to rest in the peace that comes from God's approval. Let us share the way of peace, so others may enter into the rest of Jesus, the Prince of Peace. Without faith, nobody can please God.

Father, as I enter your Word today, I ask you to freshly ignite my devotion to your holiness. I will cleave to your Word and live in your ways. Help me reach the lost for you, as the one who saves souls is wise. I will follow you all the days of my life. Help me, Lord Jesus. Let me dwell within the great depths of your peace.

June 23

FORGIVEN TO LOVE

For that very reason I was shown mercy so that in me,
the worst of sinners, Christ Jesus might display his immense
patience as an example for those who would believe
in him and receive eternal life.

1 TIMOTHY 1:16 NIV

He who is forgiven much, loves much! We have each had moments where we've regretted our actions or words. We, too, have felt God's love flood difficult situations and bad choices, as though we were watching him wipe our slates clean with his perfect, precious blood.

Although people don't always forgive and forget, that's exactly what Jesus does as he patiently fashions us in righteousness. Because we are forgiven, we should extend the same grace and love to others. Our patience with people releases them to powerfully change. Patience allows people to get back on track.

God, give me patience and tenderness for myself
and others. Remind me of the myriad of times you
have shown me patience, and soften my heart to extend
patience the way you do. I trust you with the outcomes,
believing that you will work things for the good.
Let me have patience as I wait for you.

June 24

SAVIOR OF THE NATIONS

Note then the kindness and the severity of God: severity toward those who have fallen, but God's kindness to you, provided you continue in his kindness. Otherwise you too will be cut off.
ROMANS 11:22 ESV

The kindness and compassion of Christ rings through this verse. The church, built in Judaism, still must rest upon faith in Christ, their Messiah, who has visited his people. Even now, Jesus awaits each one's turn in faith so he will give them his reward. Not all believers are Jewish, but through Israel came the Savior of the nations. We all have the invitation to know and remain in Jesus, and those who do will also receive his reward.

Knowing Jesus deeply cares about our intimate thoughts and heart desires should give us pause. There are unholy places in all of us. He is absolutely holy, yet he extends his eternal paradise to everyone who receives him in faith and continues to abide in him.

Jesus, Savior of the nations, thank you for including all people in your plans for salvation and eternal blessings, Jews and Gentiles alike. I am so glad you offered me your kindness. Help me to dwell in you all my days while reaching out to others who need your truth. Help me to tenderly, faithfully live out my salvation. I love you— thank you.

June 25

TEACH AND ENCOURAGE

I am fully convinced, my dear brothers and sisters,
that you are full of goodness. You know these things
so well you can teach each other all about them.

ROMANS 15:14 NLT

You have much to teach others. If the Lord is your Lord, then you are full of his goodness, and he has made you a walking epistle. As a Christian, you constantly learn and live out God's principles. We each build precept upon precept in our lives, and our understanding of the kingdom of God changes as we develop in our relationship with him.

If you have been taught something by the Lord, please share that with others, and then encourage them to share their findings with you. This is an effective way to build each other up in the faith, and it is as precious to God as it is to the body of Christ.

Jesus, I confess that I am sometimes shy about sharing how you have grown me in goodness. Help me to be an encourager and teacher for others, taking the time to listen to them do the same. You have so much to teach me through the words of others. Please help me not to forget when you want me to speak aloud what you've grown in my own heart, and when I should simply listen.

June 26

THE APPEARANCE OF FAITH

*"May the LORD now show you kindness and faithfulness,
and I too will show you the same favor
because you have done this."*

2 SAMUEL 2:6 NIV

These words were spoken by the new king, David, to the men of Jabesh Gilead after they had shown kindness toward Saul by giving him a proper burial. They knew David's reign had begun, but they chose to be faithful to their last opportunity to honor Saul. This faithfulness pleased David greatly; the king knew that a faithful heart is a trustworthy treasure.

Sometimes, faith doesn't look progressive. It isn't always expressed in the shifting of gears to keep up with change. However faith may appear, if we honor it and walk faithfully in what God has given us to tend, we will be blessed, and we will prosper in his reward.

God, thank you for your perfectly faithful nature.
Slip me into step with you, so your life and mine
look alike. I want to become your faithful servant who
honors you in what I do. Show me where this verse
applies to my life, and let me prosper, as you will it,
in actively living in sync with your good purposes.

June 27

WEAK FLESH

*He is able to deal gently with those who are ignorant
and are going astray, since he himself is subject to weakness.*

HEBREWS 5:2 NIV

Jesus understands we are weak, and he deals gently with us, because he values our fragile frames. We can feel so powerful, yet we are delicate creations. But what does Hebrews mean when it says Jesus is "subject to weakness"? Jesus, as perfect God in human flesh, cannot sin, but he can be tempted. In his time on earth, he experienced temptation as all humans do. He understands, even as he resists.

We are important to Jesus. We will always have his attention and care. Release yourself, today, and let God deal gently with you. Come to Jesus expecting his gentleness. He knows your weakness, and he will show you compassion and grace.

**Jesus, thank you for becoming flesh to resist temptation
where I cannot. I need gentleness today. Show me where
your compassionate treatment of me is growing and
healing in my life and circumstance. I'm resting in
your peace, and I covet your gentle touch.
Thank you for building this relationship with me.**

June 28

GRACED WITH DISCERNMENT

Wise words bring many benefits,
and hard work brings rewards.
PROVERBS 12:14 NLT

Sometimes, the best opportunities are simple ones. Wise speech and unrelenting effort are two examples of characteristics that shift our choices. Holding them up against our past experiences, we recognize opportunities we have taken or missed. This gives us understanding on how to choose better in the future.

How many times have the right words changed the course of your life? How many times have you pushed through to achieve a goal when you were tempted to stop short? How many times has it not worked out that way? Ponder those moments, and then take all these thoughts and hand them over to Jesus. Let Holy Spirit breathe on and in you. He will give you peace and perspective on your losses in these areas, and he will further develop you to gain more wins in the future.

Holy Spirit, you are the most successful person I know. You even raised Jesus from the grave (Romans 8:11)! You are the one who leads me into all knowledge. Let us work together, pondering what you consider success. Please put wind in my sails. Give me your perspective and wisdom, setting wise words in my mouth and strengthening me to persevere when needed. Thank you for encouraging and cultivating me.

June 29

PLANTED IN GOD'S WILL

Love never hurts a neighbor,
so loving is obeying all the law.
ROMANS 13:10 NCV

Is there a better place to plant yourself than in the center of God's will? All we need to do that is ... to love. We are all called to love. Jesus said that when we love God and our neighbors, all the law and prophets are fulfilled. This does not mean we throw the Ten Commandments out the window. Think through each of those laws. Would you lie about your neighbor or covet their belongings if you loved them? Would you put other things before God or take his name in vain if you loved him perfectly?

We can't love perfectly, but love is the perfect motivator. We can succeed and thrive as living expressions of God's love. Why? Because love does not fail. God, as love personified, will never fail you. If you want to bat 1.000 in God's will for your life, plant your thoughts and choices firmly in his love.

Heavenly Father, you are a perfect example of
unconditional, unrelenting love. Help me to love others
the way you love me. May all I do be motivated and
executed in love, so that the world may see you
clearly through me.

June 30

COMPLETED

*Those the LORD has rescued will return.
They will enter Zion with singing;
everlasting joy will crown their heads.
Gladness and joy will overtake them,
and sorrow and sighing will flee away.*

ISAIAH 51:11 NIV

Laugh until your stomach hurts! Take a dance around the kitchen! Sing in the shower! Reborn in Christ, we can be the happiest people on the earth. As a believer, this promise is for you: everlasting joy will crown your head! Gladness and joy will overtake you! Because Jesus is your strength, you can rejoice through his salvation. His strength never wavers, and neither does his righteous cloak over you.

The Lord is good. He loves you with an everlasting love, and he wants his joy to be complete in you. Through salvation, this is your promise. You may access it through Christ.

Heavenly Father, help me to understand and appreciate all I have in your salvation. Let me not take for granted what I have received from your sacrifice; instead, let me explore and revel in the joy you have set before me. Fill my heart with your joy, so I will partner with you in the eternal completion and celebration of you in me: the resurrected, eternal life.

July

They celebrate your
abundant goodness
and joyfully sing
of your righteousness.

PSALM 145:7

July 1

PRESENCE OF JESUS

*"The LORD turn his face toward you
and give you peace."*
NUMBERS 6:26 NIV

Have you ever felt alone or abandoned, left to face a challenge on your own? Jesus experienced the loss of family and companions on several occasions, but at no time was he more alone than the day he faced the cross. There, hanging to die for our sins, Jesus felt the presence of his heavenly Father escape him, and he cried out, "My God, my God, why have you forsaken me?" (Matthew 27:46).

Jesus underwent this crucifixion for you. He experienced the utter absence of peace and engulfment of loneliness so you will not have to do so. It was because of his offering that he could promise you his presence. Jesus, the Prince of Peace, will never leave you or forsake you. He is your Emmanuel: God with you, always. Jesus will always be with you, to the end of the age.

Heavenly Father, where could I go from your Spirit? Wherever I am, you are there. Bathe me in your sweet love. Wrap me in your peace. Sing your song over me. I set aside this time to abide in you. I will rest in the warmth and protection of your love. Thank you for your sacrifice and your constant presence.

July 2

POWERFUL AND SILENT

Use patience and kindness when you want to persuade leaders
and watch them change their minds right in front of you.
For your gentle wisdom will quell the strongest resistance.
PROVERBS 25:15 TPT

Patience is a powerful, silent tool for change, healing, growth, and unity. Your ability to carry this fruit in your daily life makes a difference not just for today, but for the future. Continually resting in this fruit gives you a level-headed perspective that evades others when issues get hot.

You know that when you trust Jesus, not circumstances, you are acting under the power of the Holy Spirit. Your patience is a fruit of that empowerment. With patience, you allow God's work to grow in every area you give him, be it political, spiritual, or material. In every realm of your life, you have what it takes, because you have who it takes: Jesus.

God, please give me your powerful and silent patience. Help me to trust you and plumb the depths of what patience means, and what your purposes are for it. Then, I can present a case for you to the world. I will love others and honor them in words and choices, and I will become an agent of your purposes on the earth. Help me to be your salt and light and to plant this desire in others. I choose your design for persuasion, and I trust your outcomes. Thank you for your patience with me!

July 3

RUN, DON'T WALK

"One should be kind to a fainting friend,
but you accuse me without any fear of the Almighty."
JOB 6:14 NLT

God tells us to never judge another man's servant. In this passage, Job, servant of God, asks his friends to quit assuming that he had deserved his sudden tragedy. Job's friends were later instructed to approach him for forgiveness and request his prayers for restoration with God.

How many times have we pondered a person's input into his or her own difficult situation? How many times have we bitterly regretted our circumstances, wondering if we brought it on ourselves? To regain peace and holiness, resist those tempting judgments. Run directly to Jesus for insight. He gives us hopeful, wholesome, and helpful attitudes. He tells us how to pray for people who hurt, how to support them, and how to release mercy and grace over people and situations that desperately need his helping hand—and that includes ourselves.

God, I have assumed things about people and not gone to you for instruction before praying, or helping, or forgiving. Please forgive me; none of my excuses are holy. Help me to walk away from my way and to adopt your own. I want to add grace to my life and others. Help me to aid fainting friends and to forgive those who have poorly treated my own discomfort or pain. Your blood covers all. Let me be a solution, not a source of pain.

July 4

COMFORTING RULES

Everything God created is good, and nothing is to
be rejected if it is received with thanksgiving.
1 TIMOTHY 4:4 NIV

In this passage, Paul instructs Timothy to not get hung up on a list of rules, but to rather follow God in purity and truth. What were the rules illustrated? "Do not get married," and "Eat only certain foods." Paul didn't dictate Timothy's diet or marital state. Rather, he straightforwardly pointed out that demonic influence had taken hold of Christians through their own form of Christian superstition. We too make up rules to give ourselves comfort and safety, but every rule we add to what God has declared provides a layer of distance between us and our creator.

When we follow rote rules, we stop listening to God. Every one of these deceptive layers becomes an opportunity for lies and loopholes to slip into our lives and displace the genuine article of intimacy with Jesus. He wants to have a conversation with us, not just give us a list of rules. Doesn't that seem like the real Jesus?

God, I am sorry for the extra safety measures I've incorporated into my faith instead of following you in truth. Please forgive me! Peel away the unneeded rules, showing me where you and I need to be more tender and real. Direct me, and help me to stand on your Word for verification. I want to have nothing standing between us, so we can enjoy this journey together.

July 5

PRAYER MAKES CHANGE

I prayed to the Lord my God and made confession, saying,
"Ah, Lord, great and awesome God, keeping covenant and steadfast
love with those who love you and keep your commandments,
we have sinned and done wrong, acted wickedly and rebelled,
turning aside from your commandments and ordinances."
DANIEL 9:4-5 NRSV

Even in our faithlessness, God extends his hand to lead us to the faithful way. As long as there is breath in our lungs, he offers his children a chance to come into the fire of fellowship, showing us things we do not know, and often cannot comprehend. Notice that Daniel was not praying strictly for himself, but for his nation as well. Your prayers, fervently and continually brought before God, are heard, no matter how big or small the request.

Prayers change the atmosphere of a room. They make a difference in all situations, families, politics, and very hearts of the persons for whom you pray. Ask Jesus what he wants you to pray, then listen. Your words do matter. In Jesus' presence, you will better understand the difference you make.

God, there is a lot going on in the world, and I don't think you want me to ignore it. Let's talk, today, and I will echo what you ask me to pray. I have stumbled, but you are faithful. Make me a link of grace between you and the people for whom you want me to pray.

July 6

TENDER AUTHORITY

Let your gentleness be evident to all.
The Lord is near.
PHILIPPIANS 4:5 NIV

Have you seen how differently one child can be treated by another when a parent or older sibling is present? A bullying child might speak nicely, or a shy one might have the heart to speak out. There is something about having authority nearby that makes interactions more equitable and righteous.

Jesus has made all things. He is the authority and protector of us all, and his ultimate authority is always present. When we remember Jesus is present, our hearts grow tender, and we do what makes God proud. That is what this verse is about; remember that the Lord is always near, and he cares about your interactions. He will bless your gentleness to others.

Tender and just God, give me the grace to live a holy, gentle life in your presence. Let me not get down on myself or others for their lack of gentleness, but rather focus on your heart and how I could bless it, since you are always smiling on me and waiting to bless me. Thank you for giving me an ever more tender heart. I submit myself to you, knowing you are going to gently and lovingly mold the vessel of my life.

July 7

CUT THE STATIC

We keep on praying for you, asking our God to enable you
to live a life worthy of his call. May he give you the power
to accomplish all the good things your faith prompts you to do.
2 Thessalonians 1:11 NLT

Have you ever felt your calling was too big for you? In a way, it's true. God doesn't give us goals we could accomplish without him stepping in and making things happen. Here are two ways to learn what you should do and how to actively seek God's glory in it.

First, you must live in faith. This pleases your heavenly Dad immensely! His pleasure is never diminished in any failures you might experience as you pursue him. Second, your yes to God gives you license to say no to whatever would sidetrack you from your identity or calling. In this case, self-control expresses itself in remembering your "Yes, God," and dismissing what would otherwise create white noise to muddle the sound of his voice.

God, I create a lot of static on my end of our line.
Let's sit down and discuss (me listening to you)
my identity and the plans that you have for me.
Cross off my list anything that I don't need to bother
with. Let's just focus on what is important for you
and me. I love you. Thank you for an easy,
well-fitting yoke that is suited just for me.

July 8

LOVE MOTIVATED, LOVE EXPRESSED

We have come to know and have believed
the love which God has for us. God is love, and the one
who abides in love abides in God, and God abides in him.

1 JOHN 4:16 NASB

God is love, and everything he does is motivated by love. Everything he says is love, audible and resonating in our beings. Jesus' nail-torn hands leave fingerprints of love upon everything he touches. The Holy Spirit breathes love into every Christian's heart. Everything God makes is love expressed.

You are God's "I love you" to the earth. When you know this, you dwell in God's love, feasting upon it and flooding the people around you. Everything you do becomes a grace-covered echo of God's beautiful intentions for the world. You are the living, breathing yes and amen of Christ's love.

God, I would like to spend time in your presence, basking in your love. Transform me so that I will be the echo of love the earth desperately longs to hear, even those ears that do not appear to care. Let my echo bring more of your children home to your love.

July 9

APPLES OF GOLD, SETTINGS
OF SILVER

A man has joy in an apt answer,
And how delightful is a timely word!

PROVERBS 15:23 NASB

"Apples of gold in settings of silver" is a biblical metaphor that describes the use of the correct words for the circumstance. In tough circumstances, be they daily or catastrophic, everyone needs encouragement. If you have been on the receiving end of a timely word of encouragement, you understand the instant rush of joy, hope, and comfort.

Not all encouragement is created equal; the best comes from our Lord. We can place apples of gold in settings of silver when we ask the Lord for the words to say to encourage others. Sometimes, God is saying something very special to a person, something you might not think of on your own. When you feel God's prompting to speak, don't hold back. You will become the vehicle for a timely blessing.

Heavenly Father, thank you for your timely words that bring hope and joy. Help me be in tune with your Holy Spirit so that my golden words can carry silver hope and joy to others. Thank you! Through your Word and your church, your refreshing encouragement blesses your children.

July 10

RECREATED

But now in Christ Jesus you who once were far away have been
brought near by the blood of Christ. For he himself is our peace,
who has made the two groups one and has destroyed the barrier, the
dividing wall of hostility, by setting aside in his flesh the law with
its commands and regulations. His purpose was to create in himself
one new humanity out of the two, thus making peace.
EPHESIANS 2:13-15 NIV

In Christ, we freely have access to all we need. When you
accepted Christ, you became a new creation. The old is gone,
and the new is your reality. Christ in you is God's hope for
glory upon the earth, and you have been transformed by this
truth, including the heavenly perspective you have adopted in
your thinking.

You no longer have to strive to obtain peace: it is already
yours. Lean into Jesus, using the full access you possess. By
Christ's death and resurrection, he grafted you into the tree of
life. Live abundantly! When you feel you lack what God has
supplied, come to him. In Jesus, you have peace for your day.

Heavenly Father, thank you for holding nothing back
from me, including the blood of Christ. In faith, I
boldly come to you, trusting that you will be present
with me. You don't leave me alone, and you always give
me peace. Thank you for your presence and for the fruit
produced by our time together. Please exchange my
worries for your love and peace. I trust you.

July 11

PAIN AND PATIENCE

You have followed what I teach, the way I live, my goal,
faith, patience, and love. You know I never give up.
You know how I have been hurt and have suffered, as in Antioch,
Iconium, and Lystra. I have suffered, but the Lord saved me
from all those troubles. Everyone who wants to live
as God desires, in Christ Jesus, will be persecuted.

2 TIMOTHY 3:10-12 NCV

Without patience, our best attempts at changing the world
can become strings of trial and error. For greatest impact, we
must ably abide in our situations, letting Jesus' salt and light
shine through us.

What is the key to having patience? Verse 11 above says,
"The Lord saved me from all those troubles." It doesn't mean
Jesus rescued Paul from each physical situation, but rather that
he rescued his heart from the pain and suffering he experienced. This is good news! We don't have to remain hurt by
our past, and because we are healed, we can move onward,
patiently expecting a good reward for our efforts.

God, show me what pain in my heart needs to go.
Help me to release my grip on the abuses to my heart.
I ask you to save me from them. I humbly receive
your compassion, healing, and blessings.
Thank you for giving me the ability to complete
my calling as I abide with Jesus.

July 12

JUST LIKE DAD

*"If we are being called to account today for an act
of kindness shown to a man who was lame and are being
asked how he was healed, then know this, you and all the
people of Israel: It is by the name of Jesus Christ of Nazareth,
whom you crucified but whom God raised from the dead,
that this man stands before you healed."*

ACTS 4:9-10 NIV

Affection, warmth, consideration, understanding, hospitality, friendliness, compassion—there are many, many words to describe being kind. At home, at church, in the workplace, in any café or at any bus stop, there is a chance to act kindly. It can be a soothing word or a handclasp, working late at the office or staying home with a sick child. Every decision gives us opportunity.

If we are to be charged with the crime of kindness, let us be found unequivocally guilty in all we say and do. This brings glory to our heavenly Father, and we will reap our reward in due season, if we do not lose heart.

**Dad, I want to imitate your kindness. Like a kid
wearing her papa's shoes, I want people to smile and
say that I look like you, my Father, whom I adore.
I want to be kind to others, giving them what they need
rather than what they deserve. Let your kindness spring
up in me. I love you; help me to be a loving chip off the
ancient block: you, my heavenly Father.**

July 13

PURPOSE

We keep on praying for you, asking our God to enable you
to live a life worthy of his call. May he give you the power
to accomplish all the good things your faith prompts you to do.
2 THESSALONIANS 1:11 NLT

God's spirit lives inside of you as a believer of Jesus Christ.
What a gift! In that treasure, God's spirit is living and active
and prompts us in life. That little nudge you feel? That calling
you can't ignore? God is speaking to you through his spirit.
When you follow that lead, the reward is great. There is something so satisfying in working hard in goodness, knowing that
God has lead you there. You said yes and you are doing what
you were meant to.

If you're in a place where you need direction, ask God. He
will give you all you need to sustain you in your pursuit of his
purpose for your life. You do have purpose, dear friend, and
you are worthy to pursue it.

Father God, thank you for giving me the gift of
your spirit, living and active inside of me. Help me
to press into that voice, knowing you will guide me
and nudge me down the path you have laid out for me.

July 14

LOVE EQUALLY

"A second is equally important:
'Love your neighbor as yourself.'"
MATTHEW 22:39 NLT

Most have read this verse before or seen it in a frame somewhere. Sounds easy enough: "Love your neighbor as yourself." Take a minute to let that command sink in. As it settles, do you see what God is really saying? That neighbor you don't like. That coworker who annoys you. That friend who only talks about herself. You are meant to see them as you see yourself. Love without condition. Love expecting nothing back. Care and respect them as you would yourself.

Not as easy as it sounds, right?

God never told us this would be easy, but he did give us guidelines to follow. This is one of them: Love others as you love yourself. The next time you look in the mirror, picture their face instead of yours, and treat them accordingly.

Jesus, remind me I am seen the same in your eyes
as that person that doesn't quite sit right with me.
You have asked me to love without constraint and I want
to do this, Father. I want to love others as I love myself.
Help me to show someone love today in
a brand-new way. I can only do this through you.

July 15

PURCHASED

He is so rich in kindness and grace that he purchased
our freedom with the blood of his Son and forgave our sins.
EPHESIANS 1:7 NLT

We are free because of the work Jesus did on the cross. God sent his one and only Son down to earth to live as we do—in human skin, feeling emotion, and tempted with our same sin and fleshy desires. Jesus loved others very well, and then was betrayed, suffered, and died. For you ... for all of us. When he died on that cross, he saw your face among the many. Then he rose from the dead, praise Jesus, and resides in heaven!

He did that so we could be free in his sacrifice! What a loving, kind, and grace-filled Jesus we serve. That he would see us in our brokenness and sin and still chose this over and over again. You are worth it to him, child of his, and he would do the same thing over again if it meant you got to walk in freedom.

I praise you today, Jesus, as I reflect on the ultimate price
you paid for my sin! Thank you for loving me so well and
allowing me to walk in freedom. May I serve you today
in remembrance of what you did for me.

July 16

DEVOTION

*What can I give the LORD
for all the good things he has given to me?*
PSALM 116:12 NCV

One of the gifts the Lord has given us is the gift of grace. He expects nothing from us when he has given us the world. And yet that is a question we wrestle with; how do I repay God for the gift of freedom from sin? The gift of his unconditional love?

The answer: *devotion* to him. *Follow* him. *Pursue* him. He desires a relationship with you above all else and that is attainable if you allow him in. Today, take time to ask him to come into your life. Invite him in and he will walk with you every step of the way. You will find that being devoted to him is the best gift you can give yourself.

**God, I know you don't expect repayment,
but I desire to walk with in step with you as I go through
my day today. You have given me so much and I know
you want my heart. Help me give that to you today,
Lord, and above all else may I seek your face.**

July 17

BE GOOD

Because you have these blessings,
do your best to add these things to your lives: to your faith,
add goodness; and to your goodness, add knowledge.
2 PETER 1:5 NCV

Whatever your blessings look like, take them as gifts from God. He is such a loving, gracious father! Even when we can't see the whole picture, may you feel that love today. Part of the uncertainty when we can't see the whole picture is the idea of *faith*. Faith in a God of who has your best interest at heart and who loves you wholeheartedly. He asks us to spread that faith and his love to others. The best way to do that: In goodness, in loving others, in *showing* them the love of Jesus instead of just telling them. This happens through truly being his hands and feet.

Once that foundation of goodness is laid, knowledge seeking usually follows. Those you are showing goodness to want to know more and you can teach them the ways of the Bible and who God says he is. Knowledge, goodness, and faith go hand in hand. What a beautiful gift to give back to God … showing others his love in tangible ways!

You are so good to me, God. I want to show others your goodness and help teach them about you. Give me your words of wisdom, Father, and encourage me to be brave in my loving actions towards others.

July 18

A LISTENING EAR

Like a gold ring or an ornament of gold
is a wise reprover to a listening ear.
Like the cold of snow in the time of harvest
is a faithful messenger to those who send him;
he refreshes the soul of his masters.
PROVERBS 25:12-13 ESV

To be a friend who *refreshes* is the best kind of friend. One who listens to you. Helps you when you need a hand. Blesses you in tangible, real ways. What a kind way to live! In Proverbs, a listening ear is paralleled with a gold earring. How valuable and rare!

Yes, to be that kind of person might be a rarity but one God encourages us to emulate. In conversations this week, remember to open your ears and open your heart to hear what the person across from you is saying. There is so much blessing to come when we close our mouths and listen with our ears, pouring into those we love through the gift of hearing what they are choosing to share.

God, I want to be the kind of friend that
chooses to listen when someone seeks me out.
Help me to remember how rare it is to have people
in life who truly want to love in this way.
Help me be a refresher, in your name,
to those I am loving this week.

July 19

OVERFLOW

But the gift is not like the trespass.
For if the many died by the trespass of the one man,
how much more did God's grace and the gift that came by
the grace of the one man, Jesus Christ, overflow to the many!
ROMANS 5:15 NIV

When Jesus died on the cross and rose again he did for you. For me. For each person you see in your day-to-day life. For the beggar on the street. For the abandoned orphans. For the homeless man you pass. For the neighbor you try to avoid. For the young, old, wise, and disrespectful. His gift of freedom did not come with a price tag or a qualifier. He died so that we might live! Each and every one of us regardless of who we are or what we've done or not done.

To see his blood spill out to the many that don't yet know him, we have work to do. To see his abundant overflow to the unreached, we need to step us as believers and encourage them in his love for them! We serve a kind and loving God, show someone that love today.

God, I know you died for me and every other person I will encounter today. Help me to remember I have a job to do here in this world—to share your love with everyone so your overflow will reach the masses! I want to encourage others in their walk with you. Help me to do that today in your name.

July 20

SING, SING, SING!

*They celebrate your abundant goodness
and joyfully sing of your righteousness.*
PSALM 145:7

There are some church services, or Christian celebrations, that are so full of the Holy Spirit that it's beautifully over-whelming. Have you experienced that? In a remarkable way, believers are coming together to celebrate all that God has done in their lives! Dancing, singing at the top of their lungs in praise, crying tears of joy for his abundance of grace and sacrifice. How happy that sight must make our Father in heaven!

Today, find a praise and worship song and joyfully sing out to the God who loves you (he does not care what you sound like! It is music to his ears!) This God adores you and cherishes you. Who is so good that he will never abandon or forsake you. Who is proud to call you his son or daughter. What a good, good Father!

**Father, thank you for loving me so well.
Today I want to spend time praising you in song!
I thank you for the gift of your goodness and love.
I'm forever thankful for the ways you love me.**

July 21

DEVOTED FOR ETERNITY

Afterward the people will return and devote themselves to the
Lord their God and to David's descendant, their king. In the last
days, they will tremble in awe of the Lord and of his goodness.
HOSEA 3:5 NLT

Salvation in Jesus Christ is such a gift. A gift God gave us
to allow a bridge to happen between his ultimate sovereignty,
and fear, and a life lived in conjunction and relationship with
his Son, Jesus. God knows us so well in our human flesh to
know our greatest need as sinners was Jesus! Once you're a follower of Jesus, it doesn't guarantee ease. To follow him means
applying ourselves, seeking Him out, and truly become *willing*
people to do this work.

Doing the work God asks us of means devotion to the
promises he has given; the promise of an eternity with him
when we follow Jesus, expanding his kingdom and preaching
the truth to unbelievers. May we help others to tremble in the
spirit of the Lord and his ultimate sacrifice in goodness!

God, I want to do your hard work.
I want to daily devote myself to your promise
and your cause. I want to tell others of your goodness!
Help me be a vessel for you today!

July 22

LOVE AS GOD LOVES

"I give you a new command: Love each other.
You must love each other as I have loved you."
JOHN 13:34 NCV

"Love each other as I have loved you." Baffling, right? How? How do we show this kind of love to others? How can you possibly love another as God loves us? In order to understand his love, we must seek him. So dive into the Word, and find verses and parables that show the love of Jesus. Seek knowledge! Go back to the Old Testament and see the fear of God and his promises to us.

There are very common people in the Bible that Jesus loved really, really well and performed miraculous encounters with! We are to show the same kind of love. Feels impossible but nothing is when we seek God first. Start small; start with opening your Bible and asking for wisdom and direction. Move up from there and keep going. Keep pressing in to learn the love of God and continually invite the spirit in to show you where to step next.

God, thank you for loving me so well.
I want to obey your command and try to love
others well too. Give me vision and wisdom on how
to do this and open my heart to that kind of love!

July 23

LOVE OF ETERNITY

Do not love the world or the things in the world.
If anyone loves the world, the love of the
Father is not in him.

1 JOHN 2:15 ESV

Our world today is just cluttered with *stuff*. Material possessions, technology, reality-TV love—more and more and more. That isn't a bad thing, but it can be a slippery slope. It is so easy to get caught up in the desires of this world and forget God's commands to not love the things of this world. When we die and go to eternity, none of this will come with us. Not our homes, our cars, our material things. Nothing. So God asks us to focus on the internal; our heart posture, our love to others, our pursuit of him and his love.

Let this kind of love be your focus instead on how much stuff you have or don't have.

God, in a world so focused on things,
help me to stay focused on the kind of love
that matters. Yours. Help me to pursue you
above all else and stay grounded in your love.

July 24

TRUTH IN THE WORD

You shall love the LORD your God,
therefore, and keep his charge, his decrees,
his ordinances, and his commandments always.
DEUTERONOMY 11:1 NRSV

The Word of God can be a powerful tool in a life that can otherwise be challenging. He instructs us to keep his commandments *always*, which is impossible without first gaining wisdom and knowledge on what those are. Then, because we are sinners, we will continue to sin. But there is hope because, by focusing on the Word of God and his teachings, and ignoring those sins that can so entrap us, we starve those out and suffocate them, letting in light and goodness from the Holy Spirit and truth in the Word.

Love God, seek the truth in the Word of God, and keep his commandments in the forefront of your life.

Jesus, may I seek you first in this world.
Help me to gain wisdom and insight into
your commandments and may
I pursue them wholeheartedly.

July 25

LET GO

"I say to you, love your enemies.
Pray for those who hurt you."
MATTHEW 5:44 NCV

One of the very hardest commandments we are given from the Lord—to love our enemies and pray for those who hurt us. Do you want to cry out in frustration and throw your hands in the air? How can he possibly want something so difficult for us? Then we remember Jesus. We remember him, bleeding and dying on the cross, and saying, "Father, forgive them, for they know not what they do" (Luke 23:34 ESV). The ultimate enemy. You. Me. Them. Persecuting Jesus and him paying the ultimate price for us.

In love, and grace, and forgiveness, we pursue those who are the most difficult for us to love. We put their needs in front of our own. We forgive and move on. We let go and let God.

God, show me the enemy I am meant to love and
forgive. Give me wisdom with how to best do this and
do in your loving way. I want to follow you, obey you,
and show others your unfailing love.

July 26

AFFIRMING WORDS

Let us think of ways to motivate one another
to acts of love and good works.
HEBREWS 10:24 NLT

When you receive an encouraging word from someone, it can carry you in instrumental ways, motivating you to continue choosing goodness; to continue choosing love and pouring that out on others. Just as you have received encouragement in your life, we are asked to pay that forward. To motivate others and bless them through words of affirmation.

Each time you do this, remember who it is that you serve. Remember who it is you are trying to show to others … Jesus. His perfect love and his perfect sacrifice were poured out for you and everyone you encounter. It really is simple: He asks us to love others and do good works. Sometimes we just need someone to remind us.

Jesus, I want to love as you do. I want to treat others as you would. I want to love others as myself. Put people in my life to motivate me, Lord, use them in my life and let me hear your voice in their encouraging words.

July 27

BROTHERS AND SISTERS

Love one another with brotherly affection.
Outdo one another in showing honor.
ROMANS 12:10 ESV

Have you ever watched an oldest sibling and a middle or youngest play together? There is usually one trying to outdo the other in some way; win that game, make things fair, be the one to obey. As brothers and sisters in Christ, we should have a similar motivation but in a more adult-like, healthy way. A sharpening of our character that should happen when we surround ourselves with believers.

We aren't meant to condemn others and make them feel bad about themselves. Pursuing a love like Jesus' love means honoring our brothers and sisters as his children. It also means loving each other unconditionally and encouraging each other. We are meant to hold each other accountable, but always in the love of Christ.

God, thank you for giving me brothers and sisters who can hold me accountable and help sharpen my character. May I pursue you with discernment in those areas of my life! I ask that you continue to show me how to best love my brothers and sisters in your unfailing love.

July 28

LOST

*"What do you think? If a man owns a hundred sheep,
and one of them wanders away, will he not leave the ninety-
nine on the hills and go to look for the one that wandered off?"*

MATTHEW 18:12 NIV

We all have people in our life who have "wandered." They have lost their way in the midst of a difficult circumstance, a broken relationship, hurt feelings, or some other hardship. Seeing that story unfold can be extremely tough and, oftentimes, we end up feeling at a loss as how to show them the loving grace God calls us to display as believers.

God will help. Just as the verse in Matthew says above, we are instructed to leave the "ninety-nine" to reach that one. God values that one life, that child of his, the same as all the others. Leaving the "ninety-nine" might be leaving the comfort of our home, the safety of our job, or some other form of security, in order to go and find the *one* life that God desires to come back to him.

**God, I want to help in your pursuit of your
children that are lost. Guide me in the right direction
to show them love in the way of Jesus.
Give me discernment about their situation,
their heart towards you, and how to best love them.**

July 29

LOVING CORRECTION

Whoever loves discipline loves knowledge,
but whoever hates correction is stupid.
PROVERBS 12:1 NIV

Whether it is in your job, your faith walk, a relationship, school, or athletics, having the ability to accept a failure or criticism and then move on is critical to your growth. Baseball players are pretty good at brushing off disappointment. When they slide into second and the ump calls them out, they hop up and brush off their pants. When strike three is called, to the boos and hisses of fans, a great ballplayer realizes it's just part of the game.

In the game of life, we fall short. We get corrected and criticized. Those who succeed at playing the game of life learn from their mistakes and let them go. Failing at something does not make us failures; it gives us experience for the next time. People who are smart accept correction, learn from it, and move on.

God, help me to receive correction with grace.
Let me see it as a tool to become better and realize
that I will not grow without it. Once I take away
the lesson, help me to let go of criticism.

July 30

DISCIPLINED THINKING

You are good, and what you do is good;
teach me your decrees.
PSALM 119:68 NIV

Wherever you are at in your life, may you feel the goodness of a God who loves you! He is so very good, even if we can't see the story he has written for us unfold in the way we'd like. His mysteries that are intertwined in our story are not ours to know. But his goodness is.

Teaching ourselves to claim good, claim victory over sin, speak truth over lies all take practice, patience, and a lot of prayer. It feels like a disciplined practice and a constant pressing into his Spirit. One tool we have at our fingertips is the Word of God. Getting into the Word every day will equip you with tools you need, your armor to take each curve in your story with more ease and trust.

Jesus, remind me that you are living and active.
That your Word is truth. That I have a tool to arm myself
with in every step of this journey of life. I praise you for
your goodness, thank you for loving me as my Father.

July 31

PROTECTOR

LORD, don't hold back your tender mercies from me.
Let your unfailing love and faithfulness always protect me.
PSALM 40:11 NLT

Oftentimes we think of protection as armor from something that we don't want to happen. We pray for protection from illness, from tragedy, from hardship, and yet, God might have a different story already written for our life. A life that might not be void of tragedy. In the circle of life and sin of humanity, it is inevitable that life will be hard. However, in the same breath of hardship come God's tender mercies, which are new every morning. He does not hide them. He does not take them from you.

If you are in a season of hardship, look to our faithful Father and his promises to you. Wake up, knowing he sees you, hears you, and knows your heart. We serve a loving God. He will not fail you, even in your worst circumstance. Instead, he will cover you with his mercy.

God, thank you that you are a tender, loving Father.
That you know me better than I know myself.
May I always see you as my protector,
the upholder of my head, and may I feel
your mercy no matter where I am.

August

God gave us a spirit
not of fear but of power
and love and self-control.

2 TIMOTHY 1:7 ESV

August 1

HIDE-AND-SEEK

His massive arms are wrapped around you, protecting you.
You can run under his covering of majesty and hide.
His arms of faithfulness are a shield keeping you from harm.
PSALM 91:4 TPT

We want to run and hide from so many things in life, thinking that if we can run, that difficulty will surely be gone when we choose to come back. We run because of fear. We run because of anger. We run because of indifference. We run, hoping someone will chase us. Hoping someone will come find us. If you don't know Jesus, where are you running? Who are you running to?

God knows. He knows you. You matter to him. You mean something to the creator who molded you from dry clay. And he is not beyond whatever you are facing today. He tells you to run to him and he promises shelter and protection. He promises you he will meet you in that place and give you peace. Run to him, friend, run to the one who will wrap his arms around you so you can rest.

What a faithful father you are, God!
I'm grateful to you for your love, protection,
and shelter from all of the things of this world that
could scare me. With you, I'm safe. With you,
I know I'm loved no matter what I'm facing.

August 2

LIMITLESS LOVE

But you, O Lord, your mercy-seat love is limitless,
reaching higher than the highest heavens.
Your great faithfulness is so infinite,
stretching over the whole earth.

PSALM 36:5 TPT

The world is a huge place and yet we often feel we are the only ones suffering. Our circumstance stretches before us like an insurmountable mountain, and success appears unattainable. But God! God is not contained. He does not have boundaries. He says to have faith even as small as a mustard seed and we can move mountains with that faith (Matthew 17:20). The God we serve, and who loves us, is passionate about the pursuit of people and his faithfulness is never changing.

The next time you are standing at the base of your mountain, looking up at the highest peak, know who is standing next to you, cheering you on, shedding his mercy and faithfulness on you, encouraging you and urging you forward.

To know that your love spans the entire earth,
God, is a powerful reminder to me of your sovereignty!
Let me trust that as I face my day today.
Thank you for your love and mercy.

August 3

TESTS AND TRIALS

We say they are happy because they did not give up.
You have heard about Job's patience, and you know
the Lord's purpose for him in the end.
You know the Lord is full of mercy and is kind.

JAMES 5:11 NCV

The story of Job is one of dedication and loyalty until the very end, despite great suffering and pain. Satan and God are having a talk up in heaven when Satan claims he can make one of God's believers betray him. Curse upon curse is sent down to Job to get him to deny and rebuke God. He shaves his head, tears his clothes, and mourns for his great loss, but never once does he deny God. He does not get angry at God. He is sad, and frustrated, and seeks counsel from unwise friends, but he never betrays God. This is where human emotion comes in. Our Father created us, and he knew how painful those emotions can be. He sent Jesus here to experience those same human emotions we have! Jesus experienced all of those and more in his suffering.

"And you know the Lord's purpose for him in the end." You have a purpose, dear friend. Just as Job did, you do too. So hold fast to God's mercy and kindness. Set your eyes on the one who made you with a specific purpose in mind.

God, thank you for giving me a purpose, even if I don't yet know what that is. Thank you for taking time with me, molding me to who I am meant to be. May I have a heart like Job when I am tested. Help me to keep my eyes up towards you!

August 4

SUPREME JUDGE

For I, the Lord, love justice,
I hate robbery in the burnt offering;
And I will faithfully give them their recompense
And make an everlasting covenant with them.

ISAIAH 61:8 NASB

One of the areas often ignored, or wanting to be softened, when describing the loving God we serve is a God of justice. Not often is the God who will put all things right someday, a God who is easily accepted. As humans, we enjoy our freedom, and sometimes want to do what we want without any payment. It can be a slippery slope and yet God is a God who "loves justice" and will be faithful in his promise to us.

We walk in thankfulness for Jesus Christ, coming and taking the place for our sin and dying for us. There will come a day when he returns and the new world will be established. Let us be faithful in our pursuit and relationship with Jesus, deepening our understanding of right and wrong in the world we live in.

God, thank you for being a loving yet just God.
May I keep my eyes on you today when I make
decisions and confess and repent,
in the name of Jesus, when I need to!

August 5

GLORY

*All of God's promises have been fulfilled in Christ
with a resounding "Yes!" And through Christ, our "Amen"
(which means "Yes") ascends to God for his glory.*

2 CORINTHIANS 1:20 NLT

All throughout the Old Testament we are given hints about this "Messiah," this "Savior" who would someday come to save our human selves. Reading the Gospels sheds light on who this Savior is—Jesus Christ—who came down as a human baby, experienced much of the same things we do today in our human flesh, never sinned, and paid the ultimate price for our sins; he died on a cross after suffering immensely. The glory and praise belong to God the Father and Jesus Christ for our freedom today!

What a joy it must be for our amens and shouts of praise and singing to be heard above. What a warm sound it must be to hear our desperate prayers, whispered in the middle of the night. What a smile it must bring to see us witness to a friend in the name of Jesus, doing God's work for his kingdom. What a glorious task we are left with as believers: to spread the love of this amazing Messiah who saved us. Glory to you, God!

**Jesus, thank you for the price you paid for me,
a sinner, so I might fully live. I want to spend my
days praising and thanking you, grateful for this gift
of eternity and freedom. You are good, Father,
and I praise and give you glory!**

August 6

LEGACY

"Only the living can praise you as I do today.
Each generation tells of your faithfulness to the next."
ISAIAH 38:19 NLT

Family trees can be really interesting. Where people come from, what their heritage is, who came from where and ended up where they did. Sometimes they contain mystery and questions. At other times they might shed light on an unexplained hair color that popped up in a grandchild. When you're staring at a family tree, you're staring at a long lineage of a beginning somewhere, and also ending somewhere.

Your hope would be those loved ones would be with you in eternity, together forever. What you're doing today matters. To your little babies, to your spouse, to your friends, and other family members. You have a legacy to leave in Jesus and that is perhaps our greatest calling as brothers and sisters in Christ.

I praise you for the family and friends you've given me, Father. Help me to remember my calling here—to preach your name and share the gospel. I want to leave a legacy of other believers in my family, Lord, and show them your love through my example of living my life. Help me to stay focused on the prize that is eternity with you!

August 7

LOVE OF A FATHER

He arose and came to his father.
But while he was still a long way off, his father
saw him and felt compassion,
and ran and embraced him and kissed him.
LUKE 15:20 ESV

The picture the verse above paints is a beautiful one. A son, rising and moving towards his father, but the father also sees him, and he doesn't walk, but *runs* towards him to meet him. To reach him first. To not let his son feel shame and regret but instead to shower him with the finest, forgiving and forgetting all.

This parable parallels the love of God! A God who created you with the finest in mind. A Father who loves you without boundary, forgiving and forgetting all when he sent his son, Jesus, to die for our sins. We can walk in freedom, knowing when we repent, we are truly forgiven. God never walk towards us. He would run, without abandon, to reach us first. He pursues us even when we let him down. He desires a relationship with us even when we shut him out.

How grateful I am that you don't give up on me,
Father God! Thank you for loving me in the best way.
For knowing my heart and loving me despite
my faults. I'm thankful to be called your child
and praise your name today!

August 8

CROOKED PATH

"I will bring the blind by a way they did not know;
I will lead them in paths they have not known.
I will make darkness light before them,
And crooked places straight.
These things I will do for them,
And not forsake them."

ISAIAH 42:16 NKJV

Have you ever been lost in the car? You drive around and around, passing the same house a few dozen times, hoping the next turn you make will be the right one. You desperately want a sign, a compass, someone or something to point you in the right direction, encouraging you that you're headed the right way.

Thankfully, for believers, we have a compass who never leads us astray: Jesus Christ. Instead of driving aimlessly, we have a goal and purpose in the name of Jesus. No longer do we need to walk blindly, hoping we are headed somewhere, we can step confidently knowing we are going exactly where we need to be going. When you feel that nudge, trust your compass. When you feel lost, open the living Word of God to get direction. He hears your prayers and sets signs in your path so you always know the turn you are taking can be trusted.

Jesus, thank you for being my compass and directing my path. May I continually search you before trying to do this life on my own! I want your will for my life and to be steered where you want me to go even when it might feel scary or unknown. I want to trust you!

August 9

HUMBLE SPIRIT

Let it be the hidden person of the heart,
with the imperishable quality of a gentle and quiet spirit,
which is precious in the sight of God.

1 PETER 3:4 NASB

In today's world of social media and seemingly end-less attention on self and accomplishments, we need to be reminded that a humble spirit is pleasing to the Lord. Our heart and the intention behind why we do something matters. How we act in front of others and behind closed doors is seen by the only audience who truly matters.

Thankfully, we have the Bible to remind us of the fruits of the spirit, one of them being gentleness. This quality can be displayed in many ways, but it is a choice we make in every situation we face. How we react, interact, and teach matters to the people we encounter. May our hearts today be genuine in our relationships with others.

God, help me to have a gentler spirit when I need it. I know you've given me gifts that are unique to me and I want to discern when to use those gifting and how to use them effectively. Remind me to dig into the Word when I need answers, and seek you in quiet prayer.

August 10

BLESSINGS

*"May the Lord bless you
and protect you.
May the Lord smile on you
and be gracious to you.
May the Lord show you his favor
and give you his peace."*

NUMBERS 6:24-26 NLT

Imagine every day someone laying their hand on their forehead and blessing you before you start your day. You wake up, roll over, and before you've even poured your coffee for the day, you've got someone whispering this prayer over you.

What a gift to start your day that way! The good news is that you can. Every day you can start your day in communion with the Lord. Before anything else, invite his Spirit into your life to guide your day and steer you. Invite his holy presence to uphold you and sustain you in your trials. Ask him to walk with you as you encounter various people in conversation. What a loving God we serve, one who says he will be there with us through everything!

**Lord, bless me today, please. I invite your presence
into my life and everything I do today. I ask your Spirit
to guide me and uphold me, may I pursue a joyful heart
and seek you first. Thank you for being a loving Father
who walks with me in my everyday routine.**

August 11

ONE BODY

Is there any encouragement from belonging to Christ?
Any comfort from his love? Any fellowship together in the Spirit?
Are your hearts tender and compassionate? Then make me truly
happy by agreeing wholeheartedly with each other, loving one
another, and working together with one mind and purpose.

PHILIPPIANS 2:1-2 NLT

The church is spread out all over and seen very differently in various parts of the world. Some worship in homes together. Some are outside in a field. Some do life together and don't have a church. Some worship on their own time, in their own way. Some are in a building with lights and a twelve-person band. And yet, in Christ, we are all one body of believers, together. With the same purpose and goal. To love Jesus and preach to those who are lost and don't yet know him.

When we get down to the root of what he asks of us, it really is that simple. Loving each other, and loving each other well, united in body and mind to expand his kingdom. How connected the church could look if we kept our hearts and mind focused on the purpose God sets before us.

God, I want to be a unified body with my brothers
and sisters in Christ. Help me to declutter the noise
and see my fellow believers through your eyes.
Help me to love them, and love them well,
showing others your love in a radical way!

August 12

INTEGRITY

*God prepared David and took this gentle shepherd-king
and presented him before the people
as the one who would love and care for them
with integrity, a pure heart, and the anointing
to lead Israel, his holy inheritance.*
PSALM 78:71-72 TPT

How humbling it must have been for David to be called by God to lead Israel. Psalms tell us that God presented David as the one to love and care for them with integrity and a pure heart. You can probably think of people in your life who display integrity, who seem pure of heart. They are most likely people others look to for guidance. A person of trust and loyalty, similar to David, having characteristics that please God.

The good news is that we aren't all meant to have the same qualities and gifts. God created us as people to be a mishmash of his sons and daughters, all working together for a greater purpose, each with unique characteristics and strengths. We are all broken, and sinners, even David! Yet God can still do big things with our lives if we pursue him.

God, help me to use the gifting you gave me for the greater good of your kingdom! I want to work on my spirit, and the areas of sin in my life, always bringing them to the cross and laying them down at your feet. Thank you for being a God who created me uniquely, help me to find purpose in my day today and confidence that I'm doing what I need to do in following you.

August 13

PERFECTER OF PEACE

God gave us a spirit not of fear
but of power and love and self-control.
2 TIMOTHY 1:7 ESV

Fear and anxiety can be very crippling to live with. When we live in a constant state of stress and worry, everything feels bigger than we are. Even bigger than God. Once that fear is planted deep inside, the enemy will use it to debilitate you even more. He is cunning and a deceiver. He will mask that fear and make you feel like it is something else entirely, or something God has given you, which would be a lie.

Thankfully, we have the Word of God to live by. In the Bible, Timothy says fear is *not* of God. That he does not give us fear, but instead, power. Love. Self-control. We have these things because we have Christ. Satan does not have a stronghold on us when we relinquish these insecurities to God. The enemy does not stand a chance.

God, I'm grateful that fear does not come from you,
but sometimes I have a hard time recognizing that.
Help me see that love, self-control, and power
come through you in place of fear. Help ignore
the lies of anxiety and instead, keep my eyes
fixed on you, the perfecter of my peace!

August 14

UNVEILED

And we are instructed to turn from godless living and sinful pleasures. We should live in this evil world with wisdom, righteousness, and devotion to God, while we look forward with hope to that wonderful day when the glory of our great God and Savior, Jesus Christ, will be revealed. He gave his life to free us from every kind of sin, to cleanse us, and to make us his very own people, totally committed to doing good deeds.

TITUS 2:12-14 NLT

Sin looks very differently from person to person. We can easily look at another's sin and be thankful it isn't ours. We can commit sin in our flesh and brush it aside because it isn't that bad, comparatively. The only problem with doing this is God doesn't. We often try to justify what we are doing when we judge another, get angry too often, too quickly. We compare and compete in unhealthy ways. We may not be committing murder or stealing, but in the eyes of God, sin is sin.

Gratefully, God sent his son, Jesus, to die on the cross and forgive us of all sin. Wipe our slate clean. Free us from our debt. When you fully repent, asking Jesus for forgiveness, even if it is every single day, you are forgiven. Praise God for giving us such a gift in his Son!

God, help me to see my sin the way you do. The things that I so easily commit without even realizing I'm sinning because it has become such a way of life for me. I want the veil to be lifted and for me to see clearly where I am wrong. Forgive me, Jesus!

August 15

BRICK BY BRICK

In your knowledge, self-control, and in your self-control,
perseverance, and in your perseverance, godliness.
2 PETER 1:6

Building, growing, and refining our character requires patience, vulnerability, and introspection. It requires taking a hard look inside, at times, to get to the root cause. Refining is taking something specific, being picky about it, and continuing to work at it. Striving to find and be your best self—the person God, ultimately, designed you to be. It can be grueling work, almost like a mason who lays brick after brick until the masterpiece is complete.

Self-control, then perseverance, and in perseverance, godliness. This verse is a foundational verse in how layering on brick by brick in building your character is so important. God doesn't say it will be easy. You start with self-control. You keep going until you persevere, until you beat that area you needed to exude self-control. In that perseverance you will be closer to godliness, closer to refining that area of our heart that needs it.

God, thank you for giving me words of wisdom
in the Bible! I want to be more godly. I want to practice
self-control. I want to defeat any strongholds the enemy
might have in my life, and instead persevere for you!
Guide me in the direction you want me to go.
Help me prune off those areas of my heart that
aren't godly, and instead pursue you.

August 16

A FOOL'S TONGUE

The prudent keep their knowledge to themselves,
but a fool's heart blurts out folly.
PROVERBS 12:23 NIV

One of the areas of self-control that can be the most diffi-cult is controlling the tongue. When you feel passionate about something, when you feel you are right, when you want your voice to be heard, it is easy to forget to think before blurting out what it is you want to say. You've heard the age-old saying "If you can't say anything nice, don't say anything at all," and this is great advice to adhere to around controlling the tongue.

On the flip side, our knowledge and words can be used for good! God also asks us to share the gospel, to reach the unreached. We can do a lot for the unbelieving world by *showing* them the love of Jesus, not just talking about it, and by showing them that following Jesus makes your life look differ-ent. When they ask what's different about you, then comes the opportunity to use your time in the name of Jesus.

Father, help me see the difference in when to use my words and when to use my actions. I know at times I can speak too bluntly, say unkind things, or use my words to hurt. Instead, I want to be a vessel for you by speaking in truth and love.

August 17

THE GOOD SHEPHERD

When he saw the crowds, he had compassion for them,
because they were harassed and helpless,
like sheep without a shepherd.
MATTHEW 9:36 ESV

When watching the news any given night, there are usually stories of protests or bombings or a mass shooting or some other worldly conflict—on and on it goes in despair. At times, it is difficult to see brothers and sisters fighting, not recognizing who they are to one another. It is troubling to see so much anger, so much brokenness, so much injustice in the world. But … there is hope in Christ.

Jesus wants to be the ultimate shepherd. His desire is to not have *one* wandering sheep, much less millions. His love for his people is vast and he hurts, deeply, when he sees our world in shambles the way it is. We can pray. We can serve. We can find one lost soul and show them the love of God. If we all found one person, imagine the lives that could be saved in the name of Jesus.

Father, I know you hurt to see your children fight the way we do. Use me to reach the lost, Jesus! Remind me to pray. To fight in your name. To find others and show them your love. I want to do all I can to expand your kingdom, Lord, and help bring lost souls home to you.

August 18

ACCESSIBLE

He also told us about the love you have from the Holy Spirit.
Because of this, since the day we heard about you, we have
continued praying for you, asking God that you will know
fully what he wants. We pray that you will also have
great wisdom and understanding in spiritual things.

COLOSSIANS 1:8-9 NCV

The Spirit of God lives in you when you accept Jesus into your heart. Let that sink in. The Spirit of the one who created the heavens and the earth, that created you from dust, that is sovereign over all, can live *inside* of you! That same Spirit is *accessible* to you as a spirit of guidance. It is yours to invite in when you ask. What a mind-blowing gift!

The Holy Spirit is a counselor for us, giving us clarity, wisdom, and understanding. Jesus sends his Spirit to walk in step with us, the church, the body of believers, to work for him. To give us the words and discernment we need to expand his kingdom. All we have to do is ask in the name of Jesus. If something is holding you back, release it and let him in.

Jesus, thank you for giving me your spirit.
Thank you for your guidance and for the whispers
I hear that I know are coming from your Holy Spirit.
May I continually invite you in, today and every day.

August 19

SHOW THE LOVE

Above all, love each other deeply,
because love covers over a multitude of sins.
1 PETER 4:8

The best way we can show others Jesus is love. Love, love, love. In the face of sin or brokenness or waywardness, it might seem as if we need to offer words of conviction. Judgment. Even anger towards someone's lifestyle or choice. But when you read about Jesus, how he lived while he was here on earth, he got *in* with the people. He ate with prostitutes and tax collectors. He held lepers and gave food to the beggars. He didn't stand above them, finger-pointing and accusing. He put action where his words could have been. He showed them what it meant to love another, without constraint, and then showed them again when he died on the cross.

In our interactions today, may we be loving, and then go home and pray for redemption in that life we just encountered. May we show grace upon grace, and then ask to pray with them, asking the Spirit to fill them with all they need.

Jesus, I want my first emotion towards my fellow believers to be love, before anything else. I want to seek you in each situation and ask for your leading in my interactions and words.

August 20

UNLOVED

Those who say, "I love God," and hate their brothers or sisters, are liars; for those who do not love a brother or sister whom they have seen, cannot love God whom they have not seen.
1 JOHN 4:20 NRSV

Faith can be tricky for those who have never believed, or need facts to back everything up, because a part of faith is just that—faith. It's the ability to believe when you can't see what you're believing in, and walking in trust that there's a God who loves you and knows your story. When you choose to follow Jesus, you choose a lot of mystery, because God doesn't promise to tell us everything, but he does promise love. *Always love.*

We must then go and show our brothers and sisters that same kind of love; not in judgment, not in vain, not for any other reason than God is asking us to. He is asking us to trust him, blindly, and do nothing but show love to others, the way he so diligently shows us love. We, who are sinners, who deny him, who disrespect him, and idolize other things above him. He loves us despite it all, and we should strive to do the same with our brothers and sisters.

Father, I want to love the way you ask me to. For my brothers and sisters, I encounter, give me words and actions to show them your love. I don't want to walk in hate towards anyone, but instead, shower them with your radical love. Use me, Jesus, to do just that!

August 21

REMAIN

*"I have loved you even as the Father has loved me.
Remain in my love."*

JOHN 15:9 NLT

Reflect for a moment on a situation that brought so much joy, relaxation, peace, and happiness that you wanted to stay there *forever*. You may have literally said those words out loud: "Can I just stay here forever?" Most of us probably don't have a plethora of those, but for sure a few, that immediately bring us back when we reflect on them. You can feel the same emotions, a smile might start to tug at the corners of your mouth, and you relish those memories. Desiring to be in that moment is wanting to remain there. To stay. Not necessarily because of where you are but how you *feel* when you are there.

This is what Jesus says in John. Remain in his love. Sit tight in his presence. Stay grounded in his love. Connect to the Spirit by diving into the Word and communing with him. How you feel won't go away; you'll be tethered, connected, to the one person we should desire to be connected to.

Jesus, thank you for loving me—a love straight from your Father. You have shown me love in the most sacrificial of ways, by dying on the cross for me so I can be free. Help me to remain with you. To stay, when there are so many things that can distract and pull me away.

August 22

GLAD

"Then young women will dance and be glad,
young men and old as well.
I will turn their mourning into gladness;
I will give them comfort and joy instead of sorrow."
JEREMIAH 31:13 NIV

You've probably heard stories of unexplainable hope on the news, or experienced it yourself firsthand. Stories that are filled with despair and tragedy, and yet, in the midst of it, those who should be suffering are filled with joy. Filled with hope and renewal, the opposite of what one would expect.

There is no reason for that reaction. There is no understanding of why that would be happening, how that could be happening. You are able to look at your own life, or the life of someone else, in total disbelief because of their reaction. The only explanation is Jesus and his grace. Jesus, and his immense love for us, that he would take something so difficult and use it for good. He is the only one capable of such a glorious feat, and let's be thankful he can.

Father, thank you that you can take an impossible situation and turn it to good. Thank you for turning my mourning into dancing and my sadness into joy!

August 23

ABOVE AND BEYOND

"I say to you who hear: Love your enemies,
do good to those who hate you."
LUKE 6:27 NKJV

When you feel wronged, it's natural to want to make it right. That might look differently depending on your way of dealing with conflict. You may seek revenge. You may sweep it under the rug and secretly harbor it. You may have an angry outburst. The one who wronged you may become your enemy, someone you just plain try to avoid.

God, however, would say something else entirely in dealing with your enemy. He would say to "love them," and then beyond that, even, he says to "do good to those who hate you." Doesn't that just sound like a God thing to do? But what a release you feel when you let that pain, anger, resentment or wrongdoing go and give it to the Lord! Let it go and shower that enemy with a love that is unlike anything they have experienced before. God gives really good advice.

God, help me to love those who have wronged me.
Those people that I see as my enemies, Lord, I want
to love, but I also want to do good to them. I want to
show them your love in tangible ways. Guide me in
this forgiveness and love, God.

August 24

PASSIONS

Listen to me all you godly ones:
Love the Lord with passion!
The Lord protects and preserves all those
who are loyal to him.
But he pays back in full all those who
reject him in their pride.

PSALM 31:23 TPT

The job or hobbies we are most excited about, the ones we love the most, those are what we put our heart and soul into. They fuel us in a way that gives us energy. They motivate and inspire us to be our best self. They can be our report card, giving us praise or criticism depending on how we're doing.

It is with this very same passion that we should love, praise, and serve the Lord! Our greatest efforts should go towards our relationship with Jesus, the one who freed us from our bondage, and deeply pursues our hearts.

Jesus, I want to put my effort towards my relationship with you! You deserve all my praise, my time, and energy. I am my best self when I am in relationship with you and your Spirit guides me. Thank you for loving me so very well.

August 25

PROMISE OF JOY

"You too have grief now; but I will see you again,
and your heart will rejoice, and no one will
take your joy away from you."

John 16:22 nasb

This life is not going to be void of hardships; of trials and grief, of tragedy and deep sorrow. That pain is like nothing else, and it's often hard to keep peace at the forefront of your mind.

When you follow Jesus and read his Word, however, you can find peace. You are reminded of his promise: to one day come back and make all things right. To one day come back and be with us. To one day come back and wipe every tear from our eyes, heal every broken bone, and cure every incurable disease. His promises are rich with goodness, looking toward eternity with him, where joy cannot be destroyed.

Jesus, when you return, I want to be ready!
I want to be in eternity with you where my joy can't
be shaken. I know that, for now, this life is what I
have and I'm grateful. Help me to live with an eternal
perspective, so that everything I encounter can be seen
through Your eyes, Jesus. Remind me that you are the
rock that I stand on and you are always with me.

August 26

A SWEET, SWEET SOUND

We laughed and laughed, and overflowed with gladness!
We were left shouting for joy and singing your praise.
All the nations saw it and joined in, saying,
"The Lord has done great miracles for them!"

PSALM 126:2 TPT

Laughter is one of the greatest sounds in the world. An old married couple dancing and flirting. A toddler being tickled, giggling until she is crying. A pair of best friends, rolling with laughter in just being together. When you hear laughter, you can't help but crack a smile yourself. Can you imagine what God must feel when he hears his children laughing, singing, and praising him together? Can you imagine what happiness must sound like to him? Picture a room full of believers singing in harmony to show their love for him. What a joyous, beautiful sound that must be!

Raise your voice to him, however you worship. He doesn't require certain practices. He created us all uniquely to praise him in our individual way. Use whatever talents he's given you to honor him. All of our honor and praise glorify God and he delights in it. What a proud Father he must be of his children when they stand in worship!

Jesus, I want to start my day in praise for you. You have created us to be so creative in our worship styles, and I want to honor you in my daily praise. May you hear my voice and may it be pleasing to you, God.

August 27

PEARLY GATES

*"His master said to him, 'Well done, good and
faithful servant. You have been faithful over a little;
I will set you over much. Enter into the joy of your master.'"*
MATTHEW 25:21 ESV

Imagine hearing these words from God when you enter the pearly gates: "Well done, good and faithful servant, well done." Does it make your heart do a little pitter-patter? Can you even imagine? Let's hope so. This is what we should be striving for, friends. We shouldn't be concentrating on how successful we are in our job, how fantastic our home looks for morning coffee, if we've climbed the corporate ladder, or whether or not we satisfied every member of our congregation with our latest message. We should be focused on heavenly things, on our relationship with Jesus, on how well we are loving other people in his name. In all we do, are we serving and pleasing him?

God knows our hearts. He knows our humanness. He understands our imperfectness. He doesn't expect perfection. There is much grace in our relationship with him. But how thrilling would it be to hear those words and know we truly had given it our *all*.

**Jesus, above all else I want to be faithful to you.
I want to be loving to those you ask me to love.
I want my relationship with you to be at the
forefront of my heart and mind. I want to
be a good and faithful servant to you!**

August 28

PROMISES OF GOD

As they were talking about these things, Jesus himself stood among them, and said to them, "Peace to you! … And behold, I am sending the promise of my Father upon you. But stay in the city until you are clothed with power from on high."
LUKE 24:36, 49 ESV

Our God does not mess around. He doesn't make promises and then not fulfill them. He doesn't tell us life is going to be all rainbows, ponies, and happy times. No, he tells us the areas we need to work on, gives us commandments to follow, and promises *big* things … like sending a Savior to save us all from our own sin. God sent his one and only Son to come down here as a tiny, helpless babe, to suffer horrifically and die on a cross. Jesus promised that he would rise again. And he did!

Jesus will come again, as God says in Revelation, to make the world right. He will come again to judge the living and the dead, and his kingdom will reign forever. What a scary yet glorious thought! Let's praise God for giving us the Bible, a road map to follow for an eternity with him. May we seek the words on the pages as they breathe life into our soul.

Father, thank you for your sovereignty!
Thank you that I don't need to worry about tomorrow
because I walk with you. And thank you for giving me an
eternal perspective, so I can focus on my
relationship with Jesus above all else.

August 29

OUR BRIDGE

He came and preached peace to you who were
afar off and to those who were near. For through Him
we both have access by one Spirit to the Father.
EPHESIANS 2:17-18 NRSV

God knew that in all of humanness we wouldn't be able to really handle him. When you read in the Old Testament, you read of these ordinary men that God did extraordinary things with. He knew we would need saving. He knew we would need *him*—Jesus. So he made that bridge. He sent his Son to die for us so that we could close that gap to him in the Holy Spirit.

And now? Now we have access to the same Spirit of God for ourselves! When we repent of our old life, die to ourselves, and ask Jesus to be our personal Lord and Savior, we are granted that access. How incredible a gift it is!

God, thank you for knowing my weakness
and sending Jesus to die for me. Thank you for giving me
grace upon grace. Thank you for your Spirit to be living
and active in me, a sinner. How grateful I am to you
for this freedom and rescue.

August 30

VENGEFUL HEARTS

Deception fills the hearts of those who plot harm,
but those who plan for peace are filled with joy.
PROVERBS 12:20 TPT

Have you ever planned to do something not-so-nice? Thought it out on your own timing, planned out the steps, or the conversation, or the thing you wanted to say to whomever betrayed you or wronged you? This preplotting is *revenge* and it almost always ends up doing more harm than good. Revenge can take up a lot of amazing heart space that could be used for good. Heart space that could be filled with love, and joy, and peace. Peace that can make any bad situation good when you relinquish and give it to God.

We serve a God who tells us that when we "plan for peace," we are "filled with joy." If we give up whatever is ailing us, and instead ask for God's peace, he will shower joy on us! Sounds so much better than plotting revenge, doesn't it?

God, thank you for being a God who gives me peace
and joy in place of deception! Thank you for being
a Father that can take any situation and turn it to good.
Help me to let go of any ill will I harbor in my heart,
any space that is being taken up for revenge,
and instead focus on your goodness!

August 31

ALONG THE WAY

The end of a matter is better than its beginning;
Patience of spirit is better than haughtiness of spirit.
ECCLESIASTES 7:8 NASB

Sometimes we want to get right to the end result, particularly when in pain, discomfort, or the unknown of a particular situation. We want to see if our hard work, our suffering, our strife is going to be worth something in the end. Our natural tendency to want to know when, how, and why sometimes trumps the journey, overtaking every beautiful and difficult moment along the way. The treasure, however, is oftentimes in the journey. In the self-discovery along the way. In the trust and hope and dependency on the Lord as you've never experienced. In the revelations you discover on the path. In the redeeming love of Jesus.

Before jumping right to the end, stop and take a breath. Soak it in. Even in your pain, you are growing. Even in your suffering, God is there. Even in your confusion, he puts one foot in front of the other. Trust that there is character growth taking place. Have faith that he will guide you. Know his love will not waver.

Father, I want to trust you with everything in me. This particular situation is difficult, but I know you are good, and I release this to you now. I want to grow in this journey with you. I want to learn something about myself but also about you in this.

September

Because you are
my helper,
I sing for joy in the
shadow of your wings.

PSALM 63:7 NLT

September 1

STEADY AND SLOW

The Lord is not slow in keeping his promise,
as some understand slowness. Instead he is patient with you,
not wanting anyone to perish, but everyone to come to repentance.
2 PETER 3:9 NIV

We are often in a race in this game of life. We move quickly, jumping from one thing to another, expecting more and more, desiring the next best thing. This is most obvious when we are waiting on God. When it *feels* like we are waiting on God, at least.

Let's remember that God isn't slow. He isn't on our timetable; we are on his. He is waiting for us to come around, to see what he sees, and to release it to him, asking for forgiveness. Then we can clearly see his plan for us. When you're moving too fast, you see nothing but a blur, and there he waits. He is patient. Loving. He never leaves us. He just waits until we hit a wall, and we cry out to him to save us. He will gladly open his arms to let us climb right in.

God, you are so steady and patient. Never leaving me even when I'm moving too quickly to pause and see you, see what you're doing in my life. Please forgive me, Lord. Thank you for waiting for me every single time.

September 2

ON THE CROSS

But he was pierced for our transgressions,
he was crushed for our iniquities;
the punishment that brought us peace was on him,
and by his wounds we are healed.

ISAIAH 53:5 NIV

"By his wounds we are healed." Wounds that we can't even comprehend. Suffering that is beyond our imagination. A death that was brutal and horrific—for you, for me, for each one of us. No favorites here; all of humanity was saved when Jesus died on the cross.

There is no greater sacrifice. The next time you are asking for forgiveness, think of the way Jesus was pierced. Take in the punishment, all of it, that he endured for us. Reflect on his wounds and his tremendous gift of freedom for us all in his name.

Jesus, your love is greater than anything I can ever imagine. Your sacrifice is beyond comprehension and I'm so grateful. I don't tell you enough how thankful I am for your saving grace and ultimate sacrifice! How blessed my life is because you saved it.

September 3

THE CALM IN THE STORM

A hot-tempered person stirs up conflict,
but the one who is patient calms a quarrel.
PROVERBS 15:18 NIV

Have you ever been involved in an argument that was already heated and you added gasoline to it? Did it then escalate to something way beyond what it started as, and you later knew it was because of your fuel? Our tempers can get the best of us at times. We have a tendency to go into fight-or-flight mode. We may not want to "lose," so we fight back. We want to defend and justify.

The next time an argument is on the horizon, take a breath and invite the Holy Spirit in. Ask for patience and peace and he will grant it. Sometimes we need a supernatural intervention so our flesh doesn't act the way we'd want to. We need an intervention and God says he will do that for us! A patient voice amidst the fighting ones is a welcome sound.

Father, I want to be more patient in my relationships
and conversations. Please give me your peace, patience,
and guidance as I go through my day today.
I know I can't do this on my own.
I need your welcoming, intervening Spirit.

September 4

TENDER LOVE

Brothers and sisters, we urge you to warn those who are lazy.
Encourage those who are timid. Take tender care of those who are
weak. Be patient with everyone.
1 Thessalonians 5:14 nlt

God was so creative when he made humankind. He created us in his image, but no two of us are exactly the same. We all have strengths, differences, varying gifts, and personality traits. We're a giant melting pot of individualism and it's glorious.

As our creator, God knew exactly what he was doing and where we would struggle! He also gave us tools to help one another on the journey. We are to encourage each other in our gifts, sharpen each other when necessary, and be accountable to one another as brothers and sisters. Take a look inside today and see where you may need to lend an encouraging hand to someone. Be tender, child of God, for we are all weak.

Father God, I thank you that you're all-knowing and created us each with a purpose. I'm thankful to be in this melting pot of your children. Use me today where my gifting is and help me to encourage and be tenderhearted to those who need it most today.

September 5

THE HEAD OF THE SNAKE

The God of peace will soon crush Satan under your feet.
The grace of our Lord Jesus be with you.
ROMANS 16:20 NIV

Just as you can't be in peace and turmoil at the same time, Satan does not stand a chance if you are choosing God. Where peace resides, inner struggle does not. It is so easy to let the enemy in with his lies, telling you to worry, or be anxious, about certain things. He is a master manipulator, filling your head with disgusting thoughts that do not glorify God in the least. It is easier to give in, to let him continue to fill your head with anxiousness, but God says, "Choose me!"

God says he will give you peace if you let him. He will "crush Satan under your feet"—no denying what Romans says. *Crush* him, that's what God will do. Do not give in to the lies. You are a child of God and he delights in you. God wants to have *all* of you, even your worry or fear, so let it go.

God, I want you to crush Satan out from under me! He does not belong there, but you do! I ask for your holy presence in my life. I desire your thoughts instead of the influence of the one who deceives me best.
Thank you, Jesus!

September 6

ENDURANCE

We say they are happy because they did not give up. You have heard about Job's patience, and you know the Lord's purpose for him in the end. You know the Lord is full of mercy and is kind.

JAMES 5:11 NCV

Running any sort of race, whether it is a 5K or a marathon, takes preparation. You need to set up a running schedule, buy some good running shoes, set your alarm, and be ready to get sweaty. There are plenty of mornings you don't want to run, you'd rather just hit the snooze button. You will have obstacles along the way; shin splints, rainy weather, shoes that just won't cooperate. Then race day arrives. No matter the weather, you gear up, because you've been preparing for this. You want to see it to the very end. You want to know that your hard work has paid off. You want to feel the satisfaction in the end because you made it!

This is happiness. Not giving up and pursuing something for an end result. This is how we need to approach our relationship and life's journey with Jesus. He is a loving, kind, merciful Father who will not forsake us. Be patient with yourself; be patient with him. He will not let you down.

God, I want to look at my relationship with you as one of endurance. In whatever situations I face today, remind me that this race is for you! That I'm putting in the hard work now to live forever in union with you.

September 7

MIRACULOUS

*When I was with you, I certainly gave you
proof that I am an apostle. For I patiently did many
signs and wonders and miracles among you.*

2 CORINTHIANS 12:12 NLT

Reading the Bible, you learn of all the miracles Jesus performed while he walked in our shoes for thirty-three years. He cured a blind man of his sight, woke Lazarus from the dead, healed lepers, and made Peter walk on water. Time and time again he performed miracles. Can you even imagine what it would have been like to see Jesus in all that glory? To watch the reactions of the unbelievers? To see the transformation of their souls right before your eyes?

There is such good news in this too: miracles did not die when Jesus did. They are all around us if we keep our eyes and ears open. They are in the healing power of the Spirit, in the laying on of hands by our brothers and sisters, and in the people in your life who bless you. Jesus is living and active and he wants us to believe as they did then. Trust in his miracles today!

**Jesus, I know you are still here, performing miracles
all around me. Open my heart to them, and help
me trust that you're active now, Jesus, as you were then.
Use me however you need to, so I can be a vessel
for your kingdom.**

September 8

THE WAY OF THE LORD

Remember, our Lord's patience gives people time to be saved.
This is what our beloved brother Paul also wrote to you
with the wisdom God gave him.
2 PETER 3:15 NLT

Once you first learned of Jesus, how long did it take you to start following him? Were you young and accepted what your parents taught you and then discovered more of him slowly along the way? Were you wayward and God showed up in a vision and you immediately fell to your knees in repentance? Were you a curious college student who took religion classes, participated in theological debates, and eventually realized you couldn't dispute the truth in what you learned? Imagine, for a second, if God gave you only one chance to follow him and you said no. Where would your life be today?

Thankfully, we serve a very patient and loving Father. A Father who knows every crevice in our heart, every wayward thought or pending question. A Father that says he will wait for us, no matter the cost or path we take. A Father full of wisdom and understanding, love and acceptance. How grateful we are for this kind of unconditional love!

God, thank you for giving me a chance. For being patient with my questioning, knowing I would eventually follow you. I'm forever grateful to you for your unwavering loyalty to me. I will spend the rest of my days following and choosing you!

September 9

BLIND FAITH

May the Lord lead your hearts into a full
understanding and expression of the love of God
and the patient endurance that comes from Christ.

2 THESSALONIANS 3:5 NLT

We will never fully understand the mystery of God. He will guide us and encourage us, equipping us with what we need to endure, but he is a God of mystery and will remain so. This is an integral part of faith—choosing to continue following when we don't understand.

Eventually, this practice of faith allows us to release the need to know and be able to fully trust where he will bring us. He will lead us to understanding, as much as we need him to, and fill our hearts with peace to overflowing.

God, may you lead me into fully trusting you in every situation I face. Instead of trying to do it on my own, may I turn to you first, and allow you to mold my heart into greater understanding. Help me to have faith, blindly walking in obedience to you!

September 10

NOURISHING

*Like newborn babies, you must crave pure spiritual
milk so that you will grow into a full experience of salvation.
Cry out for this nourishment,
now that you have had a taste of the Lord's kindness.*
1 PETER 2:2-3 NLT

When babies are first born, they have a natural instinct
to feed. Their tiny little lips start puckering and they know
immediately what to do on a breast or bottle. It is incredible
to witness! It is not a learned trait, just something they know
how to do minutes after entering this world. Once they start
getting that nourishment, they crave more and more, desiring
to eat until their little tummies are full and they bodies are
being filled.

So it is in our relationship with Jesus! Once we know him,
we experience his lovingkindness, and we walk in relationship
with him, we want more and more of him. He hears our cries
for more, knows what our spirits crave, and fills every void
in our life with the fullness of him. How beautiful it is to be
known and seen so very well!

**Jesus, thank you for loving me in the many ways you do!
Thank you for knowing what I need before I even do.
Thank you for showing me more and more
of who you are when I seek you out,
allowing me to fall deeper in love with you.**

September 11

BOLD AND BRAVE

Most of the brothers, having become confident
in the Lord by my imprisonment, are much more bold
to speak the word without fear.

PHILEMON 1:14 ESV

Martyrdom still exists today. People all over the world are dying for the name of Jesus. Some are on a mission field and fear for the safety of their life and the life of their family. Some are persecuted daily. Some are hunted. Some are in the wrong place at the wrong time and are asked if they follow Jesus. They respond with a yes and are punished, or killed, for their answer. It's easy to hope you would respond the same way if you were singled out. Would you?

Speaking the name of Jesus without fear isn't easy to do in every situation, but following Jesus isn't supposed to be easy. We do a lot more for his kingdom when we speak out in boldness than we would for saying nothing at all. When you believe and follow Jesus, you're standing firm on the belief that you will live eternally with God, so sharing this with others should be a high priority. This life is an eyeblink, so let's tell others there's so much more to come! In your conversations today, may you be bold in proclaiming the name of Jesus.

Give me your words today, Jesus. In humility, may I share your good news with someone and may they be left wondering and wanting more. I want to be confident in my faith, Lord, and show another your selfless love!

September 12

PICK OF THE LITTER

He said to him, "Why are you asking Me about what is good?
There is only One who is good; but if you wish
to enter into life, keep the commandments."
MATTHEW 19:17 NASB

Many who haven't heard the gospel assume that by just being a "good person" one will go to a "better place." Have you heard that logic before? It makes sense, really, because there is so much evil, and so many unkind people in the world, that if God were going to take his pick, he'd pick the "good" ones.

There is no fault in that mode of thinking for those who have never heard about Jesus Christ. But our job, as followers of Jesus, is to share the good news with others, the truth about salvation in Jesus, that by dying to our old self, we are made new in Christ.

God, help me to teach others the truth about you.
Give me your Holy Spirit, your words, so I can be loving
and good in my actions to others so they ask about you.
I want to obey your commandments,
living a life worthy of following you.

September 13

MARRIAGE

The daughters of kings, women of honor,
are maidens in your courts.
And standing beside you,
glistening in your pure and golden glory,
is the beautiful bride-to-be!
PSALM 45:9 TPT

One of the best parts of a wedding is when the bride is about to walk down the aisle. She is beautiful in her gown. On her arm is someone she loves, her dad or a father figure, giving her away. Most times all eyes are on the bride. But have you ever looked at the groom in that moment? At the end of the aisle is a man who's waiting to start a new life with a woman he adores—a woman he cherishes and is excited to call his. The only man who has ever cared for her the way he's planning to is walking her down the aisle. What an honor being unified to someone in that way!

This psalm is a beautiful illustration of Christ's love for the church being that of a wedding, a bride and groom. Of the unity between Jesus, and our hearts, being fully submitted and satisfied with one another. Just as a husband and wife pick one another day after day, in loyalty and love, so must we do the same with Christ.

God, thank you for the relationship between us as your church and your Son. Thank you for the unity and connection we are able to have. May we choose you, every day, Lord, through it all.

September 14

TOGETHER

*We know that all things work together for good
to those who love God, to those who
are the called according to His purpose.*

ROMANS 8:28 NKJV

If you've ever participated in a race or walk for a certain cause, you know how much work and planning goes into it. You watch as each person fulfills their role and, seamlessly, everything falls into place. One person is at the starting line to ensure walkers know where to start, another makes sure numbers for shirts are pinned on at registration, the caterers are busy under the tents with food, and volunteers are handing out waters along the course. Everyone has a purpose, a place, and understands their role to make the race a success.

We, too, have a role to play in the kingdom of God. Each one of us was created with much thought, consideration, and effort as a piece of the giant puzzle of God's creation. If we, as believers, came together for good because we love God, imagine what could happen!

**God, help me understand my purpose here—why you
made me the way I am, why you gave me certain gifts.
I want to use all of my talents for good, Jesus!
Give me opportunities and fellowship with other
believers so we can work together to expand
your kingdom and spread your love!**

September 15

HUMILITY

He has told you, O man, what is good;
and what does the LORD require of you
but to do justice, and to love kindness,
and to walk humbly with your God?

MICAH 6:8 ESV

It can be easy to live in a place of self-righteousness. You love Jesus, and you know right from wrong and abide in that. You feel you have good advice for people and others seek you out to get wisdom from you. Yet in helping, you may come across as judgmental or unloving, as if you have a know-it-all attitude. What it can come down to if you're in that place is your heart posture. What is your heart stance towards God and others? Are you giving that advice in the Spirit or from yourself? Are you depending on Him or yourself?

Seek justice as God asks us to do. Live with a sense of right and wrong. *Choose* to do the right thing. *Love* to be kind. Desire to show love to others. Truly commit acts of kindness to others. Finally, walk humbly *with* God. Don't do this life on your own, don't even try. Walk with him, in humility, truly understanding you are nothing without him.

God, I want to be humble in my heart posture towards you and others. I love when people seek me out for wisdom, but I often try to answer in my own way, instead of truly seeking you first. Help me to commit my answers to you and wait for your reply, so I can know in my heart your words are coming out of my mouth.

September 16

ACTING IN YOUR GIFT

*Every good gift and every perfect gift is from above,
coming down from the Father of lights with whom
there is no variation or shadow due to change.*

JAMES 1:17 ESV

When you do something really, really well, it makes you feel good. You feel as if you're accomplishing something important and just know, in your hearts of hearts, that you were truly made to do it. You feel a sense of worth and purpose. To feel that way is a beautiful gift! To know you're doing exactly what you were created to do.

It is easy to give yourself credit in those moments. To forget that God has showered those gifts on you, with intention, and he deserves the glory. But when you're walking in your purpose, that God designed, there is nothing you'd rather be doing. When you're acting in your gifting, you know it, and God rewards you for it. Let's be sure to give him credit where credit is due. There is nothing worth purpose in this life without him.

**God, thank you for the gifts you've given me!
Help me to continue to discover what those are and
do them well. I praise your name and give you the glory
for the areas in my life where I act in my gifting,
thank you for giving me purpose.**

September 17

GOD IS GOOD, ALL THE TIME!

God, let your goodness be given away to your good people,
to all your godly lovers!
PSALM 125:4 TPT

God doesn't have a reserve tank of goodness that dries up eventually. His goodness can't and doesn't end. Let that truth settle for a minute. Because we live in a world where we can't always see his goodness. We doubt it, and I think he understands why. We turn on the news and see mass killings. We do life with people who have destructive behaviors. We know someone with cancer, or someone who has lost a child. We have a lot of questions and not always a lot of answers.

We had an enemy even before the fall of Adam and Eve. We live in a fallen world, but there is also a God of justice. A God of goodness. A God who is faithful. A God who love us unconditionally. A God who promises answers someday. A God of mystery but ultimately, love, goodness, and gentleness towards us as his children. Trust that. Trust him. Let that truth settle on you today.

God, I know you are good, above all else,
you are a good, good Father. I'm so grateful for that.
When I'm confused, help me to see you are there.
When I can't understand this world, remind me
you are good and loving. When I have questions,
let me seek the truth in you!

September 18

PAY IT FORWARD

From your kindness you send the rain to water
the mountains from the upper rooms of your palace.
Your goodness brings forth fruit for all to enjoy.
PSALM 104:13 TPT

You know the concept of paying it forward? You do a kind act for someone and, in turn, they pass that kindness on to another person, and so it continues. Kind act after kind act. Spreading goodness and service on to people all over. Imagine the aftermath of something like that—the warmth that provides to someone's heart, the smile that brings to another's face, the enjoyment so many would get from that blessing. This is fruit as described in the Bible. What we do here, in the name of God, produces lasting effects. Fruit that will last. Fruit to be enjoyed.

Any goodness we do in faithfulness to God is going to produce fruit. That fruit will take root, shaping another's life and having a lasting impact. In turn, that fruit will shed seeds that will be planted somewhere else, in the name of God, and those seeds will turn to fruit in another life, and so on, blessing after blessing. Do not doubt that his goodness is in you, friends, meant to be passed on and shared.

**God, thank you that you are good and that I can
spread that goodness to others in your name. I want
to be a person that produces lasting fruit, God.
Help me to see that your desire is the same for me.**

September 19

COMMANDMENTS

"Why do you call me good?" Jesus asked. "Only God is truly good.
But to answer your question, you know the commandments:
'You must not murder. You must not commit adultery.
You must not steal. You must not testify falsely. You must
not cheat anyone. Honor your father and mother.'"

MARK 10:18-19 NLT

Most of us know the Ten Commandments, the big ones,
at least. We know we shouldn't kill. Shouldn't steal. Shouldn't
commit adultery. There are more about not worshiping idols,
not swearing in the name of God, remembering the day of
the Sabbath and keeping it holy, not coveting anything your
neighbor has. In these commandments are huge life lessons
that we need to pay more attention to.

So often sin is ignored in today's culture. We honor only
the big ones, casting aside the sin that most frequently gets us:
anger towards others, judgment, lying, comparison. How we
need to get on our knees in repentance and lay these sins at
the cross of Jesus! God is so good, friends, and he desires our
everything. The sin we commit in secret? He knows. The sin
we harbor in our heart? He feels it. He wants to release you
from that bondage, so let it go today.

Jesus, forgive me for the sins I haven't yet repented
of. The sins I think I do in secret that I have no
accountability for. The sins I harbor and won't let go of.
Forgive me, Father, and release me of that chain.

September 20

IT WAS GOOD

Then God looked over all he had made,
and he saw that it was very good!
And evening passed and morning came,
marking the sixth day.
GENESIS 1:31 NLT

God created the heavens and the earth in six days. As he created, formed, and molded, he said the same thing: "It is good." Think of the creator of the universe looking out at you, saying, "You are *good*," because this is how he first designed everything. For good. For good purpose, for good reason, for good cause. Everything worked together for good. And then we fell. And sin entered. And the enemy walks around prowling after victims, our brothers and sisters, who are deceived by his scheming.

There is such power in the name of God; this is the good news of today! That the living, active Word of God is available to us, to direct our lives and breathe freshness into our souls. We can act in the Holy Spirit. The same spirit that created everything can live inside of us when we invite him in. There is nothing about this that isn't good, friends! God knew what would happen and still gave us a way out—the way of Jesus Christ.

Father, thank you for planning everything with purpose.
For creating everything for good, knowing we would
fail, and then giving us Jesus so we can still walk in
goodness and freedom! We are thankful for your
goodness, mercy, and justice, Father God!

September 21

PLANS TO DO GOOD

If you plan to do evil, you will be lost;
if you plan to do good, you will receive
unfailing love and faithfulness.
PROVERBS 14:22 NLT

Have you ever watched one of those movies where the plot is all about revenge? They are all kind of the same plot; one wrongful act is committed, that person is discovered for their wrongdoing, then the person who was wronged has to commit all kinds of horrific acts to get justice. One lie after another, one horrible act after another, and yet, in the end you end up feeling worse for the person trying to bring justice because they are in over their heads. They are now not only hurt by what was initially done to them, but they lost themselves along the way. Each time they tried to get even, they ended up in deeper and deeper lies, deceit, anger, and pain.

This does not need to be our movie reel. We have Jesus. We have a Savior. We have someone who says, *Stay on my path and I will shower you with goodness and love! Do not conform to this world, do not plan to do evil and end up lost. Stay the course, child, and I will guide you towards freedom.*

Father God, thank you that you know my story already.
That I have a choice to make in my actions towards
others. I want to choose you, Jesus. I want to pursue
you in the plan of my life. Help me to come to you
first before trying to act in my flesh.

September 22

SIMPLICITY IN LOVE

Let all that you do be done in love.
1 CORINTHIANS 16:14 ESV

Following God can seem overwhelming at times. There are a lot of rules when you read the Bible. A lot that others tell us we need to abide by. A lot of judgment, a lot of ridicule, a lot of sermons. Really, though, the crux of the Bible can be boiled down to one simple truth: *Everything we do should be done in love.*

Everything. Not some things. Everything. If we approach every person, each situation, every action in love, we cannot fail. It may mean we don't always feel good about the way things are handled. It may mean that, at times, we feel trampled on in humility. Pursuing love at all times might be draining. But God will fill you up. He will sustain you. Where you give love, more love will be given. When your love tank feels empty, God will shower you with more than you need.

Father, I desire that my attitudes, actions, and heart be full of love before anything else. Help me to see the simple truth of what you ask—that I love and love well.

September 23

DISPLAYED

He brought me to the banqueting house,
and his banner over me was love.
SONG OF SOLOMON 2:4 ESV

Picture yourself as a guest in a palace. You enter the gate on a horse, doors being opened for you, trumpets playing welcoming you down the walkway. You walk through the big, heavy door and know you are the guest of honor as you are greeted, bags taken, coat removed for you. You stand there waiting for what's next. You are ushered to a seat at the table where you are served a huge assortment of food—all you could ever want or desire in a meal. You are showered with goodies and then, above you, a banner is unrolled. The banner covers the entire banquet hall, with beautiful colors, a huge display that leaves no place untouched by its material. When the banner is unrolled, you feel love; a banner of love was laid out for you.

This is the love of Christ. This is his work on the cross for us. This is what he displayed in the ultimate sacrifice for us, the best love we could ever receive or ever desire. A love we can only try to fathom. A love that is truly beyond us.

Jesus, thank you for dying on the cross for me.
For showing me love like I've never before experienced.
Thank you that your love is new every day for me,
as your child, as a sinner. Thank you for making me
the guest of honor at your table.

September 24

OBEDIENT LOVE

"Whoever has my commands and keeps them is the one who loves me. The one who loves me will be loved by my Father, and I too will love them and show myself to them."

JOHN 14:21 NIV

Raising a child or training a dog is sometimes very similar. You teach them your rules, you give them consequences, and you hope they obey you. You may test them by giving them a task to follow. You see if he will retrieve the ball and bring it to you. You see if she will put her shoes away when she gets home from school. If they obey and follow your example, you feel proud. You feel as if you've actually accomplished something. You might feel something else too; you might feel *love*. You might feel loved because they're following your example. They're listening to you and doing what you ask, which is the ultimate compliment.

Imagine how God feels when he sees his sons and daughters acting out his commandments. When he sees us showering all of his children in love and goodness. When he sees us pursue him, first, and extend his grace to others.

God, I want to always act in love. When I disobey, may I repent to you, so I can be forgiven and move on in your love toward my brothers and sisters.

September 25

HE HEARS THE DETAILS

May the Lord cause you to increase and abound in love
for one another, and for all people, just as we also do for you.
1 THESSALONIANS 3:12 NASB

Do you have that person in your life who is just plain difficult to love? Maybe you have tried, and failed, multiple times
to rise above and show them love no matter how they treat you
back. You have prayed, and prayed, for God's love to intervene
and act on behalf of him. Yet each time you have an encounter
with that person, you fall short. Every. Single. Time.

This can be discouraging, for sure, but there is hope
through dedicated, specific prayer. God tells us to pray for an
increase of love and he will give it. Praying for a specific desire
is something God welcomes, and if you've tried to act in your
own free will, and failed, what harm is there in turning it all
over to God? It's amazing when we pray for specifics and
see God bless us with an answer to that prayer, and he will,
friends. He will.

**God, thank you that you are a Father who hears
my prayers. When it's difficult for me to ask for love
towards a person, may you give me an increase of
your love. When I don't know what to pray for,
give me specific words and people to lay at your feet.**

September 26

JOY IN THE SHADOW

*Because you are my helper,
I sing for joy in the shadow of your wings.*
PSALM 63:7 NLT

God is our greatest cheerleader. He watches as we take flight in a calling he has put before us and he gently encourages us, urging us forward and cheering us on. The God of the universe, the creator of everything, the one living on the throne of righteousness, knows us and cheers us on.

What a privilege and an honor to know that once he sets us down a path, he will not let us stray without first urging us forward for his mission, putting stepping-stones down for us to walk on. What confidence we can have when we know he is our helper. What joy we can proclaim when we know we are in the shadow of him leading the charge. There is no one else we should want to follow. Let him hear your shouts of praise and joy for who he is!

Father God, thank you that you help me in times of trouble and times of joy. Thank you that I walk safely in the shadow of your wings, every day, and that you are my shield and protector.

September 27

AUTHORITY IN LOVE

Obey your leaders and act under their authority.
They are watching over you, because they are responsible
for your souls. Obey them so that they will do this work with joy,
not sadness. It will not help you to make their work hard.
HEBREWS 13:17 NCV

We've all had that boss that is difficult to follow. A person who is supposed to lead and encourage, and instead just shouts orders and treats you with disrespect. Bosses like that can make it very difficult to come into the workplace with joy. It makes you want to treat them the same way. And it can be draining to always be the bigger person. But have you ever thought what it's like to come to work in their shoes? To have that much responsibility, that much at stake? Have you tried to get to know them as people, understanding that what they may have going on at home is coming to work with them every day?

As believers, we are called to a great purpose in love. We are encouraged to obey our leaders, do our work with joy, and understand that nothing good will come from trying to make their jobs more difficult. As you approach your day today, ask for grace and understanding for your boss or coworkers.

God, I need grace today. Help me to approach people with joy and love, even when I'm not getting that back. I want to obey your commandments, God, above all else in my life, even when it's tough.

September 28

ALL JOY

Indeed, you are our glory and joy.
1 THESSALONIANS 2:20 NIV

How beautiful it would be to live every day in the assurance of one thing no matter what: Jesus is our glory and our joy. Come what may, that is the truth we cling to in every circumstance. That our joy is not found in the things of this world—our home, our children, our job, or social status. Those things will vanish and be left here when we die. None of that truly matters. But that our joy is made complete in only one thing … Jesus Christ.

When you've experienced extreme difficult, tragedy, or sadness in your life, this concept is made apparent. Can we rise above our circumstance, in the name of Jesus, and still find joy in him? Can we wake up every day and choose him? Choose joy? Think on this the next time you are tested in various ways. Where does your joy truly live?

**Jesus, I know my joy can only come from you.
Especially in times of trial, Lord, may I look to you
as the perfecter of my peace and joy. There is nothing
else here that can fill me the way you do. I've tried
and failed and always come back to the truth:
you are my constant source of joy.**

September 29

ETERNAL JOY

The kingdom of God is not a matter of eating and drinking but of righteousness and peace and joy in the Holy Spirit.
ROMANS 14:17 ESV

We live in a society that constantly desires more, more, and more. More is supposed to mean more of everything, including happiness that comes from attaining. Attaining more stuff does not bring lasting happiness. It may provide a brief moment of joy when it is first acquired, but that vanishes, leaving an empty hole that only looks like it needs to be filled again with someone else.

When we believe in eternity, in Jesus, in a life beyond what is right in front of us, our perspective shifts and we see the truth in desiring more. That "more" isn't going to be coming with us to heaven. That nothing of this world will be. That our joy doesn't come from more stuff, or more recognition. No, our kingdom with the Father is about our hearts. Our joy comes in the form of the Holy Spirit, of living in unity with that Spirit, or bringing others to Christ for his kingdom. God's people matter, not the stuff in this world.

God, help me to recognize that my heart can only be filled with your Spirit. That living with you is the only thing that will bring true, lasting happiness and joy in my life. Help me get rid of the clutter in my heart and only focus on expanding your kingdom in love.

September 30

SINCERITY

The goal of this command is love, which comes from
a pure heart and a good conscience and a sincere faith.
1 TIMOTHY 1:5 NIV

You've probably seen the ads, or watched a pastor on TV filling the screen with questionable theology. Or maybe you've heard a remark from a fellow believer that made you sit back and wonder. It isn't our place to judge, at all, but sometimes we need to sharpen one another in love. Sometimes we need a gut check on our faith and the sincerity of it. Sometimes we ourselves stray and need someone to steer us back to Jesus. Sometimes we feel like wandering sheep with no shepherd.

If we're acting in the love of Jesus, and coming at everything with a pure heart, that can only come from Jesus, and a sincere faith, then we're doing our job as believers. We're loving others the way Jesus desires us to love and we can rest at night with a clear conscience, knowing we're relying on God to fill us, direct us, and fill us with his overflowing love to pass down to others. We're not meant to do this life on our own. God will not lead us astray if we pursue him in sincerity.

God, I desire to have a heart that is pure in love for
others. I know I won't be perfect. In my humanness
I will sin, but I want to keep pursuing you with sincerity.
Thank you for directing my actions.

287

October

"I will betroth you
to me in faithfulness.
And you shall know
the LORD."

HOSEA 2:20 ESV

October 1

PEACEFUL WALLS

He grants peace to your borders
and satisfies you with the finest of wheat.
PSALM 147:14 NIV

We all desire peace—peace among nations, peace among our kids, peace among coworkers and friends, and peace in our homes. A great tool we have for creating peace is prayer. Praying over our "borders" that we have around us every day: the walls in our homes, our cars, our office building. There are places the enemy wants to destroy. He wants to break us down, but God says no.

God tells us he can grant us peace and it's never too late to start asking for that prayer. There's so much unrest in the world, so much that the enemy is wreaking havoc on. Sometimes there's nothing else to do but get on your knees and pray. Be proactive in that prayer of protection around places in your life that are important. Ask for a hedge of protection and God's supernatural peace to always be present.

God, thank you that you are a God who grants
me peace, who can fill my life with peace when I feel
I have none. I pray for protection of peace in these
places in my life (name them out loud) and that
the enemy would not breech that peace. He has
no place in my life, God, but you do.

October 2

JOY IN THE SPIRIT

The believers were filled with joy
and with the Holy Spirit.
ACTS 13:52 NLT

In order to have true joy in Christ, we need to invite the Holy Spirit in to dwell with us. To reside in us. To be active and present in our spirit. We can do nothing apart from the Spirit of God and yet, oftentimes, we try to find fulfillment in other ways. We fill our lives with meaningless things to try to bring joy, and we often fall short. That joy is temporary, filling us up for the briefest of moments, and fading just as quickly. Leaving us with a greater desire, a gap bigger than when we started, a hole that we feel we need to fill.

Yet we know the truth in Jesus. We know there is only one way to live and that is in conjunction with the Spirit of God. If we let that settle on our hearts, we recognize the power of that statement. The Spirit of God, the same Spirit of the living God, is a gift God has given us! Praise God today for that gift and find true joy in the Holy Spirit!

God, I'm blown away by the gifts you've given me.
I've tried to find joy in countless other ways and yet
I always come back to you and your Spirit. I ask for your
Spirit to come to me today, Lord, may I let you in so
I can experience the fullness of joy in walking with you.

October 3

PEACE WITH FAITH

When it was evening on the first day of the week,
Jesus' followers were together. The doors were locked,
because they were afraid of the elders. Then Jesus came and stood
right in the middle of them and said, "Peace be with you."
After he said this, he showed them his hands and his side.
His followers were thrilled when they saw the Lord.
JOHN 20:19-20 NCV

Wouldn't it have been great to have been one of the disciples back in the day seeing Jesus resurrected after he was beaten and killed on the cross? How great would the assurance have been to see him standing there among all of you together, showing you that he was doing exactly what he said he was going to do? Not only that but speaking to you, saying, "Peace be with you." Oh, how glorious those words must have sounded from him!

We don't have that experience, but we do have faith. We have the truth of what faith is, trusting and believing Jesus is who he says he is. Believing that he still performs miracles today, even when we can't physically see him. Jesus is the giver of peace. Through his death and resurrection, we have access to peace in his Spirit. There is no greater gift.

Jesus, thank you that you are the perfecter of peace.
Thank you that by your wounds, I am healed. Thank you
for the ultimate sacrifice you paid for my freedom.

October 4

MARTYRDOM

*I, John, your brother and companion in the suffering
and kingdom and patient endurance that are ours in Jesus,
was on the island of Patmos because of the
word of God and the testimony of Jesus.*

REVELATION 1:9 NIV

The island of Patmos was a desolate place. John was sent there for his testimony and faith in Jesus. John spoke passionately about Jesus, taught about him, and followed him with loyal conviction. This wasn't okay with leaders and they banished him. It was here that he wrote the Book of Revelation after having a vision detailing out what would happen in the end times.

When we think of current suffering in the world for our faith in Jesus, it looks very different, but still life threatening, still potentially scary, and still making us depend on Jesus to give us endurance to make it to the end. Whatever that end may look like, we cannot do it on our own. We are meant to be brothers and sisters together, sharing in the suffering and advancing the kingdom of God together.

**God, I want to be a loyal follower of you,
come what may. I want to reach the unreached and
preach your good news to others. I understand I may
be persecuted for this, and yet I want to have
confidence in you, Lord. Give me endurance.**

October 5

A GOD IN CONTROL

*That we ourselves boast of you among the churches
of God for your patience and faith in all your persecutions
and tribulations that you endure.*

2 THESSALONIANS 1:4 NKJV

When life is going well, it's much easier to have faith, patience with the unknown, and trust in God's plan. There is nothing much to worry about, nothing really to fear, nothing to get caught up on. You can float through the day-to-day, loving the way God has made your life turn out. Feeling thankful for what He's given you and how blessed you feel. At the same time, there is always the other side that is meant to derail you or give you endurance.

When your life feels out of control, when tragedy has struck, when fear sets in, this is the true test. This is when our dependence on God is most evident. Are you handling it on your own or relying on God? Are you acting out in anger or trusting his next step for you? Are you first seeking him before you leap? Endurance is not built by a quick fix. Endurance is built when we keep coming back, time and time again, putting more and more trust in God's hands and watching as he builds us up brick by brick.

**God, I thank you that you are a God who gives me
so much but also takes away. You give me layer upon
layer to build on as life happens. You are patient
and loving with me, and give me endurance from
your Spirit when I need it most.**

October 6

IN SECRET

"Woe to you, scribes and Pharisees, hypocrites!
For you tithe mint and dill and cumin, and have neglected the
weightier matters of the law: justice and mercy and faithfulness.
These you ought to have done, without neglecting the others."
MATTHEW 23:23 ESV

It is easy to do what looks right on paper. To look holy on the outside and ignore matters of the heart. To neglect certain areas of our life that are in secret, but prune those areas that others might see more easily. We want our outside to look right while inside we might be struggling. This is human nature and something the enemy delights in. He is a master deceiver and he can often keep us in this place of spinning—continuing our bad habits in secret, while outwardly working on those that might be perceived by others on the outside.

What matters to God? The heart. What we do in secret, he sees. What we think in the quiet of our homes, he hears. Our biggest impact is going to be made when our lives are lived radically enough to get others to ask the question of why we are different.

God, I want to focus on heart issues. I want my life
to be lived worthy of you. I don't want to be so focused
on the outside that I miss what truly matters and deceive
myself, thinking I'm living a worthy life.
You are my judge, God. Give me discernment about the
areas of my life where this might be true.

October 7

GOOD FEAR?

"Now fear the LORD and serve him with all faithfulness.
Throw away the gods your ancestors worshiped beyond
the Euphrates River and in Egypt, and serve the LORD."

JOSHUA 24:14 NIV

Have you ever been standing in line at a theme park for a roller coaster and been completely gripped with fear? A few minutes ago you willfully ran up to the line, excited and looking forward to riding it, but now, after standing there for a while, watching cart after cart being filled and exited, your mind fills with doubt. That first bump looks so high. That roller coaster takes forever to get up there and then it just drops. You aren't fearing that the roller coaster will derail off the track. No, it's a simpler fear, a respect almost of what the roller coaster was created to do.

This is similar to the fear of God talked about so frequently in the Bible. Different from anxiety about the future, or fear of the unknown (fear instilled from the enemy), fearing the Lord is more of an attitude of reverence for the power of who God says he is. This kind of fear is healthy fear, believe it or not, and a respect for God.

God, I want to gain a deeper knowledge of what it means to truly fear you. I only know you as the loving God that I know you are, but I know there is much more to your character that I want to know. Give me the resources and insight to build on this so I can get to know you more intimately.

October 8

GOD'S LOVE

I have always been mindful of your unfailing love
and have lived in reliance on your faithfulness.
PSALM 26:3 NIV

One truth remains above all else; God loves you, child. He adores you, in fact. There is nothing you can do, nothing you can say, nothing that can separate you from the love of Jesus. There will be many times today you are faced with lies, or unkindness, or selfishness, but one thing you can cling to, and keep going back to, is that you have a God who loves you.

Remaining mindful of that love can bring great peace when you need it most. If there is anything you hold on to today, let that thought settle in your heart. That he will never leave you or forsake you. That through each circumstance you are faced with today, he will be faithful to you in his love.

God, I thank you that you are faithful and loving.
That no matter what I encounter today, nothing can
separate me from you. You are my stronghold and shield,
my rock and redeemer. I know I will face
many challenges today. Remind me you are there,
holding my hand and loving me.

October 9

WORD OF THE LORD

For the word of the LORD is upright,
And all His work is done in faithfulness.

PSALM 33:4 NASB

In today's world of social media and blogging and fantastic authors using their gifts for good, it's fun to read encouraging words from others. God has given them such a purpose in their writing and so much growth can happen when we read something inspiring, or challenging, that we can reflect on as we go about our day.

The best source for encouragement and truth, however, still remains in the pages of the Bible. The Word of God is living and active for us to partake in whenever we want to. This verse in Psalms calls the word of the Lord "upright," and the Bible should be the first place we turn to when we need encouragement, need to be held accountable, need to be reminded of the love God has for us. Before picking up another author's word, let's go to the author who wrote the Book of Life for us.

God, it's so easy for me to pick up another book for
my source of inspiration. Remind me to seek you first,
and your Word, when I need encouragement or truth.

October 10

WALKING WITH GOD

"A bruised reed he will not break,
and a faintly burning wick he will not quench;
he will faithfully bring forth justice."
ISAIAH 42:3 ESV

As believers, we experience spiritual highs and lows. You've probably had them yourself. You leave a women's conference, where you've had three days to worship Jesus. You've spent dedicated time in his presence, and you feel extremely on fire for him. Then you come home to your daily life—feeding kids, getting up early for your job, cooking for your family of five—and soon you start to mourn that spiritual high you were feeling. You desperately try to connect to God, yet everyday life has gotten in the way of your relationship.

God tell us he will be faithful in his pursuit of us. In our weaknesses, he is strong. He knows we will falter. He knows we will fail, possibly stray, and yet he promises to keep our fire alive. He promises to always pursue us, standing there at the door knocking, waiting for us to answer. Give yourself grace, friend, and know that God has not left you. Rest in that, get back to the Word of God and the discipline of it, and cling to his truth.

God, thank you for not abandoning me when I abandon you. Thank you for your constant pursuit of my heart and for not putting out my fire. Give me motivation to keep making time for you, Lord, knowing I am better walking with you than on my own.

October 11

BETROTHED

*"I will betroth you to me in faithfulness.
And you shall know the LORD."*

HOSEA 2:20 ESV

A relationship with God is similar to a marriage. It takes time, effort, and energy. We don't always get it right; we fail miserably, and yet we know we're committed. We know that when we prayed to Jesus that he was our Lord and Savior that we meant it. We died to our old lives and were made new in him. We are no longer apart from him but with him in everything.

Being in relationship with Jesus means choosing to be faithful—faithful in our pursuit of him, faithful in our daily time with him, faithful in living out what we say we believe about him. Truly knowing the Lord is knowing him intimately, knowing him inside and out, and trusting him with it all.

**Jesus, I am in a relationship with you.
It looks differently for everyone, but I trust you
wholeheartedly and I want to come to you first when
seeking advice. I desire to know you deeper, know you
more intimately, and commit my life to you daily.**

October 12

FATHER TO THE FATHERLESS

"No, I will not abandon you as orphans—
I will come to you."

JOHN 14:18 NLT

You've heard the stories. Watched them, read about them, seen them on social media. Orphans, abandoned and alone, victimized and tortured, left with nothing and no one. Who will care for them? Where will they call home? Who will hold them and tell them they are loved?

Whether or not you grew up in a stable, loving family, you were still an orphan until God stepped in, loving you as only a heavenly Father could. He isn't our biological father, but our spiritual one, guiding us in everything we do. His sovereignty is powerful and mighty, his presence in our life necessary. He does not abandon us; even when all hope seems lost, he finds us.

God, I want to be on my knees for the orphans in this world, Lord. The ones who truly have no parents and those who are lost because they don't have you. There is so much hurt and pain in the world that I don't understand, but I do trust you, and want to |do my part to impact your kingdom. Give me a heart |for the fatherless and use me how you need to.

October 13

KINGDOM REIGNS

You are the Lord that reigns over your never-ending kingdom
through all the ages of time and eternity!
You are faithful to fulfill every promise you've made.
You manifest yourself as Kindness in all you do!
PSALM 145:13 TPT

God's kingdom never ends. The faithful, God-following men and women we read about in the Bible are with God in eternity. The people we do life with now will either be in heaven or hell when they die. The kids and grandkids and descendants of ours that haven't yet been born will live on this earth until Jesus comes back or they also die.

God's kingdom truly is never ending until he says so. And there is so much more to come according to the Book of Revelation. The Bible says God is manifested in the world as "Kindness"; what a beautiful thought. Every kind act we do, or see done to others, is God manifesting himself in a tangible way. If we can walk around in this world, doing kind acts knowing we are showing God to others, what a difference we can make. What a comforting thought!

God, you are kind and loving and gracious.
May everything I do manifest your Spirit to others. Give
me a lighter step and a fullness in my heart.
I want to show others your love in tangible ways and
let them know your kingdom will last forever!

October 14

ROADMAP

*Not given to drunkenness, not violent but gentle,
not quarrelsome, not a lover of money.*
1 TIMOTHY 3:3 NIV

The Bible can serve as a road map for life. It is full of powerful instruction, giving us specific details of what to avoid, and what to grasp wholeheartedly. We are given instruction on what sins to not commit, and what good deeds to continue blessing people with.

It can be overwhelming, at times, but it also serves as a powerful tool. A weapon against the lying and scheming of Satan, who loves to try to trick us and fool us into a way of thinking that goes against what is given as truth in the Bible. If you aren't sure, ask God for discernment, and seek first the Word of God, which will give you guidance and direction.

God, thank you for giving me your Word as a living and active tool for my use. I want to soak up knowledge of what you say to avoid—drunkenness, violence, greed, and the like—and instead focus on gentleness and patience and love. Thank you for your Word. May I use it as a road map for my life, knowing its truth and power as a tool.

October 15

GOD'S SOUNDTRACK

This forever-song I sing of the gentle love
of God overwhelming me!
Young and old alike will hear about
your faithful, steadfast love—never failing!"
PSALM 89:1 TPT

Have you ever turned on the radio and heard a song that instantly brought you back to a particular memory? Clear as day, you can feel the same emotions, picture exactly where you were when you heard it, and immediately feel as young as you did in the times you sang it out loud. Music is a beautiful way for us to create a soundtrack of our life, piecing together songs for the years we heard them.

Psalm 89 relates God's love as a song, flowing in and out of generations of believers, soothing our souls, reminding us of his goodness and faithfulness. What a beautiful picture of the love of God! A forever song that we are meant to sing together, young and old, together as one body worshiping God.

God, thank you for those in the older generation
who so faithfully serve you, and those in
the younger generation who burn with
passion for you. Thank you for this beautiful
dance we do, together, as your children!

October 16

SELF-CONTROL

So he left all that he had in Joseph's charge, and because of him he had no concern about anything but the food he ate. Now Joseph was handsome in form and appearance. And after a time his master's wife cast her eyes on Joseph and said, "Lie with me." But he refused and said to his master's wife, "Behold, because of me my master has no concern about anything in the house, and he has put everything that he has in my charge. He is not greater in this house than I am, nor has he kept back anything from me except you, because you are his wife. How then can I do this great wickedness and sin against God?"

GENESIS 39:6-9 ESV

Self-control is one of the hardest fruits to obey, especially in an area of sin we may struggle with. We might have a tendency to commit these sins in secret, thinking the effect might be different or less offensive. Our hearts can be troubled by sin and spiral, looking for a way out of the hole of sin we've fallen in over and over again.

These sins can be extremely harmful to yourself, to loved ones, and to your relationship with God. Thankfully, God is a God of forgiveness. Repenting of your sins, no matter how big or small, allows you a clean slate: freedom from the bondage to this secret sin life. Give it up to God and walk in the freedom of Jesus Christ.

Jesus, thank you for dying on the cross for my sins. Please forgive me for my sins. Whether big or small, they are the same in your eyes, and I want to be free. Thank you for your grace and redemption in my life.

October 17

WALK THE LINE

No one can tame the tongue. It is wild and evil
and full of deadly poison. We use our tongues to praise our
Lord and Father, but then we curse people, whom God made
like himself. Praises and curses come from the same mouth!
My brothers and sisters, this should not happen.
JAMES 3:8-10 NCV

You may know of someone, or be the offender yourself, who belts out praise and worship songs at church on Sunday morning and yet goes home that evening and starts bad-mouthing a mutual friend. Or there's a pastor you listen to every week, someone you gain wisdom from, only find out he's been having an affair in secret. The Bible tells us this shouldn't happen, yet we're all susceptible to sin. We're broken people leading broken lives.

If we're walking in truth, our convictions about our sin, including the way we speak about people and how we act, should bring us to our knees in repentance. Beyond that, we should then know we're forgiven and work our darnedest to not repeat that sin. It is a thin line, walking in obedience to Christ, and we need to help each other along as brothers and sisters.

God, I am guilty in my own way about
not taming my tongue, or even my negative heart
attitude towards someone. Forgive me, Jesus,
and help me to walk an obedient line to you.
I can't do this on my own accord. I need you, Father.

October 18

TRAINING

I appeal to you therefore, brothers, by the mercies of God, to present your bodies as a living sacrifice, holy and acceptable to God, which is your spiritual worship. Do not be conformed to this world, but be transformed by the renewal of your mind, that by testing you may discern what is the will of God, what is good and acceptable and perfect.

ROMANS 12:1-2 ESV

Training for a marathon is a grueling task. You need to be disciplined and thorough in your pursuit of nourishment and how you approach your workouts. Some would argue it's a purely physical discipline. But running also requires mental discipline. You have to train your body *and* your mind.

This same approach works for a life in obedience to God, a disciplined tackling of the beauty in our life—but also our sin. God says our bodies are temples he made for our spirits. Our body, and mind, need to be equally nourished, taken care of, and nurtured. Doing so requires prioritizing certain aspects of our life over others. It means nurturing our gifting in our life and getting rid of the baggage of sin we carry around. It means surrounding ourselves with good instead of pursuing evil. God is a good and perfect Father; his desire is for us to live in partnership with him.

God, thank you for giving me this body, even on days when I don't love it. Help me to pursue you both in body and mind, providing nourishment where I need it most. Oftentimes, I don't even know what my needs are, but you do, God, and I trust you to guide me.

October 19

SUPREME BOSS

In all the work you are doing, work the best you can.
Work as if you were doing it for the Lord, not for people.
COLOSSIANS 3:23 NCV

This verse could be a life verse to be read out loud each and
every day! Whether you're a student, working professional, or
homemaker, work can be something to get excited about or
work can feel mundane. We try and sometimes fail. We look
for approval and feedback. Frequently, we look for satisfaction
in the wrong places. Even mundane work needs a gut-level
check sometimes; how is your heart towards those tiresome
tasks you do every day?

God instructs us to work the best we can—to try, and when
we fail, try again. Ask yourself, who am I working for? Sure,
you might have a leader or boss who is in charge. This person
might be the one to put checks and balances in place, the one
decides whether or not you're getting a raise. But God? He's
our ultimate boss. He's the one we should be working for,
working towards. Our greatest and only satisfaction comes
from the one who created us for that work from the very start.

**God, you're the one I want to make proud,
in my daily work and my heart attitude. I want to
remember you're my audience of one and you never
leave me, even when I'm doing tasks that aren't fulfilling
my life. You fill me and I'm grateful to you.**

October 20

WALK THE TALK

If you are wise and understand God's ways,
prove it by living an honorable life, doing good works
with the humility that comes from wisdom.
JAMES 3:13 NLT

Can a person be a Christian and act ugly? It's a good question. Christians can sometimes rely on "cheap grace," living as though grace gives them license to do whatever they please. They wake up in the morning, ask forgiveness, and do it all over again. But genuine faith doesn't look like that.

Jesus died so that we would be free from sin, not so that we would be free to sin. He didn't hang on the cross so we could keep doing what we're doing without feeling guilty. If we have truly made Jesus Lord of our lives, we will look different from the rest of the world. That nudge in your heart is the Holy Spirit speaking to your conscience. Let's not neglect our actions; a poor walk can undo a lot of good talking.

Dear Lord, please forgive me for abusing your grace.
Help me to be a light in the darkness.
Let my life draw others towards you,
not away from you, and may my life honor you.

October 21

BRING GLORY TO THE FATHER

"If we are being called to account today for an act of kindness shown to a man who was lame and are being asked how he was healed, then know this, you and all the people of Israel: It is by the name of Jesus Christ of Nazareth, whom you crucified but whom God raised from the dead, that this man stands before you healed."

ACTS 4:9-10 NIV

Affection, warmth, consideration, understanding, hospitality, friendliness, compassion—these are just a few words that describe what it means to be kind.

If charged with the crime of kindness, let us be found unequivocally guilty in all we say and do. This brings glory to our heavenly Father, and we will reap accordingly, in due season, if we do not lose heart.

Father, I want to imitate your kindness. Like a kid wearing her papa's shoes, I want people to smile and say that I look you, my Father, whom I adore. I want to be so kind to others that I give according to what they need, rather than what they deserve. Let your kindness spring up in me. I love you. Help me to become a loving chip off the ancient block—you, my Dad.

October 22

BECOME AN INFLUENCER

Overseers must be ready to welcome guests,
love what is good, be wise, live right,
and be holy and self-controlled.
TITUS 1:8 NCV

Whether you know it or not, you have a sphere of influence. You constantly affect people around you with a positive or negative message. Whether your sphere of influence is your immediate family, a megachurch, or even a nation, you are called to be an imitator of Christ.

Knowing this, you live as Christ does, loving what is good and doing what is right. In living out the words of Christ, you put action to your faith, and meaningfully impact others.

Jesus, thank you for your great example of how
to be a servant-leader. Please, let me imitate you
in sincerity, not just loving with words, but also actions
that sing out glorious praises to your name.

October 23

LOYAL

Steadfast love and faithfulness will meet;
righteousness and peace will kiss each other.
PSALM 85:10 NRSV

Abba Father, our heavenly Dad, is so devoted to you! He is unwaveringly committed to your well-being, and he's got your back. God will not disappoint because he is solidly immovable. He is so for you. God isn't going anywhere, sister. He hasn't changed his mind about you. He loves and cares for you more than you could ever imagine. He is timeless and steadfast, and he is a good, kind, loving Father.

Whenever you feel alone, remember God is faithful. Know that he regards every fear or question in your mind as your own invitation to draw very near to him, standing on the promises he has for you. Feed yourself upon his faithfulness, and you will soon be satisfied and well refreshed within your soul. God will never leave you.

Heavenly Father, help me to stand on your word
and on your faithfulness. Then, if I'm off the grid or
I just don't feel in step with my faith journey, I will
remember your faithfulness, your promises, and your
continual care for me. You will always be with me.
You are always for me. That blesses my heart, Lord.
Your faithfulness makes me faith filled too.

October 24

COMMEND WHAT IS GOOD

Brothers and sisters, if someone in your group
does something wrong, you who are spiritual should go
to that person and gently help make him right again.
But be careful, because you might be tempted to sin, too.
GALATIANS 6:1 NCV

As Christians, we are responsible to one another, and we bear each other's burdens. So, when spiritual siblings get caught in sin, we are obligated to come alongside and help. We must do this with a very gentle spirit, speaking truth only in love. We do not address them according to their sin (the Holy Spirit is the one who convicts us of our sins), but call out the glory of God within them, raising them to the standard they were meant to enjoy. This calls them higher, and the kindness of God gently brings them to repentance and obedience.

Let us, as the church, speak life-giving words over one another, edifying and uplifting each other. We have the blessing of being impactful here on the earth. Our power-filled words are easily heard by sisters and brothers.

Heavenly Father, in Jesus' name, help me carry others' burdens in my life and my prayers. Give me the strength to overcome. If I see a sister straying, help me to follow your lead in coming alongside, speaking good things about her identity in you, and assisting her back out of temptation and into your marvelous light. Thank you for your grace and gentleness—and thank you for the people who have helped me in this same way.

October 25

RADIATE TRUE LOVE

Love is patient; love is kind;
love is not envious or boastful or arrogant.
1 Corinthians 13:4 NSV

It's easy to feel as if we love someone. *Love* is a word we like to throw around a lot. But what is true love, really? There is a significant difference between caring about someone and truly loving them in a Spirit-filled way.

Oh, how easy it is to lose our temper and forget to show kindness to those we love! It can be difficult not to feel envy when someone else achieves something we were working for. And it's tough at times not to boast about what's going on in our lives. But when we lean into the arms of our loving heavenly Father, he fills us with a love so real we can't help but radiate it for all to see. His love gives us a supernatural sense of patience and kindness.

Lord, help me show others your true love. A love filled with patience and kindness. I want to avoid pitfalls like bragging and jealousy, and it's only possible with you at my side. I love how you love me, and I pray that your love would be reflected in me toward others too.

October 26

CHILD OF A STRONG GOD

I love you, O LORD, my strength.
The LORD is my rock, my fortress and my deliverer;
my God my rock, in whom I take refuge;
my shield and the horn of my salvation, my stronghold.
PSALM 18:1-2 NIV

Love comes in many forms. One of the most necessary, but least talked about, is security. It's hard to feel at peace when our world is rocky and stormy, full of unknowns. But we know we can rest easy in the strong and loving arms of our heavenly Father. The Lord is our strength. Because he loves us, he is our protector, our deliverer. He is mighty and full of awesome power.

We can feel secure as we take refuge in the shelter of his love. Our strength comes when we sink into the fullness of it. We can ride out every storm, knowing his love will carry us through. He is as solid as a rock, and his love for us knows no bounds.

Lord, I am overwhelmed by the power of your love.
Help me to turn to you in my despair, knowing your
love will deliver me every time. I am so grateful
I can take refuge in your strength.

October 27

PRICELESS LOVE

Though you have not seen him, you love him.
Though you do not now see him, you believe in him and rejoice
with joy that is inexpressible and filled with glory,
obtaining the outcome of your faith, the salvation of your souls.
1 PETER 1:8-9 ESV

It's kind of a strange thing, loving someone you will never see this side of heaven. And yet, when you experience the love of your almighty Father, there is no doubting his existence. There's a joy that comes from knowing his love and from seeing it play out in your life. Though words don't do it justice, once you've felt it, there can be no denying it's something absolutely breathtaking.

So while others may think it's a little weird to love someone you can see only through spiritual eyes, you can rejoice in the knowledge that you have a love that surpasses everything else. It's one that buoys your spirits and makes you want to sing with joy bubbling up from the inside and spilling out into all areas of your life.

Lord, thank you for your incredible love. You have
filled my very soul with a joy that is truly inexpressible,
and I am no longer the same woman because of it.
I praise you for saving me with your beautiful love.

October 28

BLAMELESS

This I pray, that your love may abound still more
and more in real knowledge and all discernment,
so that you may approve the things that are excellent,
in order to be sincere and blameless until the day of Christ.
PHILIPPIANS 1:9-10 NIV

It's amazing, the many ways that God loves us. One of the
ways in which he shows us his love is by giving us knowledge
and wisdom we wouldn't otherwise possess if it weren't for his
supernatural gifts. When we press into him, we are filled with
discernment in circumstances that arise. We can better determine whether or not he'd approve of our choices because we
can rely on him to give us a command of the situation at hand.

When we allow his love to abound in us, we're able to
achieve things we wouldn't be able to do without him. He is so
good to us that way!

**Father, thank you for giving me your knowledge and
discernment. I pray that I would rely on it in every given
situation. It's my true desire to be sincere and blameless
in this life! I'm so grateful you give me the tools to do so.**

GIFT OF FREEDOM

God is so rich in mercy, and he loved us so much,
that even though we were dead because of our sins,
he gave us life when he raised Christ from the dead.
(It is only by God's grace that you have been saved!)
EPHESIANS 2:4-5 NLT

There is no greater gift than the gift of life. And our gracious Lord has given us true life indeed. Though without him we were bound for an eternity of suffering, Jesus died to restore us and give us everlasting life through him. Can you imagine the suffering he went through for us? It's mind-boggling.

And yet he died for us because he loved us, and continues to love us so well. He was the ultimate example of one who gave everything to those he loves. God saw our need, and though we didn't deserve the gift we were given, he gave it anyway, simply out of his love for us. No greater love exists than the one we receive from our Father in heaven.

Oh God, I am overwhelmed by your love for me.
I pray that my life would be a living testimony
of the deep and abiding love you've shown me,
and that others would see your mercy in me.

October 30

RENEWED DAILY

The steadfast love of the Lord never ceases;
his mercies never come to an end;
they are new every morning;
great is your faithfulness.
LAMENTATIONS 3:22-23 ESV

Have you ever wondered if God is still there? Have you turned your face toward the heavens and called out to him, asking where he is in the midst of what you are going through? The answer, simply, is that he never leaves us. His Word tells us that his steadfast love never ceases. He loves us through it all, with a love that is never diminishing, and never letting up.

The love of our Lord is a beautiful thing. It's something we can always count on, and always rely upon. We are promised that every morning is a fresh start with new mercies. He is steadfast and true, and he loves us with a fierceness that makes the enemy quake with fear.

God, I am amazed by your faithfulness. Your love
is a thing of beauty, and I pray I'd turn to you to seek
that love, even in the middle of the worst life can
throw at me. I want to rest in your precious mercy
and grace each and every day of my life.

October 31

CLOTHED IN BEAUTY

Above all, clothe yourselves with love,
which binds us all together in perfect harmony.
COLOSSIANS 3:14 NLT

Women, in general, were created with a gift for appreciating beauty. We have an eye for lovely things. For many of us, this includes clothing. Adding to our wardrobe can be such a fun thing! But the best thing we could ever put on? It's a cloak of love. When we are wrapped in love, and covered with it from head to toe, it changes everything.

Love always fits, and the bigger it is the better. It's something that looks good on everyone, and it never goes out of style. And when you wear your love for all to see, you can't help but feel peace and harmony with those around you. So when you're dressing yourself for the day, don't forget to take a moment and put the love of God on first. You'll never look better!

Lord, I pray that I'd cover myself in love,
each and every day. I praise you for giving me the
gift of love, and I pray that I'd pass it along to everyone
with whom I meet. I want others to see your love
in me before they see anything else.

November

"You gave me life and showed me kindness, and in your care you watched over my life."

JOB 10:12 NCV

November 1

TOGETHER IN CHRIST

Can anything ever separate us from Christ's love?
Does it mean he no longer loves us if we have trouble
or calamity, or are persecuted, or hungry, or destitute,
or in danger, or threatened with death?
ROMANS 8:35 NLT

God gives us many promises throughout the Bible. And one of these promises is that he will always love us. But he never tells us that accepting his gift of salvation means we will lead a life without trouble. In fact, we may face more of it simply because we have chosen to walk side by side with him.

Bad things are certain to come our way throughout our lives. But we can rely on the fact that we will get through it by turning to the one who saves us and pressing in to his deep love for us. Nothing can ever separate us from that love. Yes, there will be circumstances that try to prove otherwise, but we can always be secure in the knowledge that he loves us through it all.

Lord, your love is such a gift. Thank you for
loving me through the good and the bad in life.
I pray I'd appreciate your love the way that you deserve.

November 2

DECLARED HOLY

So God brought out his chosen ones with singing;
for with a joyful shout they were set free!
PSALM 105:43 TPT

Have you ever felt captive to the icky thoughts inside your head? Do you sometimes feel trapped by the poor choices you've made? Has life been overwhelming you with all you've endured? Rejoice, my friend, because you no longer need to feel imprisoned by it all. The Bible tells us that we are set free from what would enslave us. God has set aside his chosen ones, and that includes you!

So let it all go. Release your feelings of guilt—and your burdens—and instead be glad. There is great joy in being able to relieve yourself of the heaviness you've been carrying around. And you can do so because our God and Savior has wiped your slate clean. It's time to party. You are a free woman!

Oh God, the joy I feel because of you is indescribable. I'm so thankful you have set me free from all that burdened me. I pray I'd continue to shake off these chains and remember you came to release me from all that would keep me captive.

November 3

REJOICE IN GOD'S GIFT

But let the righteous be glad;
Let them rejoice before God;
Yes, let them rejoice exceedingly.

PSALM 68:3 NKJV

There are those that would have us believe that a life lived according to God's will means a life of doom, gloom, and not much fun at all. And oh, how much they're missing when they live under this misconception! When you are given the gift of salvation, and live under the grace of God, there is great reason for celebration, and so much to rejoice about.

When you truly begin to know this good, good Father of ours, then you begin to see how worthy he is of praise and rejoicing. There is a joy in knowing him that cannot be matched by anything else you'd find on this earth, no matter how hard you may search for it. He is simply the best, and perfect in all that he does.

God, I delight in knowing you. I pray I'd come to know you in a deeper way each day. May your joy fill me to the brim. I rejoice that you love me the way that you do. My heart is full of gladness because of you!

November 4

REAP JOY

Those who sow in tears
Shall reap in joy.
Psalm 126:5 NKJV

Loving God and having a real relationship with him doesn't mean we won't go through times of trial. There are things you will experience that may bring you to your knees with sorrow and sadness. And yet the Bible says that when we sow in tears, we shall reap in joy. So what exactly does this mean?

Our work here on earth needs to be done regardless of what we are feeling emotionally as we do it. We are promised the greatest joy we will ever know with our Lord and Savior. So we may weep through our sowing of our day-to-day tasks and duties, but a joyful harvest is coming. As we struggle, we can rest assured, knowing that our time of jubilation is coming. Those tears may fall, but the day is near when they'll turn into joy.

Lord, thank you for getting me through times of trial with your promise of joy in the days to come. It's only because of you that I can push through and work, knowing that you're the giver of the greatest joy anyone can ever experience.

November 5

NEW OPPORTUNITIES

*Dear brothers and sisters, when troubles of any kind
come your way, consider it an opportunity for great joy.
For you know that when your faith is tested,
your endurance has a chance to grow.*

JAMES 1:2-3 NLT

It's kind of hard imaging having trouble be an opportunity for joy, isn't it? In fact, it's our instinct to feel just the opposite. And yet we are asked to view it that way despite those instincts. That's because, when times of trouble come our way, we become stronger in the long run. We are stretched in new ways, learning and growing as we go. And that's something to rejoice over!

If we always stayed just the way we are today, we'd never experience personal growth. But when we look at tough times as an opportunity to change for the better, we can begin to feel thankful for these times. We can delight in our rough patches, relying on the Lord to get us through it all.

**God, it's hard to look at times of trouble in a positive
light. Help me to find joy in the midst of suffering,
and to know that as I grow emotionally, I am turning
into the person you have created me to be!**

November 6

SOURCE OF HAPPINESS

Go ahead and celebrate!
Come on and clap your hands everyone!
Shout to God with the raucous sounds of joy!
PSALM 47:1 TPT

When you're feeling euphoric, doesn't it make you want to sing with gladness? Your feet start tapping along, and soon your whole body is getting into the feeling. David felt the same way all those years ago as we wrote what we now know as the Psalms. Take a look at his words. Don't they feel like they could have been written in a modern-day song in today's world?

Knowing the true joy that comes from a loving relationship with God isn't something new. People have been clapping their hands with glee for thousands of years. And yet the joy of the Lord feels just as fresh and new every time we experience it as if it were happening for the first time. So go ahead and sing if you're feeling the joy of the Lord. He's a good Father—and worthy of our praise!

Father, I've never known exhilaration like the feeling that comes from knowing your love. Thank you for the incredible gift of your overwhelming joy. I want to sing your praises all the days of my life.

November 7

SUBSTITUTION

Looking to Jesus the pioneer and perfecter of our faith,
who for the sake of the joy that was set before him
endured the cross, disregarding its shame, and has
taken his seat at the right hand of the throne of God.
HEBREWS 12:2 NRSV

Can you imagine enduring the worst kind of pain possible, and suffering mightily, all for the sake of joy? It doesn't seem to make sense, does it? It doesn't seem right to know awful pain in order to gain great joy. And yet that's exactly what Christ did for us. He gave everything he had, and suffered in extraordinary ways, because he knew that *we* would experience the greatest kind of joy possible if he did so.

So smile, laugh, rejoice! You have a God who loves you so much that he went through something awful so *you* wouldn't have to. Christ suffered so we can live forever with him in heaven, and that knowledge alone is an incredible source of joy.

Lord, you endured the cross for me,
and at times I can scarcely believe how much
you went through for me. I'm humbled,
and I rejoice daily because of what you did.

November 8

KEEP YOUR EYES OPEN

Let the skies sing for joy! Let the earth join in the chorus.
Let oceans thunder and fields echo this ecstatic praise
until every swaying tree of every forest joins in,
lifting up their songs of joyous praise to him!
PSALM 96:11-12 TPT

Look around you. If you keep your eyes open for it, you can see the entire world rejoicing in the knowledge that our God is oh so good. You can hear in the rolling thunder during a rainstorm, as it booms loudly and the skies light up with lightning. You can see it in the gentle sway of the long grass in the cow pasture as the animals munch on their lunch. As the tide laps against the shore, it soothingly sings a love song to the Lord over and over again.

Sounds of praise are all around us. Let's join in the chorus together! Each and every place our sight lands should be a reminder of the great beauty God has put together for us. Let's sing a joyful song and rejoice together in the knowledge that we are loved greatly.

Father, I'm awed by the world you've put together for us.
I can't help but feel joy as I take it all in!

November 9

PURSUE GOD

A joyful heart is good medicine,
but a crushed spirit dries up the bones.
PROVERBS 17:22 ESV

We all have a medicine cabinet at home. It's the spot you go to for the bumps and bruises, the aches and pains that life brings our way. Bloody knee? Slap a Band-Aid on it. Feeling a headache coming on? There's a pill for that. Tummy troubles? There's a cure for that too. But there's a medicine that's even better than any over-the-counter pharmaceutical you could take. And it's available at any time—you'll never run out!

The joy that comes from a deep and real relationship with the Lord is like medicine to your very soul. There's no better cure for the aches and pains that sorrow can bring you like turning your face to him and soaking in his love for you. You can rejoice in knowing he is for you. He wants you to know elation like you've never known before. God loves you!

Lord, there's no better medicine for my soul than turning to you. I'm so glad you make yourself so available to the ones who seek you out. I want to sing with joy because of your great love.

November 10

FULL POTENTIAL

Make my joy complete by being of the same mind,
maintaining the same love, united in spirit,
intent on one purpose.
PHILIPPIANS 2:2 NASB

These words, written so many years ago, really say it all, don't they? You can experience happiness without allowing the Lord into your life, but your true joy cannot be complete until you're living in accordance with him and his desires for you. Even better, these words were written by a man living in prison at the time. Paul was a man who knew what joy was, despite his circumstances.

When we're united together as Christians, intent on the purpose of spreading the love of our Savior together, our joy knows no limits. It becomes complete as we let him into our lives, opening up our hearts to him, and relying fully on him for everything we need. It's a feeling you won't find anywhere else.

O Lord, I want my joy to become complete
through you. It's my heart's desire to give myself
over to you fully. Help me to encourage other
believers to be of like mind, so that together
we can change the world for your kingdom.

November 11

LONG FOR THE LORD

Let my passion for life be restored,
tasting joy in every breakthrough you bring to me.
Give me more of your Holy Spirit-Wind
so that I may stand strong and true to you!

PSALM 51:12 TPT

Picture a mountain of calorie-free chocolate cake, served up to you at the end of a delicious dinner. Or maybe you prefer salty over sweet, and a big bowl of salsa with chips is what beckons you. Isn't your mouth just salivating at the thought of it? Imagine indulging at any time, knowing that it's good for you and doesn't come with any repercussions. You know what's even better than any of that? The sweet taste of the joy that comes from the Lord.

And just like the imaginary treats at the table, you can dive in any time without worry. It tastes great and it's good for you (it's like an advertiser's dream come true!). The best part is that you'll never run out of the great joy that the Holy Spirit brings, and you'll continue to crave more with every passing moment.

Lord, I want to taste the sweetness of the joy
that comes from knowing you. As each day passes,
I crave more of you!

GO DEEPER

His anger lasts only a moment,
but his favor lasts a lifetime!
Weeping may last through the night,
but joy comes with the morning.
PSALM 30:5 NLT

When you're in the middle of a painful situation, it can feel as if it's taking forever for it to pass. Time almost stands still as you wait for the pressure to ease up. And yet, we have something to look forward to. Joy is coming! The pain of the night may bring you to tears, but there is light ahead. And that light is bringing with it a time of rejoicing for you.

Have you ever experienced the worst kind of sorrow? There is hope for you. Joy is headed your way. While your problems may never disappear altogether, you will begin to see bright spots in the midst of the pain as you look to the Lord to guide you through. Trust him. He wants you to know that joy!

Lord, thank you for providing me with the hope that joy is coming, despite my current circumstances. I could not walk through this life without you by my side, loving me through the worst that this world can throw my way.

ABUNDANCE OF THE HOLY SPIRIT

May the God of hope fill you with all joy
and peace as you trust in him, so that you may overflow
with hope by the power of the Holy Spirit.
ROMANS 15:13 NIV

Wouldn't it be great to have been a fly on the wall (or an angel on the wall as the case may have been) as God dreamed us up? Picture it. He was deciding exactly how he wanted us to be, and along with the color of our eyes and the shade of our skin, the texture of our hair, and all of our personality traits, he made sure to leave room to be filled up. Wait, what? Yep. He created us to be vessels.

As vessels, we can try to fill ourselves up with everything this world has to offer. And there's a lot that's tempting. But when we fill ourselves to the brim with his joy and peace, it comes bubbling up and spilling over so we can share it with others. We're a vessel without a top, made to overflow so his joy can be seen by everyone.

Lord, fill me to the brim. I want your joy to overflow in me, spilling out onto everyone in my life.

November 14

CAST OFF YOUR WORRIES

Do not be anxious about anything, but in everything
by prayer and supplication with thanksgiving let your requests
be made known to God. And the peace of God,
which surpasses all understanding, will guard
your hearts and your minds in Christ Jesus.

PHILIPPIANS 4:6-7 ESV

"Do not be anxious about anything." Goodness, that's a hard one to wrap our minds around, isn't it? At times, it seems as if our world is falling apart. There's so much to feel anxious about! And yet, it's possible to let it go through God's grace. Have you ever heard it said that worry doesn't change anything? It's so true. But giving it to God through prayer and supplication changes everything.

It's amazing the peace you will feel when you hand over your worries to the Lord. It doesn't mean you won't think about the situation anymore, or have concern. Instead, God will take the burden from you and carry it for you—if you allow him to!

O Lord, I praise you for carrying my burdens!
I'm so thankful I can be at peace during the trials in life,
because I know you will supernaturally help me to do so.
I give you my anxiety and I'm grateful to be free from it!

November 15

QUIET TRANQUILITY

May the Lord of peace himself give you
his peace at all times and in every situation.
The Lord be with you all.
2 THESSALONIANS 3:16 NLT

Let's be honest—we live in a dark and stormy world. We could easily walk through life feeling the weight of the horrible daily news pressing down on us. It's amazing how many people shout the battle cry with the name of the Lord on their lips. And yet, we are told that our God is a God of peace. He calls for peace at all times and in every situation. And when the Lord is with us, when we allow him into our lives to guide our every footstep, we can find the peace that's missing in the world at large.

Are you looking for peace in your life? Is there a quiet tranquility lacking for you? You don't have to look any further than to turn your face toward heaven, and soak in the peace the Lord is offering you. He loves when his children call upon him and ask him to be first in their lives.

Lord, thank you for your peace.
In an uncertain world, it's something
we can count on.

November 16

HOPE

*We pursue the things which make for peace
and the building up of one another.*
ROMANS 14:19 NASB

It's easy to feel helpless when it looks as if everyone around you is angry and full of unrest. You scroll through your social media feeds and see article after article about the hate and unkindness that humans have toward one another. It doesn't seem as it there is anything you can do to change what this world has become, does it?

But there's hope! We can focus on pursuing peace. When we look for ways in which we can make this world a more positive place, we'll see those opportunities all around us. And when we actively begin to build one another up instead of watching all the tearing down that goes on, we'll see change begin to happen. We may just be the catalyst that inspires others to do the same, and spread the peace that comes from knowing the Lord to everyone around us.

**Lord, I pray for your peace to be with me.
I want to see opportunities to spread your love
and kindness. Help me to focus on building others up.**

November 17

RESTORE MY HEART

As a prisoner for the Lord, then, I urge you to live a life
worthy of the calling you have received. Be completely
humble and gentle; be patient, bearing with one another
in love. Make every effort to keep the unity of
the Spirit through the bond of peace.

EPHESIANS 4:1-3 NIV

The apostle Paul gave quite the charge when he told us
to live a life worthy of the calling we have received. That's a
tough order to fill, isn't it? When we strive to live that life on
our own, it's a constant battle to live up to that task. The good
news is that we don't have to do it on our own. The Lord will
help us accomplish things we can't do on our own—like being
humble, gentle, patient, and loving. And when we stumble and
fail at the task, we can rest easy, knowing we can get back up
and begin again, secure in the knowledge that we're forgiven
and our slates are wiped clean.

The peace of the Lord is within our grasp. We need only
look to him to bring it about in our hearts and in our daily
living.

God, I thank you for the gift of peace you've given me.
In a troubling world, it's something I can count on.

November 18

SERENITY

God is not a God of confusion but a God of peace.
1 CORINTHIANS 14:33 NCV

Let's face it—life can be confusing. We can stumble about, feeling overwhelmed and full of doubt. There are many unknowns, and we often question ourselves as we make our day-to-day decisions. But that's not how God wants us to live! He tells us that he is not a God of confusion, but of peace. We can have peace in our hearts and in our minds because that's how he desires it to be for us.

When we press into him, we begin to feel a calm that couldn't be present otherwise. If we seek him first in all we do, the unknowns begin to make themselves clear to us. And when we still feel unsure, we can look to him and know he is good. No matter what life gives us, he will see us through.

Lord, I know you're a God of peace.
When I find myself in the midst of confusing and
troubling times, I pray I would always turn to you
and seek you out, so I can experience that peace.

November 19

CONSTANT IN A CHANGING WORLD

"For the mountains may depart
and the hills be removed,
but my steadfast love shall not depart from you,
and my covenant of peace shall not be removed,"
says the Lord, who has compassion on you.

ISAIAH 54:10 ESV

The world is an ever-changing place. Years from now, we'll look back at what life looks like today and marvel at how much looks different. New technology comes in, towns develop, and the landscape of our life evolves. But one thing that never changes is the way our Lord loves us. There is nothing that can make him stop loving you. It's a comforting thought, isn't it? Even as everything else around us differs from moment to moment, God never does.

Even more, he has compassion for us. He cares about our suffering and misfortune. And though we may suffer as we go through trials, we can still feel quiet and tranquil because the peace that "surpasses all understanding" (Philippians 4:7 ESV) is available through him. He is steady and someone we can count on, even when all else fails.

God, I know I can rest easy because you
never change, and your love never ceases. Thank you
for being the calm in the midst of the storms of life.
Your peace comforts me.

CREATIVITY

May you be strengthened with all power, according to his glorious might, for all endurance and patience with joy.
COLOSSIANS 1:11 ESV

When you want something, it's hard to wait for it, isn't it? Something has stirred your heart, sparked a desire, created a longing in you. You want it to happen right now, as soon as possible! At times you're like that kid waiting to tear open the presents at Christmastime. Then you wait. And sometimes you wait some more. Sometimes, you just keep on waiting, and waiting, and waiting again. It feels as it it's never going to be your turn to take off the wrapping of your gift. It's not easy to do, and yet we are called to be patient in the waiting.

Thank goodness we can call on God to be strengthened with his power in the waiting. When we do, he will give us the endurance and patience in the waiting. He even says we will be joyful as we wait! The day is coming when we will finally be able to tear into that gift. In the meantime, we can look to him to give us the tools we need to find patience.

Father, thank you for helping me to be patient, because I couldn't do it without you!

November 21

ANTICIPATE THE GIFTS

Be joyful in hope, patient in affliction, faithful in prayer.
ROMANS 12:12 NIV

Do you ever find yourself reading the Bible, and something written there stops you in your tracks? Reading Romans 12:12 can be one of those times. *Seriously, God, you want me to be patient in affliction?* you ask. *That honestly seems like an impossible task.* The good news is, nothing is impossible for him.

In the midst of affliction, our flesh doesn't want to be patient. But the Lord himself gives us the power to do so. While we stand by and sit down during our time of trial, we can find ourselves more tolerant of the situation, simply because God is doing a work in our hearts. When we turn to the hope found only in him, we can experience joy in the wait. What was once impossible becomes easily doable through him.

**Lord, I pray for patience in the middle of my affliction.
I know I can't be patient on my own, but you'll get me
to a place of joy while I wait for you to bring
me through this.**

November 22

REFINED

If we are afflicted, it is for your comfort and salvation;
and if we are comforted, it is for your comfort, which you experience
when you patiently endure the same sufferings that we suffer.

2 CORINTHIANS 1:6 ESV

"If we are afflicted, it is for your comfort and salvation." Wait a second. What in the world could that mean? When we suffer, it's for our comfort? And God wants us to be patient in the middle of all that! It seems like an odd thing to say, doesn't it? But if we break it down, we see that it begins to make sense.

Every time we suffer through a trial by fire, we are being refined. We are growing and being stretched, so we can become more complete and draw closer to the Lord. That should bring us comfort! And as we go through pain, we can be patient knowing that the end result will be better than the cushy path through life we could have dreamed up on our own.

Lord, thank you for knowing better than me what
I need in life to grow closer to you and who you want
me to be. I pray for patience while I wait for
your refining to be completed in me.

November 23

HELPFULNESS

Love patiently accepts all things.
It always trusts, always hopes, and always endures.
1 CORINTHIANS 13:7 NCV

When you spend a lot of time with someone you love, it's easy to start noticing all the things that bug you about them. The annoying habits, the things you'd *never* do yourself, the bothersome way they go about life—all can become a sore spot. But when you look at the definition of love, not in the dictionary, but rather through the eyes of our God, you see that true love means patiently accepting all things. Not just the good things and the easy to love things, but all the things.

Love always trust, hopes, and endures, which means that it patiently perseveres through the good and the bad. So the next time those grievances against a loved one start to creep into your thoughts once again, ask yourself if you're acting in love. God will give you patience and a true love for them if you seek it out.

Lord, help me to love others as you'd do so yourself.
I pray for patience to accept all things about the
people in my life, so I can show them a Christlike love.
Help me to trust, hope, and endure.

November 24

OVERCOME

Whatever things were written before were written
for our learning, that we through the patience and comfort
of the Scriptures might have hope. Now may the God of patience
and comfort grant you to be like-minded toward
one another, according to Christ Jesus.

ROMANS 15:4-5 NKJV

Sometimes, it's hard to get along with the people you come in contact with on a regular basis. At times, you may not even feel like trying! People can be truly awful, and sometimes it just doesn't seem worth the effort. And truly, living in peace with others can seem like an impossible task.

But Christ came and wiped away all that seems difficult or awkward. Whereas before it would have been extremely tough to live in harmony with those around us, being like-minded toward one another, he came and changed everything. He made the impossible possible. We can find patience for others because our patience comes from him.

Lord, thank you for giving me patience when I cannot find it on my own. I pray I'd always have enough patience to go around for the people in my life, so I can become like-minded with them as we share your love.

November 25

GLORIOUS SALVATION

I patiently accept all these troubles so that those whom God has chosen can have the salvation that is in Christ Jesus. With that salvation comes glory that never ends.
2 TIMOTHY 2:10 NCV

You get a call from the doctor with a troubling diagnosis. Heading out to the car in the morning, you find it won't start. After a long day at work, you happily head home, only to be stopped with a speeding ticket on your way. Life is full of troubles. And oh, how it can make you want to scream with anger! Where is God when you're going through the rough patches?

Although it can be hard to see past our own hurts, God is never far from us. In fact, he's right by our side with every step we take. And he asks for our patience as we struggle. This patience is possible because we know we have the gift of salvation. We aren't promised a life without pain during our time here on earth, but we *are* promised glory forever and ever with him in heaven. And that's worth waiting for.

**Father, give me your eyes to see
what is ahead for me, and the promise of glory.
I pray for patience as I wait.**

ATTENTION TO DETAIL

The LORD has appeared of old to me, saying:
"Yes, I have loved you with an everlasting love;
Therefore with lovingkindness I have drawn you."
JEREMIAH 31:3 NKJV

Lately, the world seems to be completely devoid of kindness. In fact, people everywhere seem to be downright mean to one another, don't they? They're bashing each other on social media because they're angry, and violence is prevalent everywhere we look. But we have a God who is the very essence of kindness. He is a ray of sunshine in a dark and cloudy sky.

Our God cares so much for us. He treasures and adores us. The Lord cares about the littlest details in our lives, and shows us kindness through his daily mercies. There is nothing about us that escapes his attention. He is a generous, warm, and considerate God, and his love is like nothing else.

Father, you are kind, and I am humbled by your mercy. When I am tempted to show my thoughtlessness to those around me, I pray that I'd be stopped in my tracks by you, and instead reflect your kindness and mercy. Thank you for loving me the way you do.

November 27

MODEL GODLINESS

Her teachings are filled with wisdom and kindness,
as loving instruction pours from her lips.
PROVERBS 31:26 TPT

When you think of the perfect woman, who or what do you picture? A famous model or actress? Someone known for their brains or leadership skills? We all have a different vision of what perfection looks like. But if there's ever a person to look up to, it's the Proverbs 31 woman. She is touted in the Bible as the model of who we should be. She's exactly who we should want to be—loving and kind, and full of wisdom.

Can you imagine people describing you as someone who pours loving instruction from your lips? It seems like the ultimate compliment to have people notice you, not for your looks or accomplishments, but for bearing the qualities of a Christ-like woman. A woman filled with wisdom and kindness.

Lord, help me to be more like the Proverbs 31 woman. I want to have qualities that reflect you when others see me. I pray for kindness to pour from my mouth, every time I speak. Give me the ability to be a person of great character, loving and caring, and full of wisdom.

November 28

FRUIT OF PATIENCE

"The seed that fell on the good ground is like
those who hear God's teaching with good,
honest hearts and obey it and patiently produce good fruit."
LUKE 8:15 NCV

It takes time to produce a good and healthy crop. It's a process. You till the soil, plant the seeds, and carefully water them for months and months. After a time, you begin to see the fruits of your labors, as your seedling turns into a little plant that continues to grow, getting bigger and stronger until it's ready to be harvested.

It's the same with our hearts. It takes time to produce our fruit. Patiently we wait as we get watered with the teaching of the Lord, through reading his Word and soaking in his presence. After being watered with his living water, we can begin to see our patience pay off as our hearts turn from black to beautiful, full of good fruit and ready for the harvest. It takes time, but it's worth the wait!

Lord, help me to be patient as my heart learns to bear good fruit. I want to seek you with every turn, listening to your teaching and guidance as I grow and develop into the woman you desire me to be.

November 29

PASSIONATE PURSUIT

Whoever pursues righteousness and unfailing love
will find life, righteousness, and honor.
PROVERBS 21:21 NLT

As women, we tend to have all kinds of interests. There are so many different facets of our personalities. Our hobbies are varied and we usually pursue them with a passion. There is much in our lives that is good to go after, but the most important thing of all to pursue? A life of righteousness and unfailing love.

In fact, the Bible tells us if those are our pursuits, we will find life, righteousness, and honor. Those are pretty stellar things to be going after, aren't they? If we desire to live a righteous life, the Lord will help us to do so, if we simply seek his direction. And if we want to give unfailing love to others, we need only turn to him and ask for his guidance, and a heart for people.

Lord, I want to pursue righteousness and unfailing love.
It's my heart's desire to find life, righteousness, and
honor. I need your help to get there! It can't be
done without you, and I pray you'll show me the steps
I need to take to attain this lofty goal.

November 30

RECEIVE LIFE

*"You gave me life and showed me kindness,
and in your care you watched over my life."*

JOB 10:12 NCV

To say that Job went through a rough patch was putting it lightly. He lost everything he had, from his family, to his wealth, friends, and more. And yet, even in the worst of it, he could still see that God was good. He knew that he was cared for in his darkest hour, and that the God he loved was one of kindness.

Even in our own times of darkness, our God is watching over us. He cares about every detail of our life, no matter how big or small. In our moments of despair, we can look to him and be comforted, because he wants you to see his kindness. He gave us life! And he gave it not to sit on high and giggle as we stumble and flail about, but rather to be a friend to us who walks us through it all.

**Father, I pray I'd see your kindness even on
my darkest days. I know how much you care for me,
and I'm so thankful for that. You're a kind
and loving God, and I'm awed by you.**

December

When they saw
the star, they rejoiced
exceedingly with
great joy.

MATTHEW 2:10 ESV

December 1

CONTINUE WITH VIGOR

At one time we too were foolish, disobedient, deceived and enslaved by all kinds of passions and pleasures. We lived in malice and envy, being hated and hating one another. But when the kindness and love of God our Savior appeared, he saved us, not because of righteous things we had done, but because of his mercy.

TITUS 3:3-5 NIV

Whether you grew up in the church, or just learned the good news of salvation through Christ as recently as last week, there comes a point in your life when you have a decision to make. Will you continue on living according to the whims and desires of the flesh, or will you give yourself over to the Lord and become new through him?

And when you make the choice to be reborn in Jesus, you realize the incredible gift of kindness he has given us all. He saved us! God rescued us from our own nature and instead instilled in us the ability and desire to become more and more like him. And that is who he designed us to be!

Lord, I want to be more like you, and I'm thankful for the renewing you've done in my heart. Thank you for rescuing me and giving me a desire to please you. Make me the person you've designed me to be.

December 2

REFLECT GOD'S TRUTH

*If anyone has the world's goods and sees his brother
in need, yet closes his heart against him, how does God's
love abide in him? Little children, let us not love
in word or talk but in deed and in truth.*

1 John 3:17-18 esv

When we accept Christ as our Savior and begin to seek
him in every area of our lives, something happens in our
hearts. As we begin to change, we suddenly begin to see needs
where we may have missed them before. We start to notice the
friend in trouble, the children who go hungry in our neighborhoods, or that single mom who could use a hand.

To deny that we see these needs around us, and to do nothing about them, would be to deny the love of God himself. We
cannot call ourselves Christians and not act when we know
what can be done to help. In fact, we should be actively searching for ways to lift up and encourage others so we can share
the love and kindness of Christ with everyone we know.

**Lord, open my eyes to see the needs around me.
Give me the knowledge to know what to do
when a situation arises.**

December 3

URGED BY THE SPIRIT

We are not saying that we can do this work ourselves.
It is God who makes us able to do all that we do.
2 CORINTHIANS 3:5 NCV

That guy cuts you off in traffic and everything in you wants to shake a fist at him (or worse!). Your food at the restaurant is terrible and the server doesn't seem all that sorry about it. The line at the grocery store is as long as can be, and the cashier appears to be taking her sweet time ringing everybody up. It can be really hard to be kind to those around us, can't it?

There are times when speaking sharply, or getting even, feels like the right thing to do. Without God in your life, guiding your words and deeds, it may well be impossible to respond with kindness. But God takes what wasn't possible before, flips it around in your heart, and gives us a newfound ability to do what we couldn't on our own. And suddenly, we can find it in us to have a kind word for those we come in contact with.

**Father, thank you for your ability to soften
my heart and make me a kinder woman. I shudder
to think about who I would be without you!**

December 4

RECONCILIATION

*Use patience and kindness when you want to persuade leaders
and watch them change their minds right in front of you.
For your gentle wisdom will quell the strongest resistance.*
PROVERBS 25:15 TPT

Have you ever scrolled through social media and noticed people "screaming" about their latest passion? When their angry words appeared before you, did it make you want to change your own position on the subject? It's not likely. On the flip side, when you see something written in a persuasive yet gentle tone, were you more tempted to check it out to learn more? It's the old "catch more flies with honey" approach.

Even thousands of years ago, wise people knew that in order to persuade someone over to their way of thinking, they'd need a kind and gentle voice to win people over. Our world may have changed quite a bit since then, but humankind is still much the same. And we are still won over by kindness. Love heals more than hate, every time.

**Lord, I pray that your words would flow from my mouth
when I'm speaking. I want others to hear you in me
when I'm around, and I hope they'll hear your kindness.**

December 5

HUMBLE OBEDIENCE

*Do not neglect to do good and to share what you have,
for such sacrifices are pleasing to God.*
HEBREWS 13:16 ESV

Does it ever feel as if your every good deed goes unnoticed? It can seem as if nobody sees the things you do, or the way you share and give to others. At times, we may even begin to wonder if it's worth it to put forth the effort anymore. But there's someone who always pays attention to the good deeds you do. There's one who sees all, and is supremely pleased by your actions. God doesn't let your goodness slip by without notice.

It can be a sacrifice to share what we have with those around us, but it's a worthy effort on our part. The God we love and serve sees what we do, and is pleased by it all. And that alone should give us the motivation we need to keep going, and keep loving others. Serving his people is a worthy cause.

**Lord, help me to have a servant's heart.
One that would seek to do good and share what
I have with others. I want my life to be pleasing to you,
with my every word, deed, and action.**

December 6

SOW A GOOD SEED

So then, as we have opportunity,
let us do good to everyone, and especially to those
who are of the household of faith.

GALATIANS 6:10 ESV

Most of us have hearts that desire to do good. But sometimes it's hard to see the ways in which we can be good to others. At times, it's not the most obvious answer. But if we look for opportunities to do good, we'll find them everywhere. There is need all around us. This world certainly isn't lacking for that. And when we open our eyes to it, it becomes apparent what we can do.

So the next time you find yourself wondering what you can do to give a helping hand, look around your community. Find a need, whether it's someone on your street, or through an organization that helps people across the world. Seek out every opportunity to sow seeds of good wherever you can! There's nothing like the feeling of knowing that you have spent your day serving others.

God, I want to have eyes to see the need around me.
Help me to see where I can help. Give me opportunities
to do more good, and a heart to follow through on them.

December 7

INVIGORATED BY THE FATHER

Remember not the sins of my youth or my transgressions;
according to your steadfast love remember me,
for the sake of your goodness, O LORD!
Good and upright is the LORD;
therefore he instructs sinners in the way.

PSALM 25:7-8 ESV

Ah, youth. It's a time to live carefree, have fun, try new things ... and make lots and lots of mistakes. Thank goodness we're forgiven for them by the Father in heaven who loves us dearly. In fact, he loves us so much that not only does he forgive us, but he also patiently instructs us in the way we should go so we can learn and not make the same mistakes over and over again!

And when we do stumble and fall and those sins creep back up again in our lives? Well, that's when he forgives our remorseful hearts all over again. God is so good to us that he wipes away all our transgressions and makes us new. He is a good Father indeed!

Lord, I am humbled by you and your goodness.
When I think of all you do for me, I am overwhelmed.
Thank you for making me new again, even after
I stumble and fall. I am a sinner, but you?
You are good, and I want to be more like you.

December 8

KEEP YOUR EYES FIXED ON HIM

Do not be conformed to this world, but be transformed by the renewing of your mind, so that you may prove what the will of God is, that which is good and acceptable and perfect.
ROMANS 12:2 NASB

The neighbors just redid their kitchen, and you can't rest until yours is done too. Sarah just got the latest "it" bag, and suddenly you also want one. Jane got a big promotion at work, and you find yourself working like a dog until you've achieved that as well. It feels good to keep up with the Joneses, doesn't it? Except when it doesn't. You see, it's a fleeting feeling of happiness, going after what those around you have. There's a high from the score, and then you're right back where you started from again.

While there's nothing inherently wrong with achieving these worldly things, it becomes wrong when our focus becomes all about keeping up. Instead, we are to transform our way of thinking, so that our focus is on the goodness of God, and living our lives as a mirror of that.

Lord, I want to live for that which is good and acceptable and perfect. Help me to seek after that, rather than the things of this world.

December 9

CELEBRATE HIS GOODNESS

I will tell about the LORD's kindness
and praise him for everything he has done.
I will praise the LORD for the many good things he has given us
and for his goodness to the people of Israel.
He has shown great mercy to us
and has been very kind to us.

ISAIAH 63:7 NCV

When something great happens to you, don't you just want to shout about it to everyone you know? You want to share the good news, letting everybody hear about what's going on. "Did you hear what happened to me?" we ask our friends. "Let me tell you all about this fabulous thing!" Our excitement cannot be contained.

There is nothing better than telling others about the many good things the Lord has done for us and given us. We should be itching to share the good news, and to tell those around us about his mercies and kindness. He deserves all our praise, for he is a good God.

Lord, thank you for being the good and
merciful God that you are. I want to tell everyone
I know how the many things you have done for me,
and share your good news.

December 10

RECEIVE MERCY

Who is a God like you,
who pardons sin and forgives the transgression
of the remnant of his inheritance?
You do not stay angry forever
but delight to show mercy.
You will again have compassion on us;
you will tread our sins underfoot
and hurl all our iniquities into the depths of the sea.
MICAH 7:18-19 NIV

Time and time again, the people of Israel rebelled against the Lord and sinned. They deliberately turned their backs on him and made foolish decisions. Today, we do the same thing. We turn our backs, and time and time again we sin against the Lord.

The good news is that our God is a forgiving one; he doesn't hold a permanent grudge against us. He doesn't stay angry forever. Instead, he wants to show us his mercy. He remains faithful, even when we're not. All we have to do is ask for his grace. God is waiting to give us the gift of compassion, if we'll just turn back to him.

Father, I'm sorry for the many ways in which
I have sinned. I'm thankful for your daily mercies.
Your faithfulness knows no bounds.

GLORIFY AND WORSHIP

God, glorify your name!
Yes, your name alone be glorified, not ours!
For you are the One who loves us passionately,
and you are faithful and true.

PSALM 115:1 TPT

It's easy to be caught up in the admiring words of others. When you achieve a certain goal, or something great happens to you, you want to take the credit. After all, you're a hard worker. You deserve some accolades, right? It's tempting to hope you'll get all the glory. But there is only one who deserves to be glorified.

Compliments are great, and there's nothing wrong with receiving one. But when we put our stock in what we achieve and think we've done it on our own, we lose sight of the one who gives us everything we have. God should be glorified for all he's done, and all he's given us. Every good thing comes from him. And it's important that we never forget it. He is faithful in his generosity, and he deserves our praise and worship.

God, you have been so faithful in the gifts you have given me, and the things you've done for me. I pray I'd glorify you and give you the praise when I'm tempted to be puffed up with accolades.

December 12

NEVER CHANGING

For his unfailing love for us is powerful;
the LORD's faithfulness endures forever.
Praise the LORD!
PSALM 117:2 NLT

If there is one thing we know, it's that nothing stays the same. Life is an uncertain thing, changing from moment to moment. However, no matter what changes you go through in life, no matter how it ebbs and flows, there is one thing you can count on. That is the Lord and his faithfulness. Simply put, his faithfulness endures forever. He is always there for us, and he's devoted and true.

We can put our faith in him because he is steadfast. He never changes, and he tells us he will be faithful. Because of that, we know it to be true. After all, he's a God who keeps his promises. So when we are filled with worry or fear about the changes to come, we can rest assured that he will be faithful to show us his unfailing love.

Lord, I am amazed by your faithfulness. I know that,
when the rest of my life feels wobbly and unsteady,
you are someone I can count on to be a constant.
Thank you for loving me without fail,
and for remaining faithful forever.

December 13

PROCLAIM THE GOOD NEWS

I tell everyone everywhere the truth of your righteousness. …
I don't keep it a secret, or hide the truth.
I preach of your faithfulness and kindness,
proclaiming your extravagant love
to the largest crowd I can find!
PSALM 40:9-10 TPT

When you're really excited about something, do you tuck it away inside and keep it all to yourself like a secret? Or does it come bubbling up from inside you, spilling over and leave you unable to keep it under wraps? It's hard to keep something really good to ourselves. We want to share the good news with everyone we see!

It's the same with the good news of Christ and the sacrifice he made for us, giving us life for eternity. It's not something to keep inside, and all to ourselves. His faithfulness is something to be shared with the world. And his extravagant love is a pretty big deal. So find a crowd and spread the word. Get the news out. The God we love is faithful forever.

Lord, thank you for your faithfulness. I don't want
to keep it all to myself. Rather, I want to share this
good news with everyone with whom I come
in contact, telling them of your
extravagant love and your steady love.

December 14

LOVED UNIQUELY

The wisdom from above is first of all pure.
It is also peace loving, gentle at all times, and willing to
yield to others. It is full of mercy and the fruit of good deeds.
It shows no favoritism and is always sincere.

JAMES 3:17 NLT

It's incredible, the way that God loves us. And we can find a beautiful description of that love in the book of James. His love is pure and without blemish. He is a peaceful and gentle God, and full of mercy. Our God is sincere and faithful. And he shows no favoritism. So does that mean he loves us all exactly the same? Not at all! He loves each of us uniquely and differently because we're his children.

The love of a father for his children means that he loves them each for their one-of-a-kind character traits—by teaching them, admonishing them, and at times getting frustrated with those that go astray. But loving uniquely doesn't mean loving one more than another. It just means loving differently! No matter what God's love looks like to you, you can count on his faithfulness.

Father, thank you for counting me as one
of your children and loving me as such.
I know I can count on your faithful
and enduring love.

IMITATE GOD

Put on then, as God's chosen ones, holy and beloved,
compassionate hearts, kindness, humility, meekness, and patience.
COLOSSIANS 3:12 ESV

As you read through the pages of the Bible, you come across the many aspects of our God. He's shown his rage, his disappointment in his people, and his wrath. There are times and situations that have called for these qualities to have made themselves known. But even more than a God of anger, he is a God of great gentleness. The way he cares for his people, and watches over even the smallest details of their lives, shows his gentle touch.

If, then, we are to emulate God in the way we live, one of the first character traits we should strive to copy is his gentleness. And with that spirit of gentleness comes a compassionate heart, kindness, humility, meekness, and patience. When we have a gentle and tender heart toward others, we can truly begin to live like our Savior, loving others in all that we do.

God, I want my heart to be changed and become more like yours. I pray that I can become more of a gentle and tenderhearted person, finding compassion for others.

December 16

RAISE UP HIS NAME

"You have also given me the shield of Your salvation;
Your gentleness has made me great."
2 SAMUEL 22:36 NKJV

When we think of a mighty and powerful ruler, we don't usually think of someone gentle. You picture someone roaring with anger, pounding a fist and screaming about what he wants. To be someone great, someone of importance, it feels as if you've got to be the loudest person in the room. But in 2 Samuel, we are reminded that it isn't necessarily so. In fact, it says that it's the gentleness of the Lord that makes us great.

Gentleness is counterintuitive to all we've been taught, and all we think we know. Yet when we stop to think about it, it makes sense. Are you more likely to listen to someone who is raging about their opinions, or someone who speaks calmly and with reason? Do you admire more someone who would squash their opponents under their thumb, or those who use a gentle and loving approach? To become great, we must first become gentle, just as God himself has been to us.

Lord, you are the greatest of them all, and yet you are gentle. I want to become more and more like you, becoming gentle in my approach to those around me.

367

December 17

THE EASY YOKE

Take my yoke upon you, and learn from me,
for I am gentle and lowly in heart,
and you will find rest for your souls.
MATTHEW 11:29 ESV

Jesus did the biggest thing anyone could ever do for another. He sacrificed his life so that we may live. Christ was a change maker, and without argument one of the most important figures in history, regardless of what you believe about him. And yet he described himself as gentle and lowly in heart. It's humbling, isn't it? We spend our days searching for ways in which we can be exalted and admired by others, and yet the man who gave us our very life was the opposite.

Where most would seek to lift themselves up in the eyes of others, Jesus had a humble and gentle heart. And he asked us to learn from him. We weren't asked to be the biggest personality in the room. He told us to take his yoke upon us and learn from his gentle ways. And through that, we will find rest for our weariness.

Lord, when I'm tempted to seek admiration from others,
help me to have your gentle and lowly heart.
I want to find rest for my soul, and I know I will
find it through you and your teachings.

December 18

LION OF JUDAH

The rage of a king is like the roar of a lion,
but his sweet favor is like a gentle, refreshing rain.
PROVERBS 19:12 TPT

When summer's sun is scorching and beating down on you, there's nothing better than the relief of a gentle and refreshing rain. It's a welcome change that brings sweet release from the heaviness of that hot sun. In the same vein, do you remember disappointing your parents as a child, and fearing the anger that was sure to come because of your bad choices? But when they showed you gentleness and favor, it was like a soothing balm to your soul.

It's the same way with our God. He is like a mighty lion, and his roar is loud and terrifying. But his favor? That's a beautiful thing. It's a relief, just like a refreshing rain. He gently reaches down and loves on you, and it's better than anything else imaginable. The searing heat is over, and the sun's beating rays have been squelched by the sweet rain that softly drops.

Lord, I thank you for the many ways in which you
have shown me favor. Your gentleness is amazing to me,
like a sweet caress of softly falling rain.

December 19

BE STRENGTHENED BY GOD

Resist him, standing firm in the faith, because you know that the family of believers throughout the world is undergoing the same kind of sufferings. And the God of all grace, who called you to his eternal glory in Christ, after you have suffered a little while, will himself restore you and make you strong, firm and steadfast.
1 PETER 5:9-10 NIV

Ugh. Self-control. It seems an impossible task to gain control over oneself and make wise decisions, doesn't it? It's so tempting to give in to the desires of our hearts. And losing self-control often feels good at the time. It's afterward that we realize how badly we feel. Thank goodness we don't have to fight this battle on our own.

God himself tells us that he will restore us. He will make us strong, firm, and steadfast. When we're tempted to lose control and start to spiral downward, he'll give us the ability to regain control over our lives. We can stand firm in our faith because he gives us the strength we need.

**Lord, I need your help with my self-control.
I'm not able to do it on my own. It's only through
you that I can stand firm.**

TOGETHER, WITH THE HOLY SPIRIT

*We can rejoice, too, when we run into problems and trials,
for we know that they help us develop endurance. And endurance
develops strength of character, and character strengthens our
confident hope of salvation. And this hope will not lead to
disappointment. For we know how dearly God loves us, because
he has given us the Holy Spirit to fill our hearts with his love.*

ROMANS 5:3-5 NLT

It would be a sad thing indeed to go through life without any strength of character. And yet, the thought of going through the tough stuff to get there is often overwhelming to us. We look at the trials of life before us and want to run from them, not plow through and endure it all. And certainly, we don't feel like rejoicing!

But we know that God loves us dearly. And he wants to build our character. He wants to help us learn self-control. God loves us so much that he sent his Holy Spirit to help us endure through the worst of our problems and make it to the other side of them, confident in our hope of salvation.

**God, thank you for giving me self-control when
I can't find it without you. I want to build my character,
and I'll be looking to you to help me!**

December 21

NAUGHTY OR NICE?

Yet he has not left himself without testimony:
He has shown kindness by giving you rain from heaven
and crops in their seasons; he provides you with plenty of food
and fills your hearts with joy.
ACTS 14:17 NIV

Let's be honest—there are times when we try to "behave" so God or others will favor us when we need it. At those times, we look a little like the children of this season, impatiently awaiting the reward of good Christmas presents. They are behaving, yes, but not for the right reasons!

It is true that great rewards await the obedient. Let us not overlook, however, the beautiful kindnesses of the Lord that rain upon us day by day. God is good, and he is kind. He meets our needs and gives us joy that overwhelms our souls. His kindness is not dependent upon our behavior, but upon his good nature. Certainly, we are blessed. So take some time this season to dwell on what God has already given you.

God, thank you for the good gifts you have given me
this year. Thank you for your kindness I have not
deserved, including the ones I thought I did deserve!
Your tireless labors of love are evident everywhere
in my life, and I am so grateful you are with me.
Thank you! I love you too.

December 22

A MARATHON OF FAITH

For examples of patience in suffering, dear brothers and sisters,
look at the prophets who spoke in the name of the Lord.
JAMES 5:10 NLT

We patiently wait for all kinds of events. Christmas, birthdays, vacations, and even customer service can see us tapping our toes or crossing out calendar days. We have enough patience to carry on until our desired events come to pass. Patience in suffering is far more difficult than simply waiting. James offers examples of patience that reached far into their keepers' faith. Prophets of God have been dropped into cisterns and lions' dens, stoned, crucified, and sawn in two.

These prophets focused their intentions and actions toward heavenly rewards that went beyond the span of their lifetimes. In the same way, our lives are worth more than the decades we live on earth, and our callings affect continual generations after we are gone. Waiting for our dailies reminds us that we are constantly training for a beautiful reward in Christ.

Lord, you have fashioned me for a marathon of faith,
one I will win if I continue to trust your goodness,
focusing on you and your goals. Thank you for working
all things to your glory and our good. Thank you for
making me a member of your body and for loving me
so gently and patiently. Please guide me in building the
church up, glorifying your name, and patiently trusting
in your rewards and goodness in my life.

December 23

SHINE ABOVE ALL

When they saw the star,
they rejoiced exceedingly with great joy.
MATTHEW 2:10 ESV

"Rejoiced exceedingly"? With "great joy"? Matthew does not want us to underestimate the power and depth of the wise men's joy! They had traveled far, following Christ's star. When that star stopped over a house in Bethlehem, they were filled with joy because they knew a great king had arrived.

Today, you give people an opportunity for joy, because you carry Jesus in you. He expresses his love through you. God wants you to shine! Shine in God's presence and goodness, which rest deep within you. Shine like that star, which announced Christ's presence to the world two millennia ago. His joy, gratitude, and deeds will blaze brightly through your own. So shine!

God, you're amazing. You live and shine in me,
giving me great hope and joy in every circumstance.
Thank you for inviting me to continually embrace your
perspective and enjoy your presence. Help me to blaze
bright and give others joy and cause for gratitude.

December 24

PRAISE FROM JOY

The angel said to him, "Do not be afraid, Zechariah,
for your prayer has been heard, and your wife Elizabeth
will bear you a son, and you shall call his name John.
and you will have joy and gladness, and many will rejoice
at his birth, for he will be great before the Lord. And he must
not drink wine or strong drink, and he will be filled with
the Holy Spirit, even from his mother's womb."

LUKE 1:13-15 NIV

Joy results in praise. Though Zechariah was a little slow at first, the end result was praise. Elizabeth had been barren many years; they as a couple knew something about waiting! These faithful people surely expressed to God their longings, sufferings, and grief. They had sincerity and vulnerability before God, and in the end, they had extreme joy and praise.

You can trust God with every emotion. Maybe Christmas is hard; you have no joy in your circumstance. Let him know your lament. Maybe it's full of joy, overflowing with praise. Maybe you're too busy to feel anything. If so, spend some time before the Lord in silence (like Zechariah had to!). Whatever your emotion, God can handle it. There are people holding on to promises, people in grief, people filled with joy, people with hope fulfilled and hope expectant. Reach out to others this Christmas, and let them express their emotions to God.

Jesus, I want to share how I feel today. Hear me and know me. Thank you for becoming a vulnerable baby for our salvation.

A LOYAL LOVE

Hold on to loyal love and don't let go,
and be faithful to all that you've been taught.
Let your life be shaped by integrity,
with truth written upon your heart.

PROVERBS 3:3 TPT

In the beginning, God constructed a salvation plan with his Son, Jesus Christ. Over the past six thousand years or more, his believers have been instructed to live in faith, hope, and love. Let's face it—God has been doing the heavy lifting in this relationship! His faithfulness is not dependent upon ours. With his sweet love, we are simply transformed by it, and our faith blossoms.

Today, we rejoice in God's faithfulness, realized in the person of Jesus Christ. He, the Son of God, the Word made flesh, came to this earth in utter humility. We will never be the same! Let us seize his loyal love and never relent. Let us respond by allowing his integrity to shape us, and truth to pen itself on the tablets of our hearts.

Lord God, merry Christmas! Thank you for coming to earth as Jesus Christ. You have been faithful to me since before my existence. You haven't been solely the Lord of my life; you are Lord of the universe. I must answer to you. Whatever the cost, I want you to forge me into the faithful servant and heir you have envisioned in your heart for me. Help me hold on to loyal love.

December 26

ENDURE THROUGH THE STORM

My dear brothers and sisters, stand firm. Let nothing move you.
Always give yourselves fully to the work of the Lord, because you
know that your labor in the Lord is not in vain.

1 Corinthians 15:58 niv

What do you picture when you think of something that
stands firm? Do you envision a statue standing tall and still,
no matter what comes its way? A statue doesn't bend and sway
under the pressure of a strong wind. Instead, it continues to
hold its posture, never moving. And that's what we can be like
too.

If we ask God for the power of self-control over our lives,
we become like statues, never bending under pressure. Strong
winds will come. The storms of life will beat down upon us.
But we can continue to stand firm through the power of
Christ. When we give ourselves fully to him, he gives us the
ability to stay strong when we wouldn't otherwise be able to.

Dear Lord, I want to be like a statue. I pray I'd be
immovable under the pressures of life. When the winds
come, I don't want to sway. Instead, I'll stand firm
knowing you've given me the power to do so!

December 27

NOT BY MY OWN STRENGTH

May you be strengthened with all power,
according to his glorious might,
for all endurance and patience with joy.
COLOSSIANS 1:11 ESV

Is patience something that comes naturally to you? Do you look at others and the seemingly silly things they do and have a happy heart as you deal with them? If so, you are a fortunate woman indeed. For most of us, patience is not a virtue that is ingrained in us from birth. Instead, it's a learned trait and something we have to work on constantly.

The great thing is that it's possible to feel real patience, even under the most frustrating of circumstances, because we're strengthened with the power of the Holy Spirit. He gives us gifts and abilities that we wouldn't otherwise possess. And in time, our hearts can truly be changed so we feel things we wouldn't have felt in the past. We can become patient women, because a relationship with God changes who we once were.

God, I pray for patience. It doesn't come to me naturally. But I know it's possible to be a more patient woman, because I can do anything through you and your glorious might. Thank you for changing my heart!

REFINED INTO A PRICELESS TREASURE

I patiently accept all these troubles so that those whom God has chosen can have the salvation that is in Christ Jesus. With that salvation comes glory that never ends.

2 TIMOTHY 2:10 NCV

As strong women, we tend to be problem solvers. We see an issue looming on the horizon and we work to get it fixed as quickly as possible. It would be unfathomable to consider accepting trouble into our lives, wouldn't it? And yet, we are told to patiently accept it. Wait, what?

When we are patient in the midst of our trials, we grow in our faith. And we can begin to see the work that the Lord wants to do in us, and the beauty that comes as a result of it. We start to feel thankful for these times of trouble, because they are refining us. And when they come again, as they will inevitably do, we can be patient as we endure. It doesn't mean we can't work to solve things. Rather, find our patience to keep going in the middle of the storm.

Lord, I will patiently accept my trials so I can see the beauty you have in the refining. Help me to endure the worst of it!

December 29

AN AUDIENCE OF ONE

*Work with enthusiasm, as thought you were
working for the Lord rather than for people.*
EPHESIANS 6:7 NLT

At times, our day-to-day work, whether that is a job, or caring for little ones at home, or serving others in a different capacity, can feel draining. God's gentle reminder in Ephesians encourages us to focus on the true audience in the work we are doing. Who sees you? Is it just the people you are serving? No, your audience is of *one*, the Lord.

God is your audience and he knows the nature of your heart as you work. He sees your selflessness and care and he is the only one who truly matters. It isn't always easy to remember that when you're knee-deep in work pressures, but remember he sees you, friend. He sees the work you put in and appreciates you for it. Hopefully this puts a bounce in your step today.

**God, remind me today that you see me.
As I work, may I feel joy in what I'm doing because
I'm serving you first and foremost.**

December 30

PURPOSE

*We keep on praying for you, asking our God to enable you
to live a life worthy of his call. May he give you the power
to accomplish all the good things your faith prompts you to do.*
2 THESSALONIANS 1:11 NLT

God's Spirit lives inside of you as a believer of Jesus Christ.
What a gift! In that treasure, God's Spirit is living and active
and prompts us in life. That little nudge you feel? That calling
you can't ignore? God is speaking to you through his Spirit.
When you follow that lead, the reward is great. There is something so satisfying in working hard in goodness, knowing God
has lead you there. You said yes, and you're doing what you
were meant to.

If you're in a place where you need direction, ask God. He
will give you all you need to sustain you in your pursuit of his
purpose for your life. You do have purpose, dear friend, and
you are worthy to pursue it.

**Father God, thank you for giving me the gift of your
Spirit, living and active inside of me. Help me to press
into that voice, knowing you'll guide me and nudge
me down the path you've laid out for me.**

December 31

TIME WITH JESUS

My beloved, as you have always obeyed,
not as in my presence only, but now much more in my absence,
work out your own salvation with fear and trembling.
PHILIPPIANS 2:12 NKJV

Self-control is not solely expressed as prudence that avoids poor choices. It is also expressed by zealously pursuing righteousness for the long haul. This active pursuit takes energy, discipline, and vision—all factors of self-control. While defeating temptation is vastly important, we need to actively seek spiritual growth, not stagnancy.

Perhaps you're considering a New Year's resolution to make up for past issues, or maybe you feel defeated by a recent failure. Instead of guilt-tripping or mentally beating yourself up, spend some extra quiet time with Jesus today. He will have his correct perspective awaiting you. God's plans for you have always been good. He knows how to keep you in step with him, and them, as you walk with him day by day.

Jesus, I praise you! You're so good. Help me to enter into your presence with praise and worship and leave everything else behind. I want to focus on you today. Help me to see the opportunities that make for a lifetime of self-control.

"May the LORD show you his favor and give you his peace."

NUMBERS 6:26 NLT